Lyric Cousins

T0386219

for Stephen Dandridge

Lyric Cousins

Poetry and Musical Form

Fiona Sampson

EDINBURGH
University Press

Edinburgh University Press is one of the leading university presses in the UK. We publish academic books and journals in our selected subject areas across the humanities and social sciences, combining cutting-edge scholarship with high editorial and production values to produce academic works of lasting importance. For more information visit our website: edinburghuniversitypress.com

Edinburgh University Press Ltd
The Tun – Holyrood Road, 12(2f) Jackson's Entry, Edinburgh EH8 8PJ

First published in hardback by Edinburgh University Press 2016

Typeset in 10.5/13pt Sabon by
Servis Filmsetting Ltd, Stockport, Cheshire
and printed and bound by CPI Group (UK) Ltd
Croydon, CR0 4YY

A CIP record for this book is available from the British Library

ISBN 978 1 4744 0292 7 (hardback)
ISBN 978 1 4744 3262 7 (paperback)
ISBN 978 1 4744 0293 4 (webready PDF)
ISBN 978 1 4744 1760 0 (epub)

Contents

Acknowledgements

In 2009 I was delighted to be invited by the English Department of the University of Newcastle to give the Newcastle Poetry Lectures. The lectures themselves were published in 2011 by Bloodaxe Books as *Music Lessons: The Newcastle Poetry Lectures*. I was and am hugely grateful to the university team, especially Professor Sean O'Brien, for this invitation; and to Bloodaxe Books for publishing the lectures but letting me retain copyright. This book expands the three original lectures; substantial portions of each remain in the present text. I haven't wilfully paraphrased where to do so would make something less clear, though even passages which appear close to verbatim have in many cases been slightly altered. However, this process of enlargement has produced a study that's not only arranged radically differently and approaching four times the original's length, but also represents my subsequent thinking on this topic. I no longer have the same things to say!

Grateful acknowledgement is made to all the authors and publishers of copyright material that appears in this book, and particularly to the following for permission to reprint material from the sources indicated:

BLOODAXE: extracts from *Crossing the Snowline* by Pauline Stainer (Bloodaxe, 2008), from *No Truce with the Furies* by R. S. Thomas (Bloodaxe, 1995), from *New Collected Poems* by Tomas Tranströmer (Bloodaxe, 2011) and from *Airmail* edited by Thomas R. Smith (Bloodaxe, 2013).

BOOSEY & HAWKES: extract from 'Come Out' by Steve Reich, © 1987 by Hendon Music, Inc, reproduced by permission of Boosey & Hawkes Music Publishers Ltd.

CAMERON & HOLLIS: extract from *Ceri Richards* by Mel Gooding (Cameron & Hollis, 2002) by permission of the publisher cameronandhollis.uk

CARCANET: extracts from *Object Lessons* by Eavan Boland (Carcanet, 1990), from *Articulate Energy and Purity of Diction in English Verse* by Donald Davie (Carcanet, 2006), from *Overlord* by Jorie Graham (Carcanet, 2005) and from *The Figured Wheel* by Robert Pinsky (Carcanet, 1996).

COLUMBIA UNIVERSITY PRESS: extract from *Revolution in Poetic Language* by Julia Kristeva, translated by Margaret Waller (Columbia University Press, 1984).

ENITHARMON PRESS and THE ESTATE OF U. A. FANTHORPE: extracts from *Selected Poems* (Enitharmon Press, 2014) *New and Collected Poems* (Enitharmon Press, 2015).

FARRAR, STRAUS AND GIROUX: extract from *Collected Poems* by Robert Lowell (Farrar, Straus and Giroux, 2007).

GWYNETH LEWIS: extract from *A Hospital Odyssey* by Gwyneth Lewis (Bloodaxe, 2010).

JOHN WILEY & SONS: extracts from *The Production of Space* by Henri Lefebvre, translated by Donald Nicholson-Smith (Blackwell, 1991) and *Philosophical Investigations* by Ludwig Wittgenstein translated by G. E. M. Anscombe (Wiley, 2009).

LUND HUMPHRIES: extract from *Art and Objecthood* by Michael Fried (Lund Humphries, 1998).

THE PROVOST AND SCHOLARS OF KINGS COLLEGE, CAMBRIDGE and THE SOCIETY OF AUTHORS AS THE E. M. FORSTER ESTATE: extract from *Howard's End* by E. M. Forster (Penguin, 1941).

NOVELLO & COMPANY: extract from 'The Dream of Gerontius Op. 38' by Edward Elgar, © Copyright 2006 Novello & Company Limited. All Rights Reserved. International Copyright Secured. Printed by permission of Novello & Company Ltd.

THAMES & HUDSON, LONDON: extract from *Mahler: His Life, Work and World* by Kurt Blaukopf and Herta Blaukopf (Thames & Hudson, © 1991).

THE POETRY SOCIETY: extracts from 'Hard Beautiful Truths' by Jay Parini (*Poetry Review* 96: 4) and interview with Anne Stevenson (*Poetry Review* 99: 4).

THE RANDOM HOUSE GROUP: extract from *Deep Lane* by Mark Doty (Jonathan Cape, 2015), reproduced by permission of The Random House Group Ltd.

VERSO BOOKS: extracts from *In Search of Wagner* by Theodor Adorno, translated by Rodney Livingstone (New Left, 1981) and *Mural* by Mahmoud Darwish, translated by Rema Hammami and John Berger (Verso, 2009).

Finally, I owe a huge debt of gratitude to Peter Salmon, musical explorer, editor, indexer, encourager and permissions-procurer extraordinaire: without whom this book would probably not have been completed, and the time spent on it would certainly not have been so enjoyable.

Introduction:
A Little Conversation

A book like this should start with a disclaimer. At least, that seems to be the convention. Introducing *Musical Elaborations* (1991), a series of lectures in critical theory that he had given at the University of California, Edward W. Said makes clear that his volume 'is meant as neither a contribution to systematic musicology nor a series of literary essays about music as it relates to literature'.[1]

The same could be said of this book which, like Said's, started life as a series of 'three consecutive lectures' given in a non-musicological context, in this case as the University of Newcastle's 2009 Poetry Lectures. On those three evenings I was speaking to an audience defined by their interest in poetry, and our lack of musicological common ground – even, our common lack of musicological ground – was one pole of the discursive space I tried to open up. The attempt was to think about music *on behalf of* poetry.

Also as in the lectures that became Said's *Musical Elaborations*, this created a particular, perhaps unconventional, focus of thought, and has led to the kind of book that transgresses tribal certainties by no means unique to musicologists. Said's Introduction identifies his standpoint as:

> someone who has had much to do with music and who over the years has been thinking about music in many of the same ways made possible by contemporary thought about literature.[2]

His 'much to do with music' had been as a regular music columnist for *The Nation*. He goes on to identify precisely this as one of the most useful standpoints for thinking about music:

> the most interesting, the most valuable, and the most distinguished modern writing about music is, to use Edward Cone's phrase, writing that self-consciously sees itself as a 'humanistic discipline.'[3]

I too am interested in writing that 'sees itself as a humanistic discipline'. Mine, though, is not a book about music per se, and I certainly don't claim it's the best way to think about that artform.

I am, in so many ways, not Edward Said. Unlike him, I'm neither a cultural critic nor a musical *amateur*. In *Elaborations* Said uses the latter term carefully, although also in its conventional sense, to suggest a kind of powerless devotion to 'an onslaught of such refinement, articulation and technique as almost to constitute a sadomasochistic experience'.[4] It's tempting to suggest that he frames the performer–listener relationship in these terms because they are the ones most familiar to him from his pioneering dissection of the cultural power relations of Orientalism.[5] A quarter of a century on, it might make more sense to reverse them. Today's concert artist arguably feels less of a *maestro* than a servant; someone who is expected to deliver reliably, and permitted to perform only the narrowing repertory of 'warhorses' that are considered commercially viable.

Also unlike Edward Said, I'm not trying to re-contextualise our thinking about music in general. I'm assuming no such overarching cultural responsibility. Instead, in this book as in the lectures it grew out of, I'm trying to write, much more simply, from a maker's standpoint. I'm thinking about music and poetry from, and because of, my experience as someone who writes poems, and who also used to be a performing musician. Though my thinking has been painstaking, and I've read widely in my search for answers or at least answering ideas, its origins are in little more than a maker's hunch. I've followed up on that hunch because it was a feeling I recognised; the kind from which, in my experience, the kind of thinking we call writing most fruitfully comes. My process, then, has been as 'makerly' as was its starting point.

That hunch presented itself as something I'd noticed; as an apprehension but not something I understood; and as the kind of 'unease' that, if ignored, becomes more and more distracting. It was also very straightforward. I simply noticed that when I'm giving a poetry reading the experience is similar to that of giving a concert. There's a kind of estrangement from the material I'm performing which is not present in speech or other forms of *telling*. It almost feels as though this material goes at its own pace; as if it goes through its own process, into which I merely fit my actions as a reader.

In *Freedom*, the American novelist Jonathan Franzen, himself no stranger to the reading circuit, captures this experience perfectly:

> The great benefit of touring *Nameless Lake* to death – toward the end, he'd been able to entertain long trains of thought while performing, able to review the band's finances and contemplate the scoring of new drugs and experience remorse about the latest interview without losing the beat or skipping a verse – had been the emptying of all meaning from the lyrics, the permanent severing of his songs from the state of sadness […] in which he'd written them.[6]

I'm not talking, here, about the special occasion of being on stage (although I will in Chapter 12). Unlike Said, I don't believe the shifting mores of Western Classical concert music performance are precisely constitutive of the form; though they are undoubtedly constitutive of its contemporary social role. In any case, most poetry performances are shabby affairs compared to the concert stage. Poetry audiences are usually much smaller even than those for Western art music. A recent trend for complaining that poets read badly is, I suspect, an unconscious recognition of this contextual shabbiness. In fact, in Britain at least, most contemporary poets read rather well. Giving readings is a regular part of their working life, and the one that brings most of those few perks the work attracts: the odd free glass of wine, a fan or two. But fine readings can be occluded by tatty venues, poor sound systems, and excessive informality in the framing occasion (such as the be-jeaned organiser who mumbles and bungles his way through an introduction written, at best, on the back of an envelope). When poets are relocated to the gleaming space of a concert hall – as the Poetry Book Society annually, from 2009 to 2016, placed ten poets shortlisted for the T. S. Eliot Prize on the stage of the Royal Festival

Hall – the professionalism and clarity with which they almost without exception read is apparent to the large audiences these occasions attract.

Despite this, what poets do in a reading just *is* much simpler than what a violinist, say, must do in a recital. The poet preparing to read and the instrumentalist preparing to give a concert don't share levels of performance anxiety. Poets don't put in hours of rehearsal. Even the very few poets who 'read' from memory are brought up short against the limits of their occasion: performing from memory is, in a sense, *all* they can do.[7]

Nevertheless, a 'good' reading clearly is something different from, say, the mechanised announcement we hear on a railway station platform. There must be some minimal but sufficient element of interpretation in a reading, just as there is in every human speech act. When James Alexander Gordon, whose reading of the football results for the BBC was a British weekly institution, retired in 2013, much fond comment remarked that one knew directly who had won from the way he inflected the first team's name. And one way to describe my original hunch about a relationship between music and poetry would be to say that I noticed myself making such interpretive gestures – inflecting my voice upward, or observing the end of a breath as marked by a comma or a line-break – with the same detachment as that with which I had been able to observe myself playing in concerts. I did not feel that I was *talking with* the audience, but that I was *delivering a text to* them. The words I was uttering weren't what I was thinking, what Said calls my 'intimate' experiences of pleasure and of my own thoughts. They were a familiar, pre-existing piece of writing. In reading them out I wasn't 'being myself', or *telling* the audience anything: even though the poems themselves were sometimes confessional.

On one level, this shows no more than that performance is a special way of going on. Though it may have aspects of spontaneity, it's an occasion when the self – particularly the performer's self – is mediated by what is being performed. That mediation may both curtail and enlarge the range of things I can do; either way, it creates a disjunction with what I do *outside* the context of that piece of music or poetry. As Said says, performance is 'an extreme occasion'.[8]

But I'm not only interested in that extreme occasion, and my hunch also had a second aspect. I felt dimly that this *going on in its own way*, that poetry turns out to share with music in performance, was connected with other qualities both genres share. These qualities, I felt, had more to do with technical, makerly concerns than with types and occasions of performance. They were more concerned with something intrinsic to how music and poetry are structured than simply with the giving and receiving of a particular experience.

I was, though, troubled by aspects of that experience: specifically by ideas about pleasure. Much thinking about both poetry and music suffers from the way in which each popularly uses the other as a term of aesthetic approbation. A 'poetic' musical passage, or a 'musical' passage of verse, is just one that the speaker considers beautiful. This sort of vague, implied-consensual epithet doesn't ask questions, as I wish to do. As a statement of received opinion and previous experience, it is of little use in trying to make something new.

Igor Stravinsky puts this a little more sternly at the opening of his *Poetics of Music* (1970):

> it is no secret to any of you that the exact meaning of poetics is the study of work to be done. The verb *poiein* from which the word is derived means nothing else but *to do* or *make*. The poetics of the classical philosophers did not consist of lyrical dissertations about natural talent and about the essence of beauty. [...] The poetics of music is exactly what I am going to talk to you about; that is to say, I shall talk about *making* in the field of music.[9]

Stravinsky's book, too, started life as a series of lectures given in an un-musicological context, as the Charles Eliot Norton Lectures on Poetry at Harvard University. They were delivered in 1939–40, fifty years earlier than Said's California lectures, and so lack the latter's critical theoretical context. Nevertheless, they too look at music in what we might call a meta-textual way. Stravinsky makes this clear when he locates his work in a period of 'profound changes [...] not [...] in the domain of aesthetics or on the level of modes of expression' but at the level of 'both the basic values and the primordial elements of the art of music'.[10]

Both Said's and Stravinsky's studies mean that some of the

terms in which I might think about (or, as Martin Heidegger would doubtless say, 'towards') music from a literary context are not entirely without precedent. Stravinsky's 'basic values and primordial elements' seem the kind of rough-hewn and even deliberately naïve terms that might apply to the commonality between music and poetry that my hunch dimly apprehended. Encouraged by these fellow-travellers, I began to think about poetry not *as* music, but *as if it were* music. This required a kind of squint. I had deliberately *not to see* the denotative aspects of poetry – in other words, what the words *mean* – in order to allow other aspects of the form to come to the fore. My suspicion was that these are the very aspects that *constitute* the form.

Initially, then, I returned to ways in which I'd first thought about poetry: as something performing a particular discursive role. In the first years of this millennium, I wanted to articulate what was then my practice. I was working on poetry with users of healthcare services. It seemed to me that, regardless of the quality of what they produced qua verse, the seriousness with which these service users read poetry and the way they rose to its occasions in attempting to *make* something, rather than simply express what they were feeling, were genuinely of a piece with the poetic project. Listening, writing and discussing in hospital day rooms, Occupational Therapy units or simply in bed, these participants allowed poetry to go on *as* poetry.[11] They didn't reduce it to entertainment; nor compromise on its more challenging elements, such as unusual vocabulary or the ideas that came out of their own highly charged experiences. Nor did service users view what they said and wrote as mere 'symptoms' of conditions they were experiencing. Unlike paintings produced in an art therapy session, their own writing, and their reactions to poems, were *actions* which they experienced as voluntary and voluntarily-shaped.

Poetry's need for discursive intactness, its need to do *being poetry*, seems to be summed up by Robert Frost's much-quoted idea that poetry is 'what's lost in translation'.[12] However, as I became interested in translation myself, I began to stretch this definition. Another paradigm for my practice and thinking was co-translation. Ideally, this takes the form of a collaboration between the original poet and their poetic peer in what is sometimes called the 'host' language. I wanted to believe in Gayatri

Chravorty Spivak's notion of translation as 'hospitality', and saw best translation practice as a painstaking *re*-discovery of each original poem.[13]

Despite the self-protectiveness of the discourse of poetry as a whole, in other words, it appeared that an individual poem might be something that could go on even without the particular, original words in which it had been written. This seemed paradoxical: surely a poem *is* nowhere else but in the words? But here metaphor came to my aid, resolving paradox into parallelism. I had learnt through my own practice how after translation some poems, particularly those in strict form, were left with very little except the succession of, and the connections between, their ideas.[14] Some poems remained of absorbing interest, even under such conditions: these I thought of as having 'good bones'. The movement of thought – which might not be philosophical but could simply be observational, for example – was the work of the poem that was carried across by translation. So what was carried across was *connection*. As 'Dem Bones', James Weldon Johnson's joyous meme of a Spiritual – and itself a song of translation – reminds us:

Toe bone connected to the foot bone,
Foot bone connected to the heel bone,
Heel bone connected to the shin bone,
Shin bone connected to the knee bone [...][15]

Connection, a form of going on: this seemed to be part of what makes a poem. This reminded me of my sense, when giving a reading, of the poem *taking its own time* regardless of my mental experiences (including reflexive ones, such as worrying about whether the poem was any good).

A poem, then, seemed to have order and a duration. I felt this was very similar to what is most evidently distinctive about music. As Stravinsky says in the second of his *Lessons*, '*sound* and *time*. Music is inconceivable apart from these two elements.'[16] A little later, he goes on: 'Music is a *chronologic* art, painting is a *spatial* art. Music presupposes before all else a certain organisation in time, a chrononomy [*une chrononomie* in the French original] – if you will permit me to use a neologism.'[17] The Marxist art critic John Berger makes a similar distinction between music and painting in *Ways of Seeing*, where – perhaps unsurprisingly – he underlines the consequences of this occupation of *material* space for the ownership of the artforms.[18]

Many aspects of music and also of poetry suggest themselves as examples of Stravinsky's *chrononomie*. Metre, rhythm, sensual experience, connection and even 'making sense' are all part of, and brought about by, *temporal ordering*. As I thought further, I found myself constantly pulled back to the familiar, broadly-technical level of such structural elements. What I 'know', whether about musical cadence or poetic metre, kept obtruding. This pull of practical knowledge was all the stronger because of the risk of looseness inherent in thinking, as I was trying to do, without the support of conventional musicology or literary studies. But in order to discover *what I meant* by my hunch I needed to find analogous ways in which music and poetry work. By definition, these could not be artform specific elements, such as melody, harmony and time-signature in music, or full rhyme and argumentation in poetry. I was looking for forms, common to both, that were both cruder and at the same time more profoundly structural.

For the Newcastle Lectures, which were published in 2011 as *Music Lessons*, I came up with *line, density* and *chromaticism*.[19] The chapters that follow will unpack some of the ways in which I use these terms; there would be no point in repeating such explorations here. Each turned out to be useful in thinking through analogies between music and poetry. Each became dense with material, and that density in turn implied a need for further clarification. So it is that, in Part I of this book, those three terms have become six: time, abstract form, line, chromaticism, density and meaning. In Part II, I've approached the idea that examples are key to this kind of enquiry from another direction. There, I look in turn at song, opera, strict form, innovation and the role of the audience.

This chance to revisit earlier exploration brings with it the opportunity to be much more detailed – and so, perhaps, precise – than I formerly had space to be. It also represents my further thinking on the topic. What it certainly is not is any kind of last word. This book is an *essay*, a thought experiment. It tests out the premise that there could be common ground between music and poetry and asks how, if it exists, such commonality might work.

Nor am I claiming to write as a historian. For example, I'm not interested in reconstructing musical prehistory; though of course I'm glad that others are. I'm thinking only from the narrow, particular ground of my own experience. My book is almost entirely concerned with Western art music and contemporary or near-contemporary Western, if not always Anglophone, poetry. This is not because I believe these are the only, or the most significant, forms of music and verse in the world today. It is, first, because they are the grounds of my own experience; the fields in which I have received what might be called a professional formation. My profound pleasure in Arabic music, my somewhat more ephemeral but equally whole-hearted enjoyment of torch song, float uneasily on a lack of real knowledge. I could no more write with precision about these genres than I could about origami or tossing the caber. But there's also a second reason for my field of focus; one with which some contemporary poets might be uneasy. Western art music and Western literary poetry are equivalent forms. Slim volumes published by Faber & Faber are *not* the equivalent of street sounds from the urban ghetto, however much their (let's admit it: still often white middle-class male) authors might like them to be. And this is not just because of where the creator of each work 'comes from': it's a matter of the discursive role each plays.

I started this Introduction by talking about 'a book like this'. What kind of book, then, *is* it? One of the things this essay evidently does is touch on more than one artform and, by implication, on the whole infrastructure of reception that surrounds each. In the years when I was thinking about a discursive role for poetry, I discovered the notion of discursive violence. In *The Other Side of Language*, a book which has influenced the whole direction of my thought and practice, the Italian philosopher Gemma Corradi Fiumara talked about how discourses – ways of thinking and writing that know themselves to be specific – compete for territory; that is, over the things they talk and write about and claim to 'know'.[20] Woe betide the book that approaches such demarked territories from other directions – from 'outside'.

I am reasonably certain that neither Edward Said nor Igor

Stravinsky read Corradi Fiumara. Yet each introduces his project with the tremendous caution, and the corresponding clarity, of someone who knows he may be seen as a discursive trespasser. Said addresses this problem directly. A 'professional [...] field', he says, may have 'a corporate or guild consensus to maintain, which sometimes requires keeping things as they are, not admitting new or outlandish ideas, maintaining boundaries and enclosures'.[21]

I too have tried to be careful. I've also tried to write to the grain of what is observable. This project was triggered by observation – by something I *noticed* – and what follows are a series of observations. I hope that is a reasonable enough – and sufficiently small – claim to make for this book. It is, finally, neither a comprehensive survey of the ways in which music and poetry come together, nor an argument for or against a single view of how they might do so. It is not an exhaustive study of opera or a history of song; it isn't encyclopaedic on poetic form or an archaeology of the Orpheus myth. Instead, it maps connections and intersections between the two artforms. These turn out to be numerous, yet often to return to, or go by way of, points already visited elsewhere. The book, then, maps a web rather than a terrain. It is, in effect, a topographical map: the kind we use for railways rather than roads.

At some points, like major interchanges, many lines of enquiry cross. Other starting points and conclusions resemble termini. Repeated cross-references between chapters make these connections transparent, and allow the reader to crosscheck related material. Like all topographical – which is to say conceptual – maps, this one is also simplified. It deliberately uses a limited set of examples and refers to them repeatedly. That isn't because the ideas it explores only have limited application, but to allow clarity in the configuration of ideas. It would be easy to obscure the already complex web of connections between poetry and musical form in succumbing to the temptation to display a superabundance of detailed knowledge: like the train buff who tells you more than you want to know, and in doing so loses your attention completely.

Notes

1. Said's lectures were given as the Wellek Library Lectures at the University of California, Irvine. Edward W. Said, *Musical Elaborations* (London: Chatto & Windus, 1991), p. x.
2. Ibid.
3. Ibid. p. xi.
4. Ibid. p. 3.
5. Edward W. Said, *Orientalism* (New York: Vintage, 1978).
6. Jonathan Franzen, *Freedom* (London: Fourth Estate, 2010), p. 204.
7. In Britain since the millennium, the chief exponents of poetry performance from memory have been Ruth Padel and the late Michael Donaghy; both with links to other disciplines where that art is de rigeur. Michael Donaghy (1954–2004), an Irish-American poet based in London, 'read' from memory as if to assert a continuity between his poetry and the performing of Irish folk music that was also part of his working life. Ruth Padel's awareness of the Classical tradition of the rhapsode stems from her early professional life as a Classicist.
8. 'Performance as an Extreme Occasion' is the title of his first chapter. Said, *Musical Elaborations*, pp. 1–34.
9. Igor Stravinsky, *Poetics of Music in the Form of Six Lessons*, Arthur Knodel and Ingolf Dahl (trans.) (Cambridge, MA: Harvard University Press, 1970), pp. 3 and 5.
10. Ibid. pp. 11 and 13.
11. I looked at this work in, for example: Celia Hunt and Fiona Sampson, *Writing: Self and Reflexivity* (London: Palgrave Macmillan, 2005); Fiona Sampson (ed.), *Creative Writing in Health and Social Care* (London: Jessica Kingsley, 2004); Celia Hunt and Fiona Sampson (eds), *The Self on the Page* (London: Jessica Kingsley, 1998).
12. 'I like to say, guardedly, that I could define poetry this way: It is that which is lost out of both prose and verse in translation. That means something in the way the word are curved and all that – the way the words are taken, the way you take the words.' Robert Frost in Cleanth Brooks and Robert Penn Warren, *Conversations on the Craft of Poetry* (Austin: Holt, Rinehart and Winston, 1961), p. 200.
13. Gayatri Chakravorty Spivak was one of the first to use this term. See her discussion in Gayatri Chakravorty Spivak, 'The Politics of Translation' in Lawrence Venuti (ed.), *The Translation Studies Reader* (London: Routledge, 2000), pp. 397–416.
14. As extensive debate remarks, this problem is peculiarly intense in English. The language, deriving from several roots, is unusually difficult to rhyme; rhyme in an original English poem cannot but direct the thought. To rhyme translations of poetry into English is

therefore almost without exception to distort them. Conversely – though it would be easier to re-*rhyme* an English poem translated into Serbian or Italian, for example – what is often lost in translation out of English is exactitude of register. Those same discrete linguistic roots make English a language rich in synonym, and synonym is made use of – in daily life as well as in literature – to convey much more than mere denotation.

15. James Weldon Johnson, 'Dem Bones'. No recording seems to exist of him singing the spiritual; a 1950 recording by The Harmonaires is one of the earliest extant. https://www.youtube.com/watch?v=GiLrnhcPQrU Retrieved 4/11/15

16. Stravinsky, *Poetics of Music in the Form of Six Lessons*, p. 35.

17. Ibid. pp. 36–7.

18. John Berger, *Ways of Seeing*, Episode 3, Mike Dibb (dir.) (London: BBC TV, 1972).

19. Fiona Sampson, *Music Lessons: The Newcastle Poetry Lectures* (Tarset: Bloodaxe, 2011).

20. Gemma Corradi Fiumara, *The Other Side of Language: A Philosophy of Listening*, Charles Lambert (trans.) (London: Routledge, 1995).

21. Said, *Musical Elaborations*, pp. xii-xiii.

PART I

Chapter 1

About Time

At dusk, the afternoon 'Express' from Bucharest to Budapest travels slowly through Transylvania, on a curving route that allows the passenger who leans out of the window to see the other carriages running ahead and behind across the plain. As it rattles past remote villages, the train starts storks from their nests and startles small boys from the trackside scrub. It's a noisy business. The rolling stock is left over from Cold War days, and the whistle sounds like something from a black-and-white movie.

The region it's passing through seems equally unchanged by the passage of time; though in fact two World Wars, as well as the Cold War, played out on this very territory. It's also where Béla Bartók was born: the part of the Banat currently in Romania, and the source and setting of his 'Evening at the Village', a little piece that I know best in his arrangement for violin and piano (see Fig. 1.1).[1]

'Evening at the Village' uses two folk tunes from this region. It gives each a lightly plangent setting, in which parallel chords descend unexpectedly to suggest melancholy, but also tender reminiscence. (Their originals can be seen in Bartók's hugely evocative collecting notebooks in the Zenetörténeti Múzeum, the Museum of Musical History, in Budapest.)

Bartók's setting evokes far away and long ago, those twin coordinates of time and space. When we were children, all the best stories started this way: 'Once upon a time, in a country far away ...' That tingling sense of excitement with which we used to enter the not-here, not-now, comes back to us as adults in the opening word of Marcel Proust's *À la recherche du temps*

Figure 1.1 Opening bars of Bartók's 'Evening at the Village'

perdu, '*Longtemps* ...', or at the opening of Dylan Thomas's *Under Milkwood*, 'To begin at the beginning ...' It is both the French poet Yves Bonnefoy's *L'arrière pays*, and the English poet A. E. Housman's 'blue remembered hills'.[2] The distance these adult versions of 'Once upon a time' create is also our connection to the stories and worlds they evoke, since it is charged with affect. Longing or excitement, glamour or loss, are invoked in the act of storytelling, which by definition starts elsewhere (not-here, not-now) in order to travel some distance towards the listener.

A journey both separates and connects two points in space and time. Train travel allows us to experience their connectedness in a peculiarly literal, even diagrammatic, way. It's like a story stripped down to the bare *and then* ... *and then* of its chronological succession. The undeviating *next* ... *next* of the railway track; the way we both are and are not *in* the surrounding countryside; the filmic slide of the view from the window; the hypnotic, cumulative rhythm of the train passing over the tracks that lets us know we're moving even if the window blinds are down: all of these make it easy for us to recognise how we move through space. But they also help us to understand the way we move through time.

It's no coincidence that Albert Einstein chose the image of a train passing a railway platform to illustrate his theory of relativity.[3] Linear *connectedness* is – even in Einstein's thought experiment, which situates observers both on the train and on the platform – a key element of time. Einstein's passenger, like the observer on the Bucharest–Budapest Express, is always in the same relation to all the parts of the train, but the bystander on the platform isn't. The train carries its 'own' space and time with it through 'the rest of' space and time.

What it also carries, therefore, is a kind of unifying narrative. In the mid-nineteenth century, it was Railway Time that standardised clocks across the UK. Until 1840, when the Great Western Railway started this process by standardising the times in all its stations, morning and evening in Cornwall kept pace with dawn and dusk in roughly the same way that they did 300 miles to the east – and several minutes earlier – at the Greenwich meridian. After the advent of Railway Time, it was 6am everywhere in Britain at the same moment, regardless of the fact that dawn arrives twenty-eight minutes later in Truro than at the Royal Observatory.

Even today, no matter how tearful the farewell on the platform, after the train is out of sight the railways tracks remain. They make a connection with the departed person, and they are a promise of possible return. When the Lisbon plane, carrying its escapees from Vichy Morocco, disappears into the fog at the end of Michael Curtiz's 1942 film of *Casablanca*, the pathos is the greater because nothing is left behind to link the two cities. Destination and departure point, and hence the story's lovers, are irrevocably separated.[4] The free world seems absolutely other; even, to be otherworldly. In 1933, Virginia Woolf experienced this extreme separation for real at Croydon Airport when she waved her sister and nephew off to Switzerland:

> We stood on the top of the roof; saw the aeroplane whirl, till the propellers were lost to sight – simply evaporated; then the aeroplane takes a slow run, circles and rises. This is death I said, feeling how the human contact was completely severed. Up they went with a sublime air and disappeared like a person dying, the soul going. And we remained.[5]

Forster calls this connective quality of time 'the naked worm'. But he is wrong when he claims, in *Aspects of the Novel*, that the *and then ... and then* of one thing happening after another is a narrative problem.[6] Time is not a purely narrative problem, either in life or within the work of art. It is, first of all, an existential problem, as the philosophers who followed Immanuel Kant argued well into the twentieth century: among them most famously Martin Heidegger in *Being and Time* and *Time and Being*, and Jean-Paul Sartre in *Being and Nothingness*.[7] Their enquiries are beyond the scope of this book; but it's worth bearing in mind the puzzles they pose about how we fit into time, or time fits into us. Certainly, whether or not time can be independent of us, we can't be independent of it. Time is always with us, a part of what we do but so necessary that we often forget about it.

Film-makers like Abbas Kiarostami or Pier Paolo Pasolini reveal this to us when they hold a shot for an unconventionally long time. By refusing filmic conventions that feel 'natural' because familiar, they show us how things *take time* to happen. Near the start of Pasolini's *The Gospel According to St Matthew* (1964) the Virgin Mary, having revealed she's pregnant, watches Joseph walk away along a ruined wall or fortified road running away from us straight across the landscape. This held shot becomes increasingly uncomfortable to watch. We first expect and then will Joseph to do something – anything – to break the tension. And so, of course, does Pasolini's rejected Mary, whose viewpoint the camera is creating.[8]

Aside from the existential, there's also a more immediate, practical reason to resist Forster's idea that time is a purely narrative problem, in other words a problem that occurs only within fiction. It's not only in stories that one thing needs to follow another to 'make sense'. The same problem applies to the organisation of arguments and mathematical proofs, and to the way one idea leads to another in a conversation, a flirtation – or indeed a poem. An order of occurrence is just as fundamental to thought as it is to story. Indeed, it is fundamental to story *because* it's fundamental to thought. After all, story per se isn't concerned with being faithful to what 'really happened'. The story has – as Richard Poirier says in *The Performing Self*, his study of writerly narcissism – 'an utterly moral neutrality'.[9] The author's thousands of tiny calculations 'are designed to serve one another and nothing else', and the resulting fiction is true to itself, rather than to anything (even intention) beyond itself. The novelist's 'naked worm of time' enters the story *because* the story is something thought and told. The storyteller's use of *and then … and then* is not more authentic than the poet's: say, because time also exists outside the story and realism demands that the story capture it. Rather the opposite. Time is an ontological as well as an organisational element of many genres, including both poetry and fiction, (only) because *they themselves* exist in time. It's why the French Oulipo-ian novelist Georges Perec, for example, talks about the need to 'seduce' the reader so that they will read a novel right through to the end.[10]

Being sequential, music and poetry, fiction and films, theatre and dance all take time to 'take place'. But, of these, music and poetry are the least able to dress up their reliance on temporal order as the need to reflect the world's *and then … and then*.[11] They offer us a particularly unmediated encounter with time. 'Music is based on temporal succession and requires alertness of memory', as Stravinsky says: in translation. What he actually says is '*la musique s'établit dans la succession du temps et requiert donc la vigilance de la mémoire*': 'music establishes itself in-and-through the way time goes on, and therefore requires the memory's vigilance.'[12] *La succession du temps* already exists in the world, and is a condition music simply adopts. Or that it adapts: '*s'établir dans*' has a particular sense of settling in, of foundations built upon.

Music needs memory to supervise – almost, to police – itself *because* it builds on these foundations. '*Vigilance*' implies necessity as well as compulsion; it suggests that musical time will collapse unless it's ordered. This sounds a bit like Ludwig Wittgenstein's private language argument. Wittgenstein argues that there can't be a language known only by its inventor, because how could that inventor confirm his or her own way of using that language? Sounds or symbols only become language by being used consistently; something which requires the 'vigilance of a memory' beyond that of the inventor of a language; of a sort of meta-speaker or -memory. In the same way, to compose or listen to a piece of music requires a meta-attention, or memory, beyond the momentary 'ear'. One can't experience a piece of music *as such* at any moment without *both* being aware of the rest of the piece that has led up to this moment *and* keeping hold of the current moment of musical experience for what is to follow.

It's not surprising that Proust would be attracted to this 'memorialising' vision of how to listen to music. In *À l'ombre des jeunes filles en fleurs*, his narrator first encounters the sonata by 'Vinteuil' that is one of the leitmotifs of *À la recherche du temps perdu*:

> even when I had heard the sonata from one end to the other, it remained almost wholly invisible to me, like a monument which distance or mist lets one see only fragments of. Hence the melancholy which accompanies knowing such works, as it does everything that takes place in time.[13]

For Proust the vigilance of memory lasts not only through a single performance, but from performance to performance of the piece, as the listener needs several hearings to understand, and to grow to love, the whole work.

But common sense wants to reject this version of musical experience. After all, we recognise that what we're experiencing is music, even if we lose concentration halfway through the complex second subject or – more concretely still – when we switch the radio on in the middle of a piece. The phrase my husband whistles while he does the washing up is music. When his five-year-old sings a nursery rhyme with half the words and much of the tune missing, we recognise this, too as music; and indeed as verse.

In fact the experience of listening to music is routinely portrayed as the mind wandering; though this might also be because, being essentially unparaphrasable, music itself gives the writer or artist nothing to portray.[14] In *Howard's End*, for example, Forster has Helen Schlegel listening, and not listening, to Beethoven's Fifth Symphony:

> the Andante had begun – very beautiful, but bearing a family likeness to all the other beautiful andantes that Beethoven had written, and, to Helen's mind, rather disconnecting the heroes and shipwrecks of the first movement from the heroes and goblins of the third. She heard the tune through once, and then her attention wandered, and she gazed at the audience, or the organ, or the architecture. Much did she censure the attenuated Cupids who encircle the ceiling of the Queen's Hall, inclining each to each with vapid gesture, and clad in sallow pantaloons, on which the October sunlight struck. 'How awful to marry a man like those Cupids!' thought Helen. Here Beethoven started decorating his tune, so she heard him through once more, and then smiled at her cousin Frieda.[15]

A symphony is not a short piece and this is just about one sixth of the space Forster devotes to Helen's daydream. Groucho Marx is altogether more succinct. In *Horse Feathers* (1932), when Chico strikes up on the piano, Groucho addresses the camera: 'I've gotta stay here, but there's no reason why you folks shouldn't go out into the lobby till this thing blows over.'[16]

However in each circumstance, whether fragmentary or not, our knowledge of music's connectedness is part of what allows us to *have* this experience of it. We take on trust the implied musical *before* and *after*. Helen Schlegel's stream of thought relies on her knowledge that the music will carry on while she returns to the symphony, drifts into reflection, and then returns to it once more ('Here Beethoven started decorating his tune, so she heard him through once more'). Relatedly, I recognise a piece the radio tunes into because I've heard it before and I know *how it goes*.

Something of this understanding of music's essential connectedness is revealed in the way we use the verb *follow* to mean *listen to* a piece. *Follow* names the *and then ... and then* of musical experience. Other terms in common use reveal the complexity, and ambivalence, of the human relationship with time in general. Digital film-maker Richard Misek isn't the first to remind us that we frame the time we *spend* in terms of our mortality: we talk of *killing* time, or being bored *to death*.[17] The temporal nature of music (and poetry) is thus an ambiguous good. Our knowledge that it is going on is both reassuring – it promises a temporal space on which we can rely in order to daydream, for example – and threatening. It *takes time*.

'Takes' is a verb that seems to want to be transitive. But we already know that it's from *us* that time is taken. In *As You Like It*, William Shakespeare has his disguised heroine Rosalind claim that the human relationship to time changes according to circumstance:

> Time travels in diverse paces with diverse persons. I'll tell you who time ambles withal, who time trots withal, who time gallops withal, and who he stands still withal.[18]

And, since she's showing off to Orlando, she proceeds to virtuoso exposition. But what changes in her examples is only the *experience of* time. What remains unchanged – in fact what causes those very experiences: that time drags, or that it's 'running away with' us – is the involuntary, and total, nature of our relationship with it. Time does indeed 'drive' us, and not we it. That we're situated within time, which both permits and limits our existence, is true of everything material of course, whether it's man-made or part of the natural world. But the human problem is that we're *aware* of our own temporal limit.

This trouble with time certainly crops up at poetry readings. Sean O'Brien's 'Welcome, Major Poet!' is very funny about the *longueurs* that poetic egos create:

> We have sat here in too many poetry readings
> Wearing the liberal rictus and cursing our folly,
> Watching the lightbulbs die and the curtains rot
> And the last flies departing for Scunthorpe.
> [...] Here it comes,
> Any century now, the dread declaration:
> *And next I shall read something longer.* Please
> Rip out our nails and accept your applause!

Stretch-limo back to the Ritz and ring home:
Bore the arse off your nearest and dearest instead,
Supposing they haven't divorced you already
Or selfishly put themselves under a train.[19]

But boredom, and its milder-mannered sister the lapse in attention, are about much more than aesthetic choice. They are, at some level, about choice itself. There's an asymmetry between the time and space of human experience. Social shame may not stop an audience member from walking out of a performance, but if he or she does go, he (or she) won't 'have' the whole piece.

To put this another way, it's hard to imagine being bored by a painting – because the viewer can simply *move away*.[20] He can do so because the visual artwork exists in its entirety in every moment. The viewer retains control of his time, and so of his experience. (Children don't, which is why they get bored in art galleries – also, interestingly, on journeys. The child in the back seat doesn't 'go' somewhere in the same way as her parent who is driving; she has no spatial *or* temporal agency. 'Are we nearly there?' is a cry of powerlessness.) In principle, the adult in the gallery could give no more than a cursory glance, and the entire artwork would be present to him. Even an object too large to be viewed all at once, such as an architectural monument, imposes no temporal tyranny on him, because he can walk round it at his own speed and in the order he chooses.

Music and poetry disrupt this freedom of experience. We feel that boredom, or moments of inattention, are imposed upon us by the piece or poem we're listening to. In fact, of course, these experiences are responses: something *we* do. With boredom we protest our lack of control over our own time; of which the very worst manifestation is our own mortality. The stakes for music and poetry, those forms that *take our time* without the alibi of narrative, are particularly high because they are exposed, as we noted in the Introduction. They bring us back to that train journey with which this chapter opened. Travel seems to resolve those two existential dimensions, time and space, by unifying them. (Thus the central contention of Bruce Chatwin's 1987 novel-essay, *The Songlines*, that travel soothes us.[21]) So perhaps it's no coincidence that we're often most acutely aware of being trapped by time as we wait *to* travel. Heidegger even sets some of the roughly one hundred pages of *Fundamental Concepts of Metaphysics* that he devotes to the ontology of boredom in a provincial railway station.[22]

Music and poetry have a relationship with the time they themselves take. Paintings, sculpture and buildings don't, generally speaking, *know* they're going to be degraded by the actions of time.[23] But – like road maps, or railway timetables – musical scores and written poems are plans for particular passages of, or in, time. The relationship both genres have to their temporal limits is reflexive. It's also formal. The elements from which they're built – strict metre, time-signature, the proportions of the whole – 'count backwards' from their end as well as from their opening. Because they are not, except in the case of 'applied music' like film and ballet scores, in hock to external material but work upon themselves, their duration – like other aspects of their form – becomes an affair of internal necessities. The opening two chords of a symphony are enough to create and limit its entire harmonic world; where it can 'go'. Formal integrity allows us to predict from its first word where (if not quite how) a sonnet will end. If I miss the opening of either work, I don't know what I'm hearing because I don't know *where I am in* it – unless, of course, I already know 'how it goes'.[24]

But surely musical scores and pages of poetry can simply be *seen*? Don't they then work in the same way as visual art? Doesn't all this talk of time as one of their ontological dimensions simply confuse the particular *occasion* of public performance with the artform itself? After all, most experiences of poetry, at least of literary verse in the West today, are those had by the private reader. Why does Theodor Adorno write dismissively, in his *Philosophy of Modern Music*, that: 'Music which has not been heard falls into time like an impotent bullet'?[25] Why, ten years earlier, should Igor Stravinsky insist that 'music is inconceivable apart from' '*sound* and *time*'?[26] Why must the British Modernist poet Basil Bunting argue that:

> Poetry lies dead on the page until some voice brings it to life, just as music on the stave, is no more than instructions to the player. A skilled musician can imagine the sound, more or less, and a skilled reader can try to hear, mentally, what his eyes see in print: but nothing will satisfy either of them till his ears hear it as real sound in the air.[27]

We can find the answer to both questions in Stravinsky's phrase, 'inconceivable apart from'. In the lecture-essay *On Modern Art*, with which he introduced a 1924 exhibition of contemporary art (including some of his own work), Paul Klee identifies the chronologic quality of language, remarking on its 'deficiencies of a temporal nature'.[28] Language is at a disadvantage, he says, because it can't be simultaneous like visual art. We *have* to 'have' it sequentially. Admittedly Klee is making certain assumptions about language functioning *as* language rather than, for example, as a textual found object, as white noise, or in any other way that borrows some but not all linguistic phenomena. He assumes its communicative function, and therefore that the sounds used for that communication must follow each other, in the order used for such communication. This book shares Klee's assumptions. And so we find that even a barked monosyllable like *Stop!* has a sound *sequence*. It's not, for example, *Tops*. Or *Pots*. A terrific contrary illustration of the importance of such a sequence is Steve Reich's *Come Out*, which in progressively decontextualising its title phrase from a public statement on his wounding by one of the Harlem Six – 'I had to, like, open the bruise up, and let some of the bruise blood come out to show them' – and eventually even from grammatical communication brings it to the point of incomprehensibility.[29]

This sequential element is always key, whether I read verse 'to myself' from the page, or a musician reads a score (with or without her instrument), or someone remembers a poem or a piece of music. To read a poem on the page *is* to read it line by line. A musical phrase, remembered, *plays through* in the mind's ear. (Not least in the torturous case of earworms.[30]) We can test out the intrinsically temporal nature of both artforms for ourselves by asking what it would mean to experience music or poetry, whether silently or out loud, without time. A kind of conceptual and temporal black hole, in which the whole of *Parsifal* or *Gilgamesh* was fantastically crushed into simultaneity? An instant – no, a nanosecond – no, not even that – of incomprehensible discord? It is, as Stravinsky says, '*inimaginable*'.

So it's 'time' now to be a little more specific about some of the ways in which the 'chronologic' of music and poetry manifests

Figure 1.2 Excerpt from score of Bach's Chorale BWV4

itself. Music students often begin by thinking about Johann
Sebastian Bach's Chorales. These short pieces appear metrically
unadventurous; characterised by heftily columnar progressions.
Hymn-like – sometimes sung, sometimes instrumental – they
can sound undemonstrative, even impenetrable, to the young
ear they're often used to train. Their texts tend to draw the kind
of general conclusions ('Thy will be done', 'In Thee we trust')
that can only be filled with meaning by particular, personal processes – for example, a struggle to understand, or be reconciled
to something – involved in *getting to the Amen*.

There can be no spiritual shortcuts, these words and their settings instruct us. Were a rehearsal room door to swing open for
a moment, or the radio briefly to tune past, we might hear an
isolated, complex chord, but we would miss its 'meaning'. For,
while the Chorales perform a series of in-fact-astonishing tensions and syntheses, we have to follow or sing *through* these
progressions in order to 'hear' them. For example, in *Christ lag
in Todesbanden* BWV 4, an Easter Chorale on Luther's words
which is also the basis of a Cantata, the ambivalence with which
the Christian contemplates Good Friday – Christ, crucified and
'lying bound by death', is not yet resurrected: on the other hand,
he *will be* – is tellingly portrayed by a queasy oscillation between
major and minor. Only faith, at this stage, can secure the closing
tierce de Picardie, that sideways slip from a minor into a major
chord to create the resolution that *by definition* sounds unearned
wherever it occurs (see Fig. 1.2).[31]

The *tierce de Picardie* is a disruption of what has gone before;
an irruption of something non-intrinsic into its musical world; a

deliberate incoherence. Like the cavalry appearing at the eleventh hour, or the tremendous coincidence in the movie's closing scene, it's a trope that expresses hope or transcendence; in Bach's Chorales, it is literally a *deus ex machina*. By contrast 'Gute Nacht', the first song from Franz Schubert's *Winterreise* D911, uses the lateral step into the major as a kind of uncanniness, a lurch into the pathos of imagined tenderness that brings both the music and the unattainable beloved too close for comfort.[32] Hope, the cadence shows us, is painful just because it is immediate.

Musical sense, then, is created horizontally, through the kinds of musical-grammatical *successions* which are every bit as formative in serialism, or in traditional music, as they are in the Western Classical harmonic tradition. Music *is* one thing leading to another; without such connection it's no more than a car alarm, a squeaking wheel, something shouted at a particular pitch. The same holds true for language, thinking about which too often suffers from St Augustine's model of words as a series of labels for things we experience. In the famous passage from Augustine's *Confessions* I, 8:

> When they (my elders) named some object, and accordingly moved towards something, I saw this and grasped that the thing was called by the sound they uttered when they meant to point it out.[33]

Bach's Chorales showed us that prayer is a process that must be *gone through*. And this is true of every form of thought for, as Jonathan Miller has said, 'Language is successive.'[34] Still, Bach's working out of the individual struggle with God does have *particular* analogies with the very varied poetries that attempt something similar to prayer: from the seventeenth-century Metaphysical poetry of George Herbert and Thomas Traherne to Herbert Lomas's late twentieth-century *Letters in the Dark* or even Donald Hall's struggle to come to terms with the death of his wife – the poet Jane Kenyon – published as *The Painted Bed* in 2003.[35] Gerard Manley Hopkins's 'Terrible Sonnets' of the 1880s even adopt a 'horizontal harmonic' strategy, a kind of tonal exchange all their own. In 'Carrion Comfort', a word order that wrenches itself away from convention doesn't interrupt, but rather intensifies, lament:

Not, I'll not, carrion comfort, Despair, not feast on thee;
Not untwist – slack they may be – these last strands of man
In me ór, most weary, cry *I can no more*. I can;
Can something, hope, wish day come, not choose not to be.[36]

The three *nots* of this first line, passing through a double nega-
tive *and beyond*, include the very first word, which refuses the
conventional 'No –' and by that refusal amplifies itself, its *ot*
catching and tangling with 'carrion com*fort*'. Reprised in the
fourth line, however, these *nots* settle back to a double nega-
tive – and they resist suicide in the barest of terms. Among many
other sound sensations crammed into these rhymed, seven-
stressed lines are repeated lips-shut *m*s and exclamatory zero
*o*s, which don't just mimic the sudden speechlessness of 'shock
and awe', but repeatedly open and shut the vowel-music of the
poem, so that we experience each word – and realisation – not
as fluent but as paradoxically gained from whatever came before
it: silence, incomprehension, the absence of God.

The notion of chronologic meaning-making might almost be
better served by a diagram than by discussion, since such discussion must necessarily superimpose a second layer of linguistic
ordering on the idea itself. In his 1999 essay *Wallflowers*, the
Irish-American poet Michael Donaghy evokes a kinship between
poetry and dancing, which he sees as choreographing space – the
dance-hall floor – rather than as individual self-expression. For
Donaghy, it's the pedi-script *outlining* the dance, rather than
dancing *itself*, which provides a way to think about abstract
form.[37] This 'diagram', like 'the unconscious effect of form', is a
kind of 'frame or scaffolding', 'really no different from the
compass and map of our own expectations as readers'. In short,
we might add, it is just like the poem on the page, or the musical
score. It is a 'map' of the poem, the music or the dance, even
though it is not that poem or music itself. Donaghy gives the
example of fellow-American James Merrill's use of the couplet
form. He suggests it is so internalised that Ephraim, Merrill's
Ouija board 'author', is able to adopt the form for 'his' dictation
in the three-volume dream-narrative *The Changing Light at
Sandover*.[38] (Of course, this begs any number of questions about
what 'spirit writing' itself *is*.)

The forms that exist in the diagram or explanation also exist within the piece itself, of course. The ratio that measures a piece is also *in* the piece; indeed, it *is* the piece. But perhaps Donaghy's idea is so attractive nevertheless because our eye-bound, screen-led culture finds it easier to conceptualise abstract form as an attribute of space than of time. From visits to historic mansions to TV home make-over programmes, we've been trained in the satisfactions of visual abstraction: tall spikey plants look good behind something massy, windows affect the feel of a room, and so on. We even manage, despite the British cantankerousness around Modernism, to see beauty, or at least character beyond utility, in Gateshead's Sage Centre, or the view across London's Millennium Bridge to the cupcake of St Pauls. So when the twentieth-century French philosopher Henri Lefebvre, attempting to reconcile 'mental' and 'real' space, claims that: 'A spatial work (monument or architectural project) attains a complexity fundamentally different from the complexity of a text, whether prose or poetry. [... W]hat we are concerned with here is not texts but texture', he is forgetting that the poem *is* not a block of marks on a page, but a chronologic entity.[39]

Space and time work in analogous ways. Two centuries earlier, in calling architecture 'frozen music', Johann Wolfgang von Goethe was rearticulating an idea that already had a long history.[40] Plato, Plotinus, Augustine, and Aquinas all suggest that the same ratios necessarily please both eye and ear. The Renaissance architect Leon Battista Alberti said, 'I conclude that the same numbers by means of which the agreement of sounds affect our ears with delight are the very same which please our eyes and our minds.'[41] A century later, Andrea Palladio used 'musical' ratios to give his buildings *harmonious* proportions. Since the eighteenth-century Palladian style is named for his neo-Classicism, it's no surprise to find the golden section, apparent in so much of that architecture, underpinning harmoniousness in music as well as buildings. The golden section's proportional division is such that the ratio between the small and large quantities is the same as that between the larger quantity and the whole: approximately equal to 1.6180339887. Consecutive numbers in the Fibonacci sequence roughly mimic the golden section, becoming more accurate as the series progresses: 0, 1, 1, 2, 3, 5, 8, 13, 21, 34, 55, 89, 144, 233, 377, 610, 987, 1597 and so on.[42] The frequency with which the 1 to 1.62

ratio recurs throughout the Classical repertoire suggests that it is so ubiquitous, so culturally powerful, that it has become significant for that reason, even if for no other. It offers the listener a sensation of familiarity, something like a sense of understanding, of 'homeliness'.

For the classically trained violinist, the 'home' form is the sonata, which dominates Classical and Romantic repertoire. Early in his or her musical formation, this structure (not itself far from the golden section in its proportions) introduces as axiomatic the principle that it is *musical materials*, and the relations between them, that generate music. You can't have the whole piece without the opening material. Sonata form works itself out. Two pieces of thematic material, or subjects, are first given in distinct but related keys, then worked over, leading eventually to a restatement in which both are now in the same key, that of the first subject. Since perfect pitch suggests there is no such thing as real transposition, this means that the second subject has undergone a transformation of *character* as well as pitch. 'Words move, music moves, / Only in time'[43] as T. S. Eliot said, in *Burnt Norton*. Given Modernism's own sense of the text as material to be worked with, and to work itself out, it's perhaps no coincidence that Eliot takes on the exploded sonata form of the late Beethoven quartets, while Basil Bunting's 'Sonatas', including *Briggflatts*, are based on early sonata form. Ezra Pound described James Joyce's *Ulysses* as a sonata, while Louis Zukovsky's *A* goes straight to the principle at the heart of sonata form by taking Bach's forms and medieval song and using them *developmentally*.

In Chapter 12 we'll turn to the idea of performance, and look at what the time-dependent nature of music and poetry entails for the *occasions* of their chronologic way of being. In other words, we'll ask *when* and *how* music and poetry happen. As yet, though, we've come no further than noting that they happen in and through time, just as human thought and lives do: just, indeed, as railway journeys do. In the next chapters, we'll look in a little more detail at *what* happens when music and poetry occur; and at the further elements these two genres have in common.

Notes

1. Béla Bartók, 'Evening at the Village', BB 103 n 1. http://www.everynote.com/piano.show/127249.note. Retrieved 25/5/15.
2. Marcel Proust, *À la recherche du temps perdu* [1913–27] (Paris: Soleil, 2011). Dylan Thomas, *Under Milk Wood* [1954] (London: Weidenfeld & Nicolson, 2014). Yves Bonnefoy *L'arrière pays*, Stephen Romer (trans.) (Chicago: University of Chicago Press, 2012). A. E. Housman, 'The Land of Lost Content' in *A Shropshire Lad* [1896] (London: Hesperus, 2008), p. 52.
3. Unlike the railway's 'pure' *and then ... and then*, a boat drawing away from a dock moves sideways as well as forwards. Road traffic makes all sorts of disruptive manoeuvres – such as turning at junctions, giving way, even overtaking. Albert Einstein, *Relativity: The Special and General Theory*, [1917] John Gahan (ed.) (Charleston, SC: CreateSpace Independent Publishing Platform, 2014).
4. *Casablanca*, Michael Curtiz (dir.) (Burbank: Warner Bros, 1942).
5. Sunday 12 November 1933 in Virginia Woolf, *Selected Diaries*, Anne Olivier Bell (abridged and ed.) (London: Vintage Books, 2008), p. 344.
6. E. M. Forster, *Aspects of the Novel* (London: Edward Arnold, 1927).
7. Martin Heidegger, *Being and Time*, John Macquarrie and Edward Robinson (trans.) (Oxford: Blackwell, 1962). Martin Heidegger, *Time and Being*, Joan Stambaugh (trans.) (New York: Harper & Row, 1972). Jean-Paul Sartre, *Being and Nothingness*, Hazel E. Barnes (trans.) (London: Routledge, 1989).
8. Pier Paolo Pasolini, *The Gospel According to St Matthew* (Rome: Titanus Distribuzione s.p.a., 1964).
9. Richard Poirier, *The Performing Self: Compositions and Decompositions in the Languages of Contemporary Life* (New York: Oxford University Press, 1971), p. 87.
10. Georges Perec, interviewed by Kaye Mortley (Ultimo, Australia: Australian Broadcasting Corporation, 1981. Remastered by France Culture.) http://www.franceculture.fr/emissions/les-passagers-de-la-nuit-seine-saint-denis-1/vendredi-hors-serie-27-perec-english-what-man. Retrieved 21/12/15.
11. Contemporary dance is often non-narrative too. But as it is almost always set to music, in this book I assume that music 'speaks for' dance.
12. Igor Stravinsky, *Poetics of Music in the Form of Six Lessons*, Arthur Knodel and Ingolf Dahl (trans.) (Cambridge, MA: Harvard University Press, 1970), pp. 37 and 36.
13. My translation. 'Mais bien plus, même quand j'eus écouté la sonate d'un bout à l'autre, elle me resta presque tout entière invisible, comme un monument dont la distance ou la brume ne laissent apercevoir que de faibles parties. De là, la mélancolie qui s'attache

à la connaissance de tels ouvrages, comme de tout ce qui se réalise dans le temps.' http://www.ibibliotheque.fr/a-l-ombre-des-jeunes-filles-en-fleurs-marcel-proust-pro_ombre/lecture-integrale/page61. Retrieved 21/12/15.

14. Something I return to in Chapter 12.

15. E. M. Forster, *Howards End* (Penguin: Harmondsworth, 1941), pp. 24–5.

16. The Marx Brothers, *Horse Feathers*, Norman Z. Macleod (dir.) (Hollywood: Paramount Pictures, 1932).

17. Richard Misek, 'Dead Time: Cinema, Heidegger and Boredom'. http://kar.kent.ac.uk/35712/1/Misek%20-%20Dead%20 Time%20.pdf. Retrieved 27/1/16.

18. William Shakespeare, *As You Like It*, III, ii, 280–4 in *The Complete Works*, Peter Alexander (ed.) (London and Glasgow: Collins, 1971).

19. Sean O'Brien, 'Welcome, Major Poet!' in *Collected Poems* (London: Picador, 2012), p. 209.

20. He can leave the picture in the next room while he's not looking at it. Bishop Berkeley (and Schrödinger) aside, that picture continues to *be* in just the same way as when he was.

21. The book was a sensation not least because its essayistic reflections were a new kind of 'novel'. Bruce Chatwin, *Songlines* (London: Franklin Press, 1987).

22. Martin Heidegger, *Fundamental Concepts of Metaphysics: World, Finitude, Solitude*, William McNeill and Nicholas Walker (trans.) (Bloomington, IN: Indiana University Press, 2001).

23. Of course there are exceptions, particularly in environmental art, which use the effects of time as an additional dimension of, or at least element in, the work.

24. The same is not the case in, for example, the text on this page, which might turn out to be a paper of 5,000, a chapter of 8,000 or a book of 80,000 words, with no particular change in texture.

25. Theodor Adorno, *Philosophy of Modern Music*, Anne G. Mitchell and Wesley V. Blomster (trans.) (New York: Seabury Press, 1973), p. 133.

26. Stravinsky, *Poetics of Music in the Form of Six Lessons*, p. 35.

27. Basil Bunting, 'The Poet's Point of View', in *Briggflatts* (Tarset: Bloodaxe, 2009), p. 42.

28. Paul Klee, *On Modern Art* (London: Faber, 1948), p. 15.

29. Written for a benefit concert to help fund the retrial of the Harlem Six, convicted after the 1964 Harlem Riots of a murder only one of them committed. Steve Reich, *Come Out* (1966), https://www.youtube.com/watch?v=g0WVh1D0N50. Retrieved 4/11/15.

30. See also Chapter 12.

31. https://en.wikipedia.org/wiki/Christ_lag_in_Todes_Banden,_BWV_4#/media/File:Christ_lag_in_Todesbanden.JPG. Retrieved 2/1/16.

32. Ian Bostridge, *Schubert's Winter Journey* (London: Faber, 2015). Bostridge talks about the 'fragility' of this *too-good-to-be-true*.
33. It was made famous by Ludwig Wittgenstein, who took it as the starting point of his *Philosophical Investigations*. Ludwig Wittgenstein, *Philosophical Investigations*, G. E. M. Anscombe (trans.) (Oxford: Basil Blackwell, 1989).
34. In a recent BBC Radio 4 interview.
35. Herbert Lomas, *Letters in the Dark* (Oxford: Oxford University Press, 1986). Donald Hall, *The Painted Bed* (Boston: Mariner Books, 2003).
36. Gerard Manley Hopkins, *Poems and Prose*, W. H. Gardner (ed.) (Harmondsworth: Penguin, 1979), p. 60.
37. Michael Donaghy, *Wallflowers* (London: Poetry Society, 1999), pp. 17–20.
38. James Merrill, *The Changing Light at Sandover* (New York/London: Knopf/Random House, 2011).
39. Henri Lefebvre, *The Production of Space*, Donald Nicholson-Smith (trans.) (Oxford: Blackwell, 1991), p. 222.
40. 'Baukunst eine erstarrte Musik nenne', the phrase used by Goethe in Johann Peter Eckermann, *Gespräche mit Goethe* (1836), appears earlier in Friederich Wilhelm Joseph Schelling's *Philosophie der Kunst* (1802–3). Johann Peter Eckermann, *Conversations of Goethe with Johann Peter Eckermann*, J. K. Moorhead (ed.), John Oxenford (trans.) (Boston: Da Capo Press, 1998). Friederich Wilhelm Joseph Schelling, *The Philosophy of Art*, Douglas W. Stott (trans.) (Minneapolis: University of Minnesota Press, 1989).
41. Leon Alberti, *On the Art of Building in Ten Books*, Joseph Rykwert, Neil Leach and Robert Tavernor (trans.) (Cambridge MA: MIT Press, 1999), book. IV, ch. 5, p. 305.
42. 'Hidden' or encoded forms seem to be beside the point in thinking about the *experience* of music and poetry. Yet golden section conspiracy theories abound, and involve the usual Modernist suspects. See for example: Erno Lendvai, *Béla Bartók: An Analysis of his Music* (London: Kahn & Averill, 1971). Roy Howat, *Debussy in Proportion: A Musical Analysis* (Cambridge: Cambridge University Press, 1983). Courtney S. Adams, 'Erik Satie and Golden Section Analysis', *Music and Letters*, 77: 2 (Oxford University Press: Oxford, 1996), pp. 242–52.
43. T. S. Eliot, 'Burnt Norton, V' in *Collected Poems 1909–1962* (London: Faber, 1985), p. 194.

Chapter 2

Abstract Form

For a poet, the notion that abstract form – not 'meaning', but pure *shape* – can play a key role in what she writes is seductive. On the one hand, it implies the possibility of developing and experimenting with the kinds of sophisticated formal patterning that we traditionally associate with verse, such as the way stanzas 'chunk' a ballad's story, or a rhyme scheme creates a network of meanings that crisscross and link up within a poem. On the other, it also appeals to something more primitive. For it suggests that poets can – and perhaps even should – do what could best be described as *play*.[1] It implies that they might 'go by feel', making judgements – for example about where to end a piece – that aren't based purely on semantic logic but pay attention to what 'feels right for', or 'works for', the poem.

'What feels balanced' is a non-denotational quality of the text; and this quality is established by our *experience* of that text. 'Balance' is a rhythmic sensation, and it is sensation that is significant here; even if the rhythm that creates it also takes an arithmetical form, such as a regular number of stresses in a line. One example of this is the poem that becomes fourteen lines long because stopping at line thirteen makes it *feel* cut short. That this feeling might simply be the result of conditioning by long exposure to the sonnet form makes no odds. Our argument isn't that abstract forms are 'natural'; and in any case it's not clear what 'natural' could mean within the man-made world of the poem. As Paul Klee says:

> The artist [...] does not attach such intense importance to natural form as do so many realist critics, because, for him, these final forms

are not the real stuff of the process of natural creation. For he places more value on the powers that do the forming that on the final forms themselves.[2]

From the outset, then, abstract form seems to have a special link with the *makerly* aspects of poetry. And this 'making' by the *feel* of a form appears to be a kind of *legitimate play*. But what *can* legitimate a man-made practice, such as this one, that doesn't claim authenticity to something beyond itself? By definition it can only 'legitimate' itself. So what legitimates a poem's 'going by feel' must be something in the nature of poetry itself. Moreover, legitimate or not, playful going by feel appears at the heart of poetry's relationship to language. Research suggests play may always be part of the relationship between language and its occasion, from rhetoric to phatic rejoinder, tabloid journalism to chit-chat at the bus stop.[3] But poetry *feels* like a special case. At every level, from the popular 'if it doesn't rhyme it isn't poetry' to the most sophisticated of literary-critical readings, we take poetry's ability to denote to be 'the least of it'. Something else, we maintain, is going on.

We need, then, to look more closely at poetry's particular relationship to language. But that relationship is complicated. Poets work with a medium that is not purely tractable. So do composers, but – as we'll see – the limits music imposes on them are only internal and organisational. Composers aren't subject to the verifying pull of external factors, such as poetry's obligation to denote. For, unlike music, language is not only aural. When it ceases to be denotative, it ceases to *be* language and becomes pure sound.

We saw in Chapter 1 how, in Steve Reich's *Come Out*, taking a phrase out of its *connective* context ultimately stops it making sense. Gavin Bryars's 1971 *Jesus's Blood Never Failed Me* illustrates a different but related consequence of sampling. This piece repeats two lines sampled from a homeless man's drunken song, until the listener can no longer hear them as communication.[4] Although the resulting work – a chaconne of chords is set below the voice – is widely seen as moving, I've always heard it as reductive. Our *listening* loss of communicative experience seems to suggest that the singer, too, is not longer doing what we can recognise as a way of using language – singing a hymn

– but is in the grip of some compulsion, or pyschosis. He has lost communicative agency. Mechanised, the language act itself becomes mechanical, and the speaker less than human.

Psychoanalytic theory makes this distinction between language and non-denotative utterance fundamental to our ability to understand the world. The self emerges, we're told, when the connective music of what the French call *lalation*, and we should probably call *la-la-la*-ing or babble, is broken up into an infant's first words. Although this musical 'babbling' gives semiotic pleasure, naming is the primal form of agency; the start of acting as a self. The biblical story in Genesis 2 of how Adam names the creatures, is a perfect metaphorical realisation of naming as the moment of agency:

> And out of the ground the LORD God formed every beast of the field, and every fowl of the air; and brought *them* unto Adam to see what he would call them: and whatsoever Adam called every living creature, that *was* the name thereof. (Genesis 2:19)[5]

Theorists like Julia Kristeva and Melanie Klein, working from psychoanalytic traditions that are only broadly similar to each other's, share the idea of some deep-seated link from the experience of connectedness – *both* between sounds and between the mother's and the infant's body – to an artistic, or even childish, escape from the responsibilities of knowing and naming.[6] In *Revolution in Poetic Language*, Kristeva says that:

> In 'artistic' practices the semiotic – the precondition of the symbolic – is revealed as that which also destroys the symbolic, and this revelation allows us to presume something about its functioning.[7]

Depending on one's intellectual orientation, this may be no more than metaphor. But what makes it interesting for thinking about poetry is the way that it *contrasts* connectedness with denotation. In Chapter 1 we saw how such connectedness plays a key role in a poem or piece of music. And by its very nature abstraction, the topic of *this* chapter, makes us think about what is and is not denotative in a poem.

At this crisscross of principles – of abstraction intersecting with denotation – we get our first glimpse of a kind of three-dimensionality within an otherwise linear picture of the poem or piece of music chronologically unfurling through time. We have looked at how language needs to be joined-up in particular ways in order to make sense. But perhaps some kinds of disconnection *also* 'mean' something. Kristeva, who has been a practising psychoanalyst, observes how analysands' language breaks away from denotative content and becomes more purely a matter of sound patterning when they get close to what is most difficult – that is, most meaningful – for them to say. In the consulting room, as in the rest of life, this *most meaningful* is both said and avoided through an apparently 'unnecessary' musicality of speech: in repetition, stammering, rhythmic phrases and content-less prompting terms, *y'know*s and *like*s. Because trauma causes the self to regress to its earliest, pre-verbal way of being, Kristeva says, the articulation of hurt and of strong emotion – of any threat to that self – bears traces of the early connectedness of utterance and sensation; of what preceded denotation. If 'true' – that is, universalisable – this would suggest that everyone experiences a link between the big emotions, such as those associated with birth, love and death, and the abstract and sensory elements of language – its 'singsong' – even if they haven't made that link conscious. It might, for example, explain the effectiveness of music and poetry in the liturgies of so many religions. (This effect may well work in both 'directions': Kristeva has suggested that her own interest in the preverbal may come from her extensive childhood exposure to Orthodox Christian liturgy.[8])

But in such speculation we run ahead of ourselves. It all seems so much simpler for musicians. As we saw in the last chapter, what Igor Stravinsky calls 'chronologic' connection is essential to music, but the medium *seems* otherwise to be purely available to itself. In fact such pure availability may be an illusion. At the very least, by existing in the physical world, music is subject to the physical laws that govern sound. Nevertheless, abstract form does seem closer at hand for the composer than it is for the poet. It seems to *be* the whole of the matter, instead of having to work 'below', or alongside, linguistic denotation.

The comparative difficulty of handling abstraction in language matters to poets for reasons that cluster around the goods abstraction offers to verse. At the most fundamental level, a poet simply wants her poem to be in control of its own formal structure. Her mind is put at ease about her craft when she can identify and use forms. In 1907, when he was in the midst of trying to revivify the Irish literary tradition, W. B. Yeats wrote that:

> In life courtesy and self-possession, and in the arts style, are the sensible impression of a free mind, for both arise out of the deliberate shaping of all things, and from never being swept away, whatever the emotion, into confusion or dullness.[9]

Poets can satisfy this need by joining existing schools of poetics, which have an already-extant repertory of poetic forms: metre and rhyme, genre, even alliteration and assonance. Literary critics, too, endorse the kinds of 'well-made' structures that they can recognise and name. 'Beauty is, or it includes, order; ugliness is or includes muddle,' as Donald Davie puts it, in characteristically uncompromising style.[10]

Of course, 'order' need not mean anything more sophisticated than making sure that a poem is divided into sections that are of roughly equal length, or that its strict metre is properly sustained. Such well-made forms can seem unambitious, but are avowedly fit for purpose. I like to picture them alongside such traditional crafts as building 5-bar gates and bean-rows from birch switches. These forms show their workings: both what's achieved and how it's done. Everyone knows, or else can find out, what iambic pentameter is, because it works in plain sight – or rather, sound. As it marshals a poem, it also provides it with a characteristically onward-striding authority that is both immediately audible, and refracted through English literary history. Sean O'Brien uses the metre in both these ways to create a solemn music for his poem 'War Graves'. This contemplates precisely whether we can escape the literary reception which by now overlays the brute facts of the Great War, in order to respect the thing itself:

> Unending noon. The harvesters 'are stalled
> Like tanks on the escarpment'. Must this be
> 'The trap of elegy', to find ourselves composed
> Entirely of literature? To have no exit
> [...][11]

Poet-critics – who as it happens include both Sean O'Brien and Donald Davie – are particularly likely to endorse such crafty forms. Their relationship to poetry necessarily includes a kind of knowing pragmatism: after all, an understanding of structure is every bit as useful in writing a poem as it is in responding to it. Another poem showing the pull these forms exert is Elizabeth Bishop's 'One Art'. Since their publication in *Edgar Allan Poe and the Jukebox*, her sixteen drafts for this villanelle have become well known.[12] They chart the poem's famous shift from free verse into this most restrictive of forms; of which it has, ironically, become one of the most-taught examples. Drafts five and eight are particularly telling. They consist of little more than the opening and closing lines, with end-rhymes for the entire poem mapped down the page.

But poetry isn't written simply for the approval of other poets. One reason the general reader may not readily notice abstract form is that it coexists with the many other things going on in verse, from the stimulus of unusual ideas to the excitement of unexpected emotion. Still, this begs the question of *why* it's less conspicuous than those other elements. Is it just because of how we've been taught to read poetry? Or is there something necessarily veiled about abstract form in language: the element of it that by its very nature refuses to *tell us* things?

Another way to frame this question may be to ask exactly what we're looking for when we search a poem for truly abstract formal elements. Emotive atmosphere and resonant allusion, for example, don't seem to *name* anything. And yet they *do* denote mood, and emotion. Charles Baudelaire's colourist collection *Fleurs de Mal* caused a sensation when it was published in 1857. The poet and his publisher were successfully prosecuted for an 'outrage to public decency'; while Victor Hugo declared that Baudelaire had created 'a new *frisson*'. So the book's adjective-laden, exaggerated new style of poetic diction was highly successful in shocking the bourgeoisie; in other words, in getting them to *hear what it was saying*.

At other times, resonance denotes – though 'slant', in Emily Dickinson's term – by making us think of something a poem doesn't actually name. It's a technique that Dickinson herself makes much use of, in order to explore metaphysical elements that cannot be directly named or articulated. In poem #996, she has:

I heard, as I had no Ear
Until a Vital Word
Came all the way from Life to me
And then I knew I heard—[13]

Sound-matches can denote, too: as, here, the missing 'ear' is packed away inside the 'heard' of the first line, then rung out by a sharp slant assonance – 'knew' – and the repeated 'heard' of the fourth.

'Abstract ideas', though sometimes set up as the enemy of the 'expressive' lyric tradition – William Carlos Williams's line, in *Paterson*, about 'no ideas but in things' has been much quoted – are contrasted, by critics and teachers, with concrete examples, that is, things from the material world.[14] Yet the *expression* of these ideas isn't abstract; the poem *tells* us the idea. W. H. Auden's 'In Praise of Limestone' interleaves the concrete world and the world of ideas, but the poem is always an *address*: there is a reader to whom world and ideas alike are being shown. So to avoid confusion, I'll call all denotation, whether of the material world or of immaterial ideas and whether direct or slant, semantic.

Pretty much all we're left with, by way of an abstract element to poetry, if we discount these semantic elements of various kinds, is whatever can be counted or measured: that is, what is *quantifiable*. Numbers of stanzas, the proportions of lines devoted to one topic or another, and the relative lengths of sections, can all be counted. So, indeed, can other formal elements within verse; including the length of a line, chromaticism, texture and density (how wide is the variation? how many elements does it comprise? And so on). In the next four chapters I'll look at each of these elements, and at the analogies between how they operate in music and in poetry.

For the moment, though, let's go back to where we started: with the question of time. We can measure blocks of time, and count up temporal occurrences. While poetry is by and large surprised to find itself thinking, and thinking about itself, in measured time, music has no such qualms. The rhythmic building blocks of a piece that we call *bars* are even named 'measures' in American English, and musicians are accustomed to 'counting the rests'; that is, literally counting up the bars and beats till they 'come in'.

This Anglophone musicians' phrase – 'come in', never 'join in' – is an hospitable, spatial metaphor that suggests nothing so much as the dance. It says music is a space they enter, not an action they start to perform, and it reminds us of musicans' physical proximity when they 'play together'. The composer Edgar Varèse claimed to have been inspired by the writings on music of the Polish savant Józef Maria Hoene-Wroński, who stated that the object of music is 'the corporealization of the intelligence that is in sound'.[15] Musicians' experiences are indeed clearly 'corporeal'. There is a lot of *doing* involved in any musical occasion, and space and time are both germane to it. Playing in the orchestra for one of Richard Wagner's hours-long operas just *is* much more tiring than playing for an opera on the classical scale, say one by Wolfgang Amadeus Mozart. Jokes aside, the viola section simply can't go out to buy coffee and resume when they feel fresher; they must *keep going*. The collective nature of the majority of musical occasions also means matters of timing are more pressing than they are in poetry.[16] In order to make a piece happen, a group of musicians must as a minimum start at the same moment, continue at the same speed and finish at the same time as each other. By contrast, the occasion of poetry need entail only a single individual reading 'to herself' in silence, who can change speed as often as she likes.

Not that the way poetry happens can ever be entirely disembodied either. Both eye and ear map the development of an argument when poets use strophes to 'paragraph' distinct thematic materials. Yeats's 'arrangements of events in the words', can be seen in his own poems, like the famous middle-period 'The Wild Swans at Coole', from 1919:[17]

The trees are in their autumn beauty,
The woodland paths are dry,
Under the October twilight the water
Mirrors a still sky;
Upon the brimming water among the stones
Are nine-and-fifty swans.

The nineteenth autumn has come upon me
Since I first made my count;
I saw, before I had well finished,
All suddenly mount
And scatter wheeling in great broken rings
Upon their clamorous wings.

I have looked upon these brilliant creatures,
And now my heart is sore.
All's changed [...][18]

This illustrates Yeats's habit of making his sentence and stanzas coeval. He routinely ends his sentences at the end of a stanza. This isn't unusual in an early twentieth-century poem ('Wild Swans' was published in 1919), and it suggests a trace of the traditional song and ballad forms the poet imitates particularly in earlier collections, such as *The Wind among the Reeds* (1899), *In the Seven Woods* (1904) and *The Green Helmet and Other Poems* (1910). More striking is how relatively rarely he ends sentences *elsewhere* within a stanza, and how this technique is apparent from the earliest work right through his prime, from 'The Ballad of Moll Magee' to 'I am of Ireland', though it is increasingly diluted in the late poems. The five stanzas of 'The Wild Swans at Coole' balance a reasonably complex rhythmic and rhyme scheme in stanzas that are noticeably longer than the portable quatrain (which we might have anticipated because of its traditional formal associations). They range across a narrative period of nineteen years, and contrasting moods of exaltation and abasement. Yet the poem's only mid-stanza sentence break is one marking roughly the mid-point of the whole poem and highlighting its *turn* from 'then' to 'now', at 'All's changed'. This alignment of sentence with meaning and with verse creates a singular, muscular and highly audible music; one that could even rise to the occasion of poetic prophecy in which Yeats believed.[19]

Of course, line-break and verse-break are nothing more than an arrangement of type on a page if they simply occur a regular number of words or lines apart: as if text were merely a kind of visual and aural wallpaper to be pasted in neat parallel 'strips'. To form part of the poem, these formal breaks *must* form part of the poem: that's to say that they must do some of its aural and perhaps even semantic work. The stanza form itself is abstract. Yet, as 'The Wild Swans at Coole' shows, there is a quasi-mimetic relationship between verse structure and meaning. It's a form of temporal mimesis. Verse-breaks like Yeats's mirror the stages of a thought, which as we saw in Chapter 1 is chronologic, and also *represent* successive moments in time. Something similar is at work in the sonnet *volta* at the end of its eighth line, when the poem turns its material right over, like a hay-bale that needs to dry on the other side in order to be finished. Similarly too, *terza rima*'s looping intellectual lope down the page spells out the connectedness inherent in a journey such as its most famous protagonist, the Dante of the *Divine Comedy*, under-takes.

Strict metre means we can even count out the beats within a line, as if we were musicians. But temporal structures argu-ably do even more work in free verse, which might otherwise be dismissed by lazy readers as unmusical or not consciously organised. In contemporary British poet Alice Oswald's chap-book-length, commissioned poems about rivers, *Dart* (2002) and *A Sleepwalk on the Severn* (2009), the *and then ... and then* of what she observes makes a map both temporal and chrono-logic of each river's winding route to the eventual ocean.[20] In Sean Borodale's poetry cookbook, *Human Work*, free verse that moves sentence by sentence down the page records the *and then ... and then* of the cooking process together with its straggling unevenness:

> This curly fan I tear into pieces, is endive, for example,
> thin, wasting sunlight: its bitter participle.
>
> I dip and shake;
> the whole world of its time flickers on and off.
>
> Tear, not chop.[21]

If quantifiable form can be co-opted like this to map a poem's argument, it can also underline its *expressive* function. The sheer length of Les Murray's Australian verse novel *Fredy Neptune* (1998) underlines the exhaustion experienced by his eponymous everyman, who has been burdened with the twenti-eth century's war guilt. Louis MacNeice's short lyric 'Prognosis' was written under the shadow of war, in the European Spring of 1939. The poem's momentum changes as it nears its conclusion. Its springy rhythm is created by the way that each quatrain forms a single question. Only in the ninth and final stanza is this pattern broken, into not one but two momentous questions – about Love, and Death – that as it were stop the laughter of the tea-leaf fortune-telling game.[22]

At first glance this aptness for expression is puzzling, because abstraction is often characterised by both admirers and detractors as standing at a particular distance from individual human experience. (Complaints levelled against Modernist architecture, for example, often have to do with the way it fails to meet standards of lived human usefulness; and cite the vertical slums that try to imitate le Corbusier's *Ville radieuse*.) Yet as we'll see, one explanation for the pull of abstract forms, such as proportion, is that – far beyond the needs of musical performance – they are fundamentally anchored in the embodied human experience. One way to handle this apparent paradox is to think about a poem as a form of cohabitation between the intentional and expressive on the one hand, and the impersonal or formal on the other. Whatever poetry appears to be *saying* – telling a story, 'confessing' emotion – it is also carrying out abstract form.

As we'd expect, these cohabiting aspects of the poem can coincide, overlap with or sometimes even confound each other. Earlier, I pictured poetic forms that are fit for purpose as similar to traditional farming crafts; now, I'm talking about constructed cohabitations. Since the work of Ferdinand de Saussure (1857–1913) and Vladimir Propp (1895–1970), the idea of the 'structural' has been loaded with both linguistic and ethnological conventions. But 'structure' is also a non-technical word meaning something built or *put together*. As that 'together' points out, plurality of elements is key to any structure; as 'put' shows us, so is intentional action.

Abstraction is conspicuous when it comes adrift. In George Meredith's *Modern Love*, longeurs such as Poem Thirteen, a generalised comment on ageing, or Eighteen, with its description of a village party – both surely only included to make up the numbers to a tidy fifty – suggest structure has got in the way of the poem's emotional tone-world. The lack of enthusiasm some readers express for Ted Hughes's last collection, *Birthday Letters*, is surely a response to its at times strangely prosaic rhythms, which make certain passages appear closer to lists of ideas, or notes, than to his earlier, characteristically through-driven lyric verse.[23]

But where abstraction *does* work, cohabitation suggests a resolution to the language-as-art paradox it throws up. That paradox goes like this: while every (other) artform – including even those, such as dance and film, that usually rely on narrative – can resort to *pure* abstraction, language arts seem bound by an opposing principle of *essential* denotation. In practice, we accept that poetry is an artform. We allocate it a special discursive role that includes much more than simple reportage. Yet it consists of nothing but language. As the American poet Brenda Hillman says, 'It is common to hear students talking about "the idea behind the poem". There is no idea "behind" a poem, I say. The words and their phrases are what we have.'[24] Ultimately, a poem is not an idea, but *itself*. Since it works with sound as well as with a complex variety of often-simultaneous thought experiences, one can't skim-read or summarise a poem any more than one can paraphrase a piece of music: music *is not* the programme note that attempts to describe it. Sound patterns are by nature non-denotative, with the conspicuous exception of mimesis. The patterning of a poems's semantic content is a numerial form: the sonnet *tells* us one thing up to its turn, and then something else; but the location of that turn is abstract, formal design.

Abstract forms can be used consciously and even pragmatically, therefore. But the power they exert over us remains somewhat mysterious. Sometimes poetry even seems to ask itself what abstraction *is*. In 'Romanesque Arches', the Swedish Nobel Laureate Tomas Tranströmer gives measured space meaning through its relation to human experience:

An angel with no face embraced me
and whispered through my whole body:
'Don't be ashamed of being human, be proud!
Inside you vault opens behind vault endlessly.
You will never be complete, that's how it's meant to be.'[25]

In 1989, when this poem was published, Tranströmer had been going against the grain of contemporary Swedish poetry for over twenty years. As he says in a 1967 letter to the American poet Robert Bly, 'One should preferably be a card-carrying Marxist. Instead, suspect elements of old-fashioned individualism, including religiosity, have been detected.'[26] The famous thought experiment that opens Rainer Maria Rilke's *Duino Elegies* was written over sixty years earlier, also against the grain of what was contemporary, then an emerging Modernity:

Who, if I cried out, would hear me among the Angelic
Orders? And even if one
Suddenly clasped me to his heart I'd shrink
From his more intense being. So beauty
Is nothing but the beginning of a terror that we scarcely endure
[…][27]

It's no coincidence that both these passages are willfully unconventional. Both, after all, are trying to get beyond familiar
thought to evoke some special apprehension. They move us
because we both can and cannot apprehend what they are
evoking. We seem to read them with a divided mind, one that
oscillates between the literal and a leap into an evocation that
we feel ourselves being nudged towards.

Writing on visual art explores this apparently mysterious
power of abstraction as feeling. In *The Hidden Order of Art*
(1967) – as its subtitle says, *A Study in the Psychology of Artistic
Imagination* – the exiled Viennese art critic and psychologist
Anton Ehrenzweig opens his chapter on 'Abstraction', 'There is
a close nexus between the power of abstraction and the creative
capacity for dedifferentiating the concreteness of surface thinking.' In other words, abstraction's 'origin in deeply unconscious
layers of the mind' creates the 'undifferentiated vision in which
the boundaries of the inside and outside world have become
uncertain'. To put it another way, abstraction is precisely that
which pulls on denotation and transforms something that is
being represented into a religious or secular symbol, or simply
into something pleasurable.[28]

This view of the deep psychological traction of abstract patterns, such as repetition, appears in Wassily Kandinsky's 1911
treatise *Über das Gestige in der Kunst*:

> The apt use of a word (in its poetical meaning), repetition of this
> word, twice, three times or even more frequently, according to the
> need of the poem, will not only tend to intensify the inner harmony,
> but also bring to light unsuspected spiritual properties of the word
> itself.[29]

A 'corresponding vibration in the heart' is set up; at least,
according to Michael Sadler's 1914 translation. By the time
such continental ideas have filtered through British reception,
for example in Roger Fry's influential study *Vision and Design*

(1920), this heightened, 'poetical' language has been replaced by talk of the artist's 'creative vision', in which 'emotional elements of design' replace the need to replicate the material world.

Such ideas about psychic mechanisms may to some extent be typical of their Modernist moment. By the 1950s, Gaston Bachelard's classic *La poétique de l'espace* synthesises a vision, or anyway a series of images, of the meanings that particular spaces hold for the person occupying them. Famously, the space his book mostly explores is the home. His mixed sources for this vision of meaningful space are telling. From the phenomenological psychopathologist Eugène Minkowski he takes the notion of reverberation, or *retentir*, which as he says 'is very apt, for in sound both space and time are epitomized'.[30] Minkowski's reverberation seems close to fellow-Russian Kandinsky's 'corresponding vibration'. From the poet Pierre-Jean Jouve, Bachelard takes the notion that 'poetry is a soul inaugurating a form', and thus that such forms allow the phenomenologist to witness the 'soul'.[31] From the psychoanalytic theorist J. B. Pontalis, he takes the idea that 'The speaking subject is the entire subject'; in other words (and they are Bachelard's own) that poetry can offer 'a phenomenology of expression'.[32] Like Kristeva and Klein, Bachelard links abstraction to connectedness:

> The atomism of conceptual language demands reasons for fixation, forces of centralisation. But the verse always has a movement, the image flows into the verse, carrying the imagination along with it [...].[33]

If some of this seems occult, if not outright superstitious, we have to ask ourselves from where else an *essential* order of measure might come. Those famous Leonardo da Vinci drawings that 'prove' various proportions against his image of a man give us one answer. It isn't surprising that artists of all kinds look for some ontology – such as the proportionate dimensions of human embodiment – to anchor the forms that enable their work; or to make it into something more than mere reportage. The search for essential truths that could stabilise the apparent abstraction of chaos is a continuing human theme.

We look for form and pattern in order to make sense of experience. But as part of that search we also have to ask ourselves whether we *discover* or *devise* such forms. What's *true*, rather than *conceptually possible*? For decades, until work at CERN around the year 2012, we didn't know whether the Higgs boson particle was a fact, or a conceptual lever. And if conceptually entailed principles are true in some special way, 'true in maths' as it were, does that mean other things can also be 'true in thought': fictional characters, for example? Geometry works both as a closed conceptual system and empirically: I really do need that number of tiles to finish the bathroom wall. But to complicate matters, when quantifiable patterns do occur in the physical world, which might be one definition of 'truth', they tend not quite to add up.

Poets might pay attention to musicians, who deal with this anomaly routinely. The problem of *equal temperament* is useful in any thinking about pure form and its inconsistencies. In summary: pitch appears to be a *given*, since certain relationships between the notes of the harmonic series – octaves, fifths, thirds, all the apparatus of a Western 'key' – are correlated by over-tones. If you sound both notes of an interval perfectly in tune together, the next note 'up' the series will sound itself. This feels like God, or the universe, giving you a tick: but is simply the result of the way each pitch pulses at a particular frequency per second, which is therefore related to the frequency of every other pitch. Especially strong relationships – frequency ratios of 1:2, 2:3 or 3:4 – constitute the harmonic series.[34] However, although pitch continues to repeat each key to an infinity of both higher and lower notes on either side of what a musician plays, and out beyond the range of the human ear, the extreme verity which produces overtones is only *local*. If you pitch several consecutive intervals perfectly, the outer notes of that series will no longer be in tune with each other. (Pythagoras was the first to understand that a *diatonic comma* is necessary between twelve consecutive perfect fifths and seven perfect octaves, because the 'cycle of fifths' doesn't quite add up. B# is *not* exactly C, in the conjuring trick beloved of music teachers. Musicians call this non-identicality, which sounds like out-of-tuneness, an 'enharmonic' change; and they locate it particularly around the accidentals, between, for example F# and G♭.[35])

Musicians have always adjusted to these natural facts. Within a key, most decent fiddle-players flatten their submediants and heighten their leading notes just as, in the wider realm of absolute pitch, they sharpen their F#s and flatten their G♭s. These notes are customarily treated as synonyms though in fact, just as there *is* no such thing as a synonym – since each alternative offers a variant meaning, resonance and register as well as sound – the hyperactive brightness of F# is *not* identical with the pitch-pine gloom of G♭. The key-character of perfect pitch makes it impossible *fully* to transpose musical material, just as we cannot perfectly translate poetic material. Even within a single language there is no such thing as a true synonym; a problem that's even more marked in translation between languages.[36] However in the Baroque era the rise in importance of keyboard instruments, with their wide range of pre-tuned notes, meant such differentiations were lost. The ringing endorsement of absolute pitch was smoothed away by a diplomatic compromise that preserved the *form* of harmonic relations, but not quite their content. Famously, J. S. Bach's *Well-Tempered Clavier* (1722) was written to demonstrate the possibilities this strategy opened up: possibilities since further enlarged by the development of equal temperament.[37]

Bach's Forty-Eight Preludes and Fugues showcase a dialectic between radical adventurism and profound conservatism, which we could say arises from the human search for existential pattern. Deep foundations enable extravagant superstructures, and to this religious composer whatever was given was not accidental but *God*-given. This meant not only that music *has* certain inalienable qualities, such as harmonic relationships, but that it *should reflect and celebrate* their evidence of Divine Order by exploring and exploiting what such harmonies can do. Harmonic form was not only a *means* of music, but an *end*. Over twenty centuries earlier, Pythagoras had posited another, similarly totalising, metaphysics in which the mathematical coherence of the musical cycle of fifths predicated an entire music of the spheres.[38] He reasoned that the moving planets sound a note according to their place along a heavenly monochord stretching from pure spirit to pure matter. This seems less purely speculative when we remember that, for Pythagoras, number characterised the entire universe, from colour spectrum to gender relations. Besides, as if to suggest they might after all be key to the Order of Things, these same number relations do occur in a range of physical contexts. For example, in the nine-teenth century John A. Newlands discovered the *law of octaves* which, though it turns out to be another of those imperfectly occurring natural patterns, gave the Periodic Table its name. In his formulation, 'When elements are arranged in increasing order of their atomic mass, [every] eighth element resembles the first in physical and chemical properties just like the eighth note on a musical scale resembles the first note.'[39]

So human meaning and abstract form are not inimical. Yet the exact terms of their relationship are often mysterious. The sonnet's octet:sestet is both proportionate, and yet just unequal enough to cause the topple which we recognise as its turn. We might think of this bifurcated form as posing – and then resolving – the problem of duality; to put it another way, of relationships. But why has the culture settled on this particular proportion for such semantic transformation? Why not balance a sonnet between ten lines and six, or seven and five? What makes eight : six so 'right'? We don't kiss and make up an average of three times out of every four; nor take three-quarters as long to divorce as to marry!

Pythagoreans might respond that the mathematical ratio of 8:6 is in some way *productive* of change. After all, 4:3 is the ratio of a perfect fourth in music, and Pythagoras called this pivotal interval, located between the fourth and third steps of the harmonic series, the *diatesseron*.[40] All of which simply begs a further series of metaphysical, ultimately extra-textual, ques-tions about the *status* of such forms in the world around us.

Edward Said, unsurprisingly, finds cultural roots for this kind of belief:

> In the *Poetics* Aristotle speaks of the drama as somehow possessing a necessary and proper magnitude or size, neither too large nor too small, neither too long nor too short. Out of this and other passages in the treatise there emerged the concept of classical unities, as well as notions of proportion, limit and constraint that have long been associated generally speaking with Western art of the period up to 1800, after which extravagances of ego, sheer size, and massive effect become common.[41]

But, whether familiarity 'naturalises' such abstract forms, or their occurrence in nature familiarises us with them, what we do know is that making them conscious turns feelings or intuitions into serious artistic strategies. What legitimates the poet's makerly play may be neither God nor science; but simply creative process.

Notes

1. Johann Huizinga's *Homo Ludens* is a theory of art, and other creative activities such as philosophy, as play: '[Play] is a significant function – that is to say, there is some sense to it. In play there is something "at play" which transcends the immediate needs of life and imparts meaning to the action. All play means something.' Johann Huizinga, *Homo Ludens: A Study of the Play Element in Culture* [1944] (London: Routledge & Kegan Paul, 1980), p. 1. This way of thinking about play continues to be influential, as the title of Stephen Nachmanovitch's *Free Play: Improvisation in Life and Art* indicates. Nachmanovitch claims that: 'Improvisation, composition, writing, painting, theater, invention, all creative acts are forms of play.' Nachmanovitch, Stephen, *Free Play: Improvisation in Life and Art* (New York: Tarcher/Penguin, 1990), p. 42.
2. Paul Klee, *On Modern Art* (London: Faber, 1948), p. 45.
3. The term 'phatic communion' was coined by Bronisław Malinowski in 1923. Bronisław Malinowski, 'The Problem of Meaning in Primitive Languages', Supplement 1 in C. K. Ogden and I. A. Richards (eds), *The Meaning of Meaning* (London: Kegan Paul, 1923), pp. 296–336.
4. From: Gavin Bryars Ensemble, *The Sinking of the Titanic* album reissue (North Elmham, Norfolk: LTM/Boutique, 2009), NL B001VG2MEY.
5. Genesis 2:19. *King James Bible*. http://biblehub.com/genesis/2–19. htm. Retrieved 2/1/16.
6. In *The Psycho-Analysis of Children* (1932) Melanie Klein discusses an infant 'position' (not 'stage': it is a state that can always be re-entered) of learning to integrate good and bad feelings and experiences: the famous 'good breast' and 'bad breast'. Melanie Klein, *The Psycho-Analysis of Children* (New York and London: Vintage, 1997).
7. Julia Kristeva, *Revolution in Poetic Language*, Margaret Waller (trans.) (New York: Columbia University Press, 1984), p. 49.
8. Interview with John Sutherland in the *Guardian*: http://www.the guardian.com/education/2006/mar/14/highereducation.research1. Retrieved 25/5/15.
9. William Butler Yeats, from 'Poetry and Tradition' in A. Norman Jeffares (ed.), *Selected Poems* (London: Pan Macmillan, 1976), p. 162.

10. Donald Davie, 'Articulate Energy' in *Purity of Diction in English Verse and Articulate Energy* (Manchester: Carcanet, 2006), p. 334.
11. Sean O'Brien, 'War Graves' in *The Beautiful Librarians* (London: Picador, 2015), p. 17.
12. Elizabeth Bishop, *Edgar Allan Poe and the Juke-Box*, Alice Quinn (ed.) (Manchester: Carcanet, 2006), pp. unnumbered.
13. R. W. Franklin (ed.), *The Poems of Emily Dickinson* (Cambridge, MA and London: Belknap Press of Harvard University Press, 1999), p. 415.
14. William Carlos Williams (1883–1963) is famously known for coining the term: 'No ideas but in things.' This one is from the hundred-line, 1927 version of 'Paterson'. William Carlos Williams, *Paterson*, Christopher MacGowan (ed.) (New York: New Directions, 1992).
15. Malcolm MacDonald, *Varèse, Astronomer in Sound* (London: Kahn & Averill, 2003), pp. 52–3.
16. Obviously, there is solo repertoire, and there are times when a musician is reading a score alone.
17. Yeats, 'Poetry and Tradition', p. 163.
18. William Butler Yeats, from 'The Wild Swans at Coole' in A. Norman Jeffares (ed.), *Selected Poems*, p. 64.
19. Yeats studied William Blake's prophetic books in his youth, decades before he wrote 'The Second Coming'.
20. Alice Oswald, *Dart* (London: Faber, 2002). Alice Oswald, *A Sleepwalk on the Severn* (London: Faber, 2009).
21. Sean Borodale, 'Garden Salad', in *Human Work* (London: Cape, 2015), p. 28.
22. Louis MacNeice, 'Prognosis' in *Collected Poems* (London: Faber, 1979), pp. 157–8.
23. Ted Hughes, *Birthday Letters* (London: Faber, 1998).
24. Brenda Hillman, *Cracks in the Oracle Bone: Teaching Certain Contemporary Poems*, The Judith Lee Stronach Memorial Lectures on the Teaching of Poetry (Berkeley: The Bancroft Library, University of California, 2008), p. 10.
25. Tomas Tranströmer, 'Romanesque Arches' in Robin Fulton (trans.), *New Collected Poems* (Newcastle upon Tyne: Bloodaxe, 2011), p. 158.
26. Tomas Tranströmer, letter of 1/7/67 to Robert Bly, in Thomas R. Smith (ed.), *Airmail: The Letters of Robert Bly and Tomas Tranströmer* (Newcastle upon Tyne: Bloodaxe, 2013), p. 68.
27. My translation.
28. Anton Ehrenzweig, *The Hidden Order of Art* (London: Weidenfeld & Nicolson, 1993), pp. 128 and 130.
29. The treatise first appeared in English in 1914 as *The Art of Spiritual Harmony*. Quoted in Mel Gooding, *Ceri Richards* (Moffat: Cameron and Hollis, 2002), p. 16.

30. Gaston Bachelard, *The Poetics of Space*, Maria Jolas (trans.) (Boston: Beacon Books, 1994), p. xvi.

31. Ibid. p. xxii. (Bachelard's citation: Pierre-Jean Jouve, *En miroir* [1954] 1972, Mercure de France, p. 11.)

32. Ibid., p. xxviii. (Bachelard's citation: J. B. Pontalis, 'Michel Leiris ou la psychanalyse interminable' in *Les Temps Modernes*, December 1955, p. 932.)

33. Ibid., p. xxviii.

34. The interval between a pair of notes whose frequency ratio is 1:2 (e.g. 440 and 880 Hertz) is an octave (in this case octave As). The interval between two notes whose frequency ratio is 2:3 is a perfect fifth (for example, 440 and 660 Hz: A and the E above it); while the 3:4 ratio produces a perfect fourth (as from E upward to the next A).

35. The present, Mercatorian or Holderian comma, was first calculated by the Chinese mathematician Ching Fang in the first century bce. In the seventeenth century, Nicholas Mercator calculated the variation between these circles of perfect fifths and perfect octaves more accurately, and William Holder pointed out that the perfect major third is also very close to being present in equal temperament. In order to enable the key relationships within an octave to ring true, these mathematicians have divided the octave into fifty-three intervals, or 'commas', rather than the twelve semitones, because fifty-three consecutive perfect fifths (3/2ths to the power of 53) very nearly equals thirty-one perfect octaves (2/1ths to the power of 53). These physical facts are genuinely, if imperfectly, universal: something that seems *prima facie* difficult for poetry, with its multiplicity of local languages, to match.

36. As the false synonyms thought up by automated translation in Les Murray's poem 'Employment for the Castes in Abeyance' illustrate. Les Murray, 'Employment for the Castes in Abeyance' in *Selected Poems* (Manchester: Carcanet, 1986), pp. 51–2.

37. Although a less welcome consequence of this is arguably a dulled pitch palate. Twentieth-century composers, from Berg to Stockhausen, made a compensatory exploration not of the *expressive* qualities of discord but of how its *systematic* use might shift the whole project of contemporary music.

38. The relationship between the tonic and the fifth step in each musical scale – the first interval, after the octave, in the harmonic series – is that between the 'home' key and its neighbour in the step-wise acquisition of key-signature sharps, then (through enharmomic modulation) shedding of flats, of key cousinship. The 'cycle' includes and relates all keys and returns to its starting point.

39. John Newlands, 'On Relations Among the Equivalents', *Chemical News*, 10, 20 August 1864, pp. 94–5.

40. There's a qualitative difference between noticing that a particular proportion is naturally occurring, and believing that this natural

occurrence confers particular metaphysical or semantic status. Arguably all we can do is resort to the old existentialist trick of being clear about the forms that are available to work with.

41. Edward W. Said, *Musical Elaborations* (London: Chatto & Windus, 1991), p. 63.

Chapter 3

Drawing the Line

Igor Stravinsky's *Rite of Spring* opens with one of the most famous solos in the orchestral canon. In fact, it starts with just one note, itself instantly recognisable within the Western tradition: a single high C on the bassoon. This is of course a wind instrument and its reedy, wooden timbre evokes the wind, reeds and woods that make up the endless Russian *taiga* (see Fig. 3.1).[1]

Like that wilderness, the opening note seems as though it could go on for ever (and it's marked with a pause sign). Instead, it lapses into a figure that resembles a turn, one of the ornaments with which musicians traditionally italicise a note.[2] But the motif is repeated, and out of it arises an answering phrase. Next comes a tonal step sideways, as clarinets add plangency. The bassoon repeats itself – there's an answering line from the cor anglais, in which an echo of hunting horns is probably no accident – and the instrumental chorus clusters round, baying and chattering.

Stravinsky's bassoon solo doesn't sound much like what we conventionally think of as tuneful. It doesn't try to charm, or

Figure 3.1 Bassoon solo from the opening of Stravinsky's *Rite of Spring*

offer the 'dying fall' of closure, and it isn't regular – something that, arguably, that makes it hard to memorise. But this is just why it offers such a useful example of linear melody. For something fundamentally melodic does remain, willy-nilly: not beautifully modulated tonal *surface*, but something apparently prior and essential. The bassoon ventriloquises the human voice.[3] Yet it doesn't do this by *timbre*, but the way the melody's singularity and its joined-up-ness combine to trace what we recognise as a *phrase*.

But *how* do we recognise it? It's no coincidence that, in Jacques Derrida's deconstruction of language and hence thought, the *trace*, the 'mark of the absence of a presence', contains a puzzle about the actual nature of correspondence between *trace* and *what is traced*.[4] We seem to make a connection between melody and what musicians do indeed call *line*: almost as if the breath passing down the long, skinny bassoon were drawing a diagram of what we hear. The comparative anthropologist Tim Ingold's work on man-made lines such as footpaths, or the warp of a carpet loom, underlines how these signify the connectedness, the *and then … and then*, of process. They aren't just *evidence* of a practice such as weaving; they are its *logic*.[5] In such traditional, collective and so repeated practices, this is the path that is by definition always taken. The path *is* the desire line.

By contrast, human activities which are formed by *specific* choices – choices made on each occasion – entail a phantom plurality, the 'paths not taken' of their discarded (or overlooked) alternatives. One thinks of the drafts in a writer's notebook, or the shavings on a cabinet-maker's workshop floor. Composition, whether musical or poetic, works like this, creating a chosen sequence out of the field of possibility. Thus, Pierre Boulez quotes Henry Miller – 'What appears now before my eyes is the result of innumerable mistakes, withdrawals, erasures, hesitations; it is also the result of certitude' – to explain a 'logic of co-ordination' by which linear form, whether musical or literary, emerges from a multiplicity of experiments, drafts and aborted openings.[6] And this distinction, between habitual and elective processes within making, evokes the distinction Ingold makes between traces and threads, two kinds of line which respectively outline and connect; and which, as he says, can turn into each other.[7]

This is one model of linearity: that of a single conceptual succession. But melody, whether it's composed or traditional, also expresses a practical, internal logic all of its own. It's a particular kind of sound-object; like the woven textile, its nature *is* connectedness. But there must be more to it than that. Composition could produce something unmelodic; the warp on a loom could be used to make open-work. Melody, like all music, is the *and then ... and then* of notes succeeding each other; but within that melody the notes come one at a time and have a stronger relationship to each other than to other musical lines going on at the same time. They are chronologically connected. Residually, and often actually, they are also connected by something internal, yet constitutive: they share a breath.

Another way to say this is that melody can usually be sung – albeit sometimes only by a virtuoso contemporary specialist, a Jane Manning or a Christine Rice – and this sing-ability is structural. It's even possible to sing the opening of the *Rite*, which has in any case been identified as transcribed folksong.[8] After all the bassoonist, too, must connect these notes in a single breath. This single breath is fundamental to the line of melody; and also of poetry.

Music and poetry meet in song, of course. As the singer-songwriter Tom Waits says, in his Rock and Roll Hall of Fame Induction Speech, 'Songs are really just very interesting things to be doing with the air.'[9] Soon after the Second World War, banned from teaching under de-Nazification, and working in the relative seclusion of Todtnauberg in the Black Forest, Martin Heidegger wrote that:

> Singing and thinking are the stems
>   neighbour to poetry.
>
> They grow out of Being and reach into
>   its truth.
>
> Their relationship makes us think of what
>   Hölderlin sings of the trees of the
>   woods:
>
> 'And to each other they remain unknown,
>   So long as they stand, the neighbouring
>   trunks.'[10]

How telling that this image of the relationship between poetry, song and thought, in which they 'grow' in parallel with each other, is *linear*. Was this inadvertent, on the part of either Friedrich Hölderlin or Heidegger? Or is this metaphor being doubled to represent *both* the linearity of each form and the analogy between them? Whichever is the case, I like the sense Heidegger gives here of the *emergent* poem or song. As so often in this contested philosopher's work, not least thanks to his speculative etymology, there is a sense of origins. He gives us a glimpse *both* of silence, the not-poem that comes before each particular poem *and* of cultural origin in general.[11]

It's easy to note how singing starts from silence, because it starts with a preparatory in-breath. In song, such physical constraints and possibilities cut across other formal and linguistic concerns. (The great tenor Enrico Caruso had a dedicated laryngologist, P. M. Marafioti, who after his death wrote a successful book, still available today, revealing the master's vocal exercises and breathing techniques.[12]) A song's first note has a peculiar resonance because of the way it emerges from silence to set a particular tonal scene within the almost infinite field of musical possibility. As a minimum, we know we are in a key or mode that includes this particular pitch. (Without formal musical training we don't *know* that we know this – but our accultured ear does.) We also hear who's singing. And beat and stress reveal the first note's rhythmic role: is it an upbeat, that articulation and prolongation of the preparatory inhalation, or a keynote, stressed by the downbeat? Either way, it projects the song to come, throwing a formal template ahead of itself. The significance of this first note is a trace, within what we might call the song's consciousness, of the archaic gesture of utterance itself.

In fact, the preparatory in-breath is predicated by all oral forms. A poem also starts with a sense of anticipation, a prickle of pre-existence. At one level, it's readers and audiences who bring this anticipatory sense to the completed poem, whether they've turned up for a reading armed with knowledge of the poet's work or are browsing a volume in a bookshop. But analogy with song also seems to suggest that this preparatory sense of anticipation might be, or have become, intrinsic to the poem.[13] One moment at which this occurs is during the writing process. The classic Green Room advice is, *You aren't nervous, you're excited.* And some poets experience anticipation within the writing process in terms quite as bodily as any stage fright. Anne Stevenson calls this, 'That pregnant feeling! It's something like turning the circle on the top of the salt cellar until the salt comes out. You just have to get the holes matching.' Les Murray says, 'Poetry builds up in your mind like a charge. If you go in too early, you'll muck it up, if you go in too late, it'll be dry … At the right moment, the poem doesn't have words. It's a pressure.'[14]

But it's the poem itself, of course, that makes any such writing process significant. The Russian émigré and Nobel laureate Joseph Brodsky urged his creative writing students to cut evidence of warming up. The start of a poem, he maintained, is too often just that. (Warming up is a practice all too familiar to musicians: sure enough, pianist Alfred Brendel called his *first* collection of verse *Fingerzeig*.[15]) For Brodsky, the finished poem should feel necessary all the way through; as if it could never have taken any other form. But this is a *specific* poetics which differs from, for example, today's North American *poetry of process*, written by figures like near-contemporaries Brenda Hillman or Jorie Graham. Among the varied antecedents of *poetry of process* we could include both D. H. Lawrence and Paul Celan: poets who, by repeatedly reworking ideas and images within a single poem, show us how poetry explores rather than defines.[16] Lawrence in particular shows us how it need not *necessarily* be clear where the 'real poem' of a poem starts. Not every poet chooses to write like Brodsky, even whose longest poems – like *Gorbunov and Gorchakov*, or 'Lithuanian Nocturne' – start *in media res*.[17] Yet the casual, hands-in-pockets openings of, say, the Robert Lowell of *From the Union Dead* aren't the norm either. His 'Work-table, litter, books and standing lamp, / plain things […]' ('Night Sweat') or 'It was a Maine lobster town – / each morning boatloads of hands / pushed off for granite / quarries on the islands' ('Water') are openings all right: they assert *here*, or *now*.[18] They also get immediately to business, with no sense of throat clearing. There is no formula for the perfect poem: only good or bad judgement, something like the 'feel' we saw at play in Chapter 2.

Yet many poets do clear their throats. Indeed, one solution to vulnerabilities such as apparent instability at the opening of a poem is to *fetishise* beginning. The traditional invocation of a muse – or its subversion, as in the famous opening of Rilke's first *Duino Elegy*: 'Who, if I cried out, would hear me then from the angel / ranks?' – is a gesture of demarcation, much like dimming the House Lights, tuning a fiddle, or asking, 'Are you sitting comfortably?' Other first lines announce the programme for the poem: '*Arma virumque cano*', 'Yes, I remember Adlestrop.' Or they employ apostrophe: 'O wild West Wind, thou breath of autumn's being', 'Tiger! Tiger!', 'Thou still unravished bride of quietness.' Even the contemporary orthodoxy that has a poem proceed from some material example towards affect or insight is really just another form of scene-setting:

> By the headstones are toys and flowers and birds
> – budgies mainly, some owls –
> with wings that mill and whirr.
> (Jamie McKendrick, 'By the Headstones'[19])

> It was the first gift he ever gave her,
> buying it for three francs in the Galeries
> in pre-war Paris. [...]
> (Eavan Boland, 'The Black Lace Fan My Mother Gave Me'[20])

However significant beginnings are, whenever something comes first something else – a middle – must come second. Arguably, breath reveals its scope more through the phrase-dependent *structuring* of a poem than in the opening gestures of *utterance*. Now the *heldness* of breath or line comes to the fore.[21]

When I worked with adults with learning difficulties, I adopted the 'transparent' strategy of writing down what they said, one phrase at a time. I recorded each new phrase as a new line. In other words thought, phrase and poetic line coincided in a 'three-ply' building block within a piece. I soon discovered that I wasn't indulging in anthropological eavesdropping. These were *dictated* lines of poetry, being composed by people who happened not to have either literacy or particularly advanced language skills. Here's a poem by the women of the St Cross Day Centre on the Isle of Wight:

'The World Tree'

Perhaps the world isn't a round ball.
Perhaps it's a tree.
The roots go down to the underworld

where anger and hate and criminals and murderers are,
and the branches go up to heaven
where God and the angels are.
That would mean that everything is joined
to everything else,
that the world is a place
where good and bad are joined.[22]

Our technique turned out to be much better suited to a poem like this one – where the material was conceptually challenging for its authors and so each phrase had been elicited relatively slowly, by questions – than to work with a fluent speaker, for example someone who is temporarily unable to write for physiological reasons, talking about a favourite subject. When an oral poem is dictated by someone whose fluency outruns their need to reflect, the key link between thought and *poetics*, the connection Heidegger identifies with his arboreal metaphor, is broken. A line is no longer a unit of thought. The 'now' of the connected line of sense spreads some distance ahead of (and behind) the word being uttered. The *chrononomie* of the poem is no longer 'real time', as what comes next is often something we already know. Phrases tend to be longer, and to be delivered not only more rapidly but in groups; these correspond to sentences and even paragraphs. The structural necessity of the phrasal unit has been lost. The result is prose:

> [...] Men are supposed to be nice to their girlfriend, but sometimes men beat their wives up.

> What should a wife do? She should go and report it to the police. It's not enough to hit him back, because he's big and strong. Men should not hit women because women are fragile. They should hit someone their own size, otherwise they're a bully and a coward.[23]

This extract is from another piece by the women of St Cross, on a topic about which they had much more to say. One of the ways can we tell that 'The World Tree' is a poem is through its discursive role. Its authors thought it was a poem and wanted it treated as such, and it performs many of the functions – condensation, record, heightening – a poem can undertake. But another way is through the chronologic supremacy of its phrasal line. If we try to run the piece together as a paragraph, we can still hear and feel the form of the poem in the balance of these phrases, their rhythmic similarity and their similarity of length and pitch:

> Perhaps the world isn't a round ball. Perhaps it's a tree. The roots go down to the underworld[,] where anger and hate and criminals and murderers are, and the branches go up to heaven[,] where God and the angels are. That would mean that everything is joined to everything else, that the world is a place where good and bad are joined.

Run together like this, the poem makes for flat, jerky writing. The equation between a line of thought and each line of the original poem is usually conspicuous; in fact structural.

So 'The World Tree' shows us the *phrase* – it's no coincidence that this term's both linguistic and musical – delivering semantic *and* semiotic unity. Far from fragmenting or weakening the simple free verse form, its reinforcing layer-cake of poetic line, line of thought and melodic phrasal unit creates that form. Indeed, arguably it's the working together of such elements that differentiates the lyric poetic and musical tradition, in its widest sense, from L=A=N=G=U=A=G=E poetry, or serial music. As well as the horizontal generation of surface, this working together creates a vertical push-me-pull-you of relationship between the parts of speech, or the pitch relations, that make music and language habitable by human meaning. 'The World Tree' may seem artless; but its 'roots go down' into the very way we use language.

Of course, dictated free verse is just one, highly specific, poetic. Phrase and line aren't *necessarily* identical in either free or formal verse. Free verse can enjamb with the best of them, while formal verse has the potential to appear *over*-defined by its metre, its lineation entirely a question of footfall. The argument for the principle of the phrasal line offers two responses to such counterexamples. One is that, nevertheless, there are enough schools of poetry in which we *can* readily see phrasal lineation at work to make a case for its significance. The other is that even apparently contrary examples may reveal a deeper lyrical logic, in which the phrase *generates* a poetic line it rests within or plays against, for example enlarging the line by enjambment, or subdividing it with a caesura.

So phrases seem to be building-blocks of poetry, as they are of speech. We readily think of Beat, or Black Mountain, poetics as predicated upon speech rhythms. But other, older prosodies also have the measure of the phrase. Anglo-Saxon and traditional Welsh forms, both of which 'pair' responding assonances across the caesura, give us the earliest examples in British verse of lines with two phrases stacked inside them, as in this passage from *Solomon and Saturn*:

> Forðan nah seo modor geweald,   ðonne heo magan cenneð
> bearnes blædes,   ac sceall on gebyrd faran
> an æfter annum;   ðaet is eald gesceaft.
>
> (For then a mother wields no power   over how he becomes a man,
> the child she conceives,   but from birth one thing will follow
> another;   that is the world's way.)[24]

It's also the motor of parallelism, that two-phrase form so hugely influential in English prosody since the sixteenth century, when the *Coverdale Psalter* was incorporated into *The Book of Common Prayer*. In parallelism, the second 'line' of the verse runs parallel to the first, both rhythmically and in one or more of a number of semantic ways. In *The Art of Biblical Poetry*, his seminal study of this technique, the American Biblical scholar and translator Robert Alter defines these as: synonymity, sometimes with verbatim repetition; intensification, often with increased specificity; complementarity; narrative consequentiality.[25]

In my own analysis, the opening of Psalm 27 shows us parallelism at work in a variety of ways:

> 1. The LORD is my light and my salvation; whom then shall I fear? The LORD is the strength of my life; of whom then shall I be afraid?
> 2. One thing have I desired of the LORD, which I will require, Even that I may dwell in the house of the LORD all the days of my life, to behold the fair beauty of the LORD, and to visit his temple.
> 3. For in the time of trouble he shall hide me in his tabernacle; Yea, in the secret place of his dwelling shall he hide me, and set me up upon a rock of stone.[26]

Here, parallelism divides a verse (verse 3) and also acts *within* each half of the verse, thus making a doctrinal point – 'The Lord is the strength of my life' *means the same as* 'of whom then shall I be afraid?' (verse 1); and to retain repetition within the half-verse but posit the reciprocity of question and answer (which make their own kind of 'parallel') at the half-verse point (verse 2).

Among the earliest English verse to be influenced by this imported form – besides the hendiadys so prevalent in Shakespearean dialogue – were the freshly composed antiphons of *Common Prayer* itself. In Matins:

> *Priest:* O Lord, open thou our lips
> *Answer:* And our mouths shall show forth thy praise.
> *Priest:* O God, make speed to save us
> *Answer:* O Lord, make haste to help us.

Repetitive rather than dialectical, the to-and-fro of versicle and response owes less to Socratic dialogue than to a sense of *rhythmic* entailment, that what-goes-up-must-come-down feeling which the regularity of a formal metrical line also produces. In other words, apart from the fact that it is read, rather than improvised, repeated or remembered, it works just like call and response in oral traditions that range across the world, from Sub-Saharan Africa to Cuba, and from Classical Indian to Québecois folk music.

All the same, as in Socratic *dialectic*, this one-step-at-a-time oscillation between approach and standstill seems to lead the mind to *something beyond* itself. Liturgy doubtless intends that to be God. Yet it's the singing human who is posited by every breath, and so at the limit of every phrase. Of plainchant, that liturgical equivalent predating Anglicanism, the Catholic composer Olivier Messiaen notes that:

> 'the ordering of movement' [...] involves the alternation of rises and falls that the Greeks so aptly called *arses* and *theses*. Now, all well-written music contains this constant alternation. Plainchant, to cite only one case, is an uninterrupted succession of *arses* and *theses*, elevations and drops, rises and falls, as was perfectly delineated by the greatest theoretician of plainchant, Dom Mocquereau.[27]

Such counterbalanced exchanges demonstrate the extent of a phrase: and how after a certain point – a sort of phrasal life expectancy – each topples over into the next. Crucially for the *and then ... and then* of poetry, this shows us how a phrase can precipitate a posterity: a *what next?* Phrasal lines seem to be so many *gradus ad parnassum*. Each rhythmic step throws the speaker, singer, listener or thinker *forward*, and so *entails* an ... *and then*; just as each step taken throws the walker momentarily out of balance, tipping them forwards beyond *where they stand*.

If there *is* no next phrase, the *next* into which we're led is the silence that lurks, like a tricky manoeuvre, at the end of each phrase. Silence seems particularly close at line-ends, whose natural porosity allows it to leak into a poem. Sometimes this produces the pleasurable prolongation of enjambment, like Edward Thomas's casual trick of timing that gives us his pause – 'No-one left and no-one came / On the bare platform' – in 'Adlestrop'.[28] But at others it generates a vertiginous *aporia* after which the next line must virtually re-start the poem. In the same poet's 'Cock-Crow', for example, this *aporia*, underlined by over-punctuation (a comma *and* a dash), is deployed to leave a space for death. And not only the mortal death that night worries brood on, as in its opening couplet's ostensible theme, but (by way of an extended metaphor about the cock crowing on the morning after the Crucifixion, and Peter denying Christ) the death of hope:

> Out of the wood of thoughts that grows by night
> To be cut down by the sharp axe of light, –
> Out of the night, two cocks together crow[29]

This end-line pause is also that silence just before dawn. And it would be easy to imagine such a silence waiting in the margins of the poem as a kind of ghost- or anti-poem, with the potential to undo or overwhelm language.

Small wonder, then, that poems often *end* as if they're pre-empting a risk of dissolution. Some gestures of ending are pre-eminently semantic completions. Douglas Dunn, for example, has a tendency to write the kind of summing-up that is also a summoning-up of poetic forces. Think of the so-quotable end of 'A Removal from Terry Street': 'That man, I wish him well. I wish him grass.' Dunn's naval verse-novel *The Donkey's Ears* ends with a terrifying bull's-eye on the very last word, 'dressed to meet the horrid sea'.[30] Strong endings can also be aurally seductive. End-rhyme is, arguably, no more compelling than internal rhyme: both establish coherence, with all this suggests of control, authority and necessity, not to mention an existential Order of Things. But end-rhyme also locks a lyric shut. Philip Larkin was a master of the poetic punch-line: 'Begin afresh, afresh, afresh', '[...] somewhere becoming rain', 'Unlucky charms, perhaps.'[31] His much-quoted 'What will survive of us is love', in 'On an Arundel Tomb' clinches, even as it undermines, a (slant) rhyme ('prove/love') which tracks straight back to Christopher Marlowe's 'Passionate Shepherd':

> Come live with me, and be my love,
> And we will all the pleasures prove,
> That Valleys, groves, hills and fields,
> Woods, or steepy mountain yields.[32]

In Larkin, the rhyme worms its way out less wholeheartedly:

> [...] The stone fidelity
> They hardly meant has come to be
> Their final blazon, and to prove
> Our almost-instinct almost true:
> What will survive of us is love.[33]

Rhyme locks this stable-door *before* the horse can bolt: and the bolts are, perhaps, drawn all the tighter because of the instability ('they *hardly* meant ... *almost*-instinct *almost* true') of the poem's triply-qualified conclusion. After all, this ending reminds us, the end of a poem is *where the breath runs out*. The end of every poem is a little death.

So – phrase by phrase – breath measures, and stages, the beginning, middle and end of a poem, as it does song. Thinking about this can shift us towards a richer understanding of poetic 'meaning'. Melody reminds us how fundamentally human the dimensions of such phrases are. When he starts to sing, breath maps a singer's body onto *both* pitch and words. The singer sings his own physical capacity – the volume of his lungs, the shape of his voice box – out into the world. These sounds trace the workings of his body more purely than does speech, which is mediated by social inflection as well as by that stuttering effect of 'thinking aloud' caused by the *psychological friction* of content on what's being said.

Yet still what we call speech rhythms, the familiar shape of voiced units, haunt the lines of every song, reproducing themselves through, and being reproduced by, breath length. Breath entails both the possibility of, and a limit to, the spoken unit, which is therefore by necessity the basic unit of communication – which is to say, of sense. A phrase *is* the length of a breath. And meaning-making mimics breathing. 'What we can say' is both what we understand (take in) and what we have breath to say (expel). The poet Tony Harrison's insistence that iambic pentameter is Yorkshire speech-rhythm might be a form of regional special pleading, but it usefully suggests how naturally metre can arise, with only the lightest top-and-tailing, from the spoken phrase.

Does breath itself have a shape as well as length? I suspect that it does, and that this is what we hear in the 'common lore' of *grammatical music*, when we can follow the shape of a conversation in a language we don't know, or despite the muffling bedroom wall. In that strange experience of understanding without understanding, we glimpse the shape of the phrase *itself*: a set of speech forms or relationships prior to any particular vocabulary. Perhaps this isn't surprising. Since breath is the medium of speech, it makes sense to think of speech as having had to evolve *within* that breath. The relationship between breath and grammatical music is particularly noticeable when it breaks down, as when children run out of breath and snatch another in the middle of a phrase while they're reporting a message or reading aloud. Or when prose dreamt up entirely on the page or in the head – whether legalese or obsessive-compulsive graphomania – forms an indigestible linguistic bolus.

In yet another example, I'm well aware that I don't use pentameter myself because I can't *manage* it. This is not to say that I'm so far from Yorkshire that I can't hear the form. On the contrary, as a reader I'm drawn to its regular, persuasive music and its historically laden accent of authority. But I can't easily read such lines aloud. A lifetime of bronchial infections means I can comfortably utter a four-stress line at most and, since I think 'in my own voice', my phrases are a little shorter than, say, Harrison's. The lines in my poems don't have more than four stresses: often they're shorter still. Although they don't correspond to phrases as simply as lines do in oral free verse form, there is still a strong correlation. I don't compose like this in order to have the poem 'go well' in public readings. It's simply the compositional music that my inner ear supplies. How I breathe is how I think. The meaning the phrasal line can carry is what I can utter.

So it seems as though, in generating and limiting the *melodic* unit, breath might outline, or measure, the *semantic* unit too. Like any marriage of the musical and the semantic, this possibility could be of vital interest to poetry. It's small wonder that the Russian Acmeist Osip Mandelstam's idea of 'composing on the lips' is so attractive to a contemporary poet like John Burnside, whose extended lyrics employ an elastic linearity to join idea to idea and image to image.[34] In North America, the phrasal unit plays an equally *propulsive* role in such sharply contrasted poetics as those of Jorie Graham or C. K. Williams, who is not a *poet of process* although his work shows us the process of psychic exploration. Each uses repeated *phrasal initiatives* to build long, urgent lines:

> I have talked too much. Have hurried. Have tried to cover the fear
> with curiosity. Also amazement. It is fear. Also know that a poem
> is, in the end, not supposed to scare you, sweet friend, reader,
> I believe you to be a person who would hide me if it came to that.
> Wouldn't you? Whoever I am or happen to be.
> [...][35]

In other words, when grammar and melody move towards coincidence, they do so through the phrasal logic of a breath: its rise and fall, its deployable extent. Charles Olson's famous 1950 essay, 'Projective Verse', says as much when he identifies the poem's movement – a kind of breath of life – with human breath, which he sees as a *generative* principle:

> I say a projective poet will [go] down through the workings of his
> own throat to that place where breath comes from, where breath has
> its beginnings, where drama has come from, where, the coincidence
> is, all act springs.

Problematically, though, he goes on to conflate this universal principle with a particular poetics:

[...] ONE PERCEPTION MUST IMMEDIATELY AND DIRECTLY LEAD TO A FURTHER PERCEPTION. [...] get on with it, keep moving, keep in, speed, the nerves, their speed, the perceptions, theirs, the acts, the split second acts, the whole business, keep it moving as fast as you can, citizen. And if you also set up as a poet, USE USE USE the process at all points, in any given poem always, always one perception must must must MOVE, INSTANTER, ON ANOTHER![36]

Olson's special-case argumentation misses the point that the line of a poem – that musical semantic unit – is itself based on breath as an *impersonal* principle. Rather as the old imperial measure of a foot doesn't correspond to a particular shoe-size, but indicates human scale in general, the phrasal line of breath in a poem isn't a record of Olson's – or your, or my – personal lung-capacity, but of human breath in general. Like no other form *except music itself*, a poem's lineation records this human grammar, and takes from it its own characteristic 'tune'.[37]

To sum up, then, the breath-scale phrase attests to the human voiced-ness of the form. But, as we've seen, poetry also carries other traces of the melodic phrasal breath. It incorporates such aspects of performativity as stylised beginnings and ends (with which to resist silence), it allows phrasal music to generate the poem, and it deploys the musical character of grammatical units and the meaningfulness of the musical elements in language.

Dada heard these originary musical elements as occurring at the level of syllables, and advocated a poetry led by them:

> I want my own stuff, my own rhythm, and vowels and consonants too, matching the rhythm and all my own. [...] I let the vowels fool around. I let the vowels quite simply occur, as a cat meows ... Words emerge, shoulders of words, legs, arms, hands of words. Au, oi, uh. One shouldn't let too many words out. A line of poetry is a chance to get rid of all the filth that clings to this accursed language, as if put there by stockbrokers' hands, hands worn smooth by coins.[38]

But this is a radical form of special pleading for a radical form of poetics. What we can say in general is that poems utter themselves one line at a time. Perhaps this is so that they can be heard clearly.[39] Or maybe it's because linearity is the only real sense that can be made of our sequential lives: think of the *and then* ...

and then of an Abbas Kiarostami movie, or the way a child tells what happened in school today. As Lewis Caroll's White Knight said to Alice in *Through the Looking Glass*, 'You start at the beginning and go on to the end.'[40] Maybe poetry's understanding of the power of enactment is so strong that it has to *adopt* linear 'life-forms'. Or perhaps the singularity of the line brings a rare experience of resolution to the multiplicity of experience.

These are speculations. What we know is that the line of breath is inflected and flexible: it's something living and human. It is not a carapace. (It's not even like the shoes of the canonical greats, which challenge us to fill them exactly or fail.) Breath slips through the cracks in the metrical pavement, yet it remains exact and elective. Far from the kind of careless reading, or writing, which the problematic term 'voice' sometimes implies, breath is an additional connector, a further logic, underpinning metre and form. Breath, it transpires, is not only the human measure within language, but its animator – giving musical sense to semantic content, and creating a grammar for sound.

Notes

1. Igor Stravinsky, 'Bassoon solo in the opening measures of the introduction, "A Kiss of the Earth"', *Rite of Spring* https://en.wikipedia.org/wiki/The_Rite_of_Spring_discography. Retrieved 1/2/16.

2. Indeed, Stravinsky notates this group-etto, each time it occurs, as part ornament (grace notes) and part metrical scoring – through *rubato*, which gives the performer temporal flexibility.

3. On a bad day it's even possible to detect Mr Punch's swizzle in the double-reed squawk.

4. This definition, given by Derrida in 1970, is here taken from Richard Macksey and Eugenio Donato (eds), *The Structuralist Controversy: The Languages of Criticism and the Sciences of Man* (Baltimore: Johns Hopkins University Press, 1972), p. 254. This thinking is a feature of Derrida's earlier work. Later roughly analogous terms with which Derrida deconstructs the metaphysics of presence include 'arché-writing', 'pharmakos/pharmakon', 'specter' and, perhaps most famously, 'difference'. Jacques Derrida, *Of Grammatology*, Gayatri Chakravorty Spivak (trans.) (Baltimore: Johns Hopkins University Press, 1976, corrected edn 1997).

5. Establishing a typology of lines of practice, his Chapters 1 and 5 identify speech, song and music as related practices, made material

by analogous forms of notation. Tim Ingold, *Lines: A Brief History* (London: Routledge, 2007).

6. Pierre Boulez, *Boulez on Music Today*, Susan Bradshaw and Richard Rodney Bennett (trans.) (London: Faber, 1975), p. 20.

7. Tim Ingold's lines are active principles, as much line-making as the record of that process. Perhaps it's not surprising that he has also published a study of such processes. Tim Ingold, *Making* (London: Routledge, 2013).

8. In 1999, Richard Taruskin caused a storm by claiming to have identified specific ethnographic sources for the 'folksong' material in the *Rite*, a notion which Stravinsky had resisted. Richard Taruskin, *Stravinsky and the Russian Traditions* (Berkeley: University of California Press, 1996). Eric Walter White describes this melody as 'borrowed from a collection of Lithuanian folk music'. Eric Walter White, *Stravinsky: The Composer and his Works* (Berkeley and Los Angeles: University of California Press, 1966).

9. https://www.youtube.com/watch?v=ETTzL8MbjL8 at 3'28'. Retrieved 27/12/15.

10. Martin Heidegger, 'The Thinker as Poet' in *Poetry, Language, Thought*, Albert Hofstadter (trans.) (San Francisco: Harper, 1975), p. 13.

11. *The Oxford Companion to Music* calls 'Song' 'an instinctive activity of the human species, a natural means of self-expression common to all races. Its origins can be traced back into prehistory, most obviously to the human fascination with rhythm and the inflections of speech.' *The Oxford Companion to Music*, Alison Latham (ed.) (Oxford: Oxford University Press, 2002), p. 1183.

12. P. M. Marafioti, *Caruso's Method of Voice Production: The Scientific Culture of the Voice* (New York: D. Appleton & Company, 1922).

13. I'm grateful to John Kinsella for reminding me that tradition simply encodes the way in which we have necessary a priori knowledge of whatever forms we humans devise: since as Kant points out, they must fit with our capacities.

14. Juxtaposed in Denis O'Driscoll (ed.), *The Bloodaxe Book of Poetry Quotations* (Tarset: Bloodaxe, 2006), pp. 28–9.

15. Alfred Brendel, *Fingerzeig* (Munich: Carl Hanser Verlag, 1996).

16. Something I tried to explore in Fiona Sampson, 'Long Sight and Reading Glasses', *Poetry* 195 (February 2010), pp. 402–10.

17. 'Joseph Brodsky, *Collected Poems in English* (Manchester: Carcanet, 2001), pp. 163–208 and 215–25 respectively. 'Lithuanian Nocturne' starts with a sea-scene and only turns back to greet its dedicatee, the Lithuanian poet Tomas Venclova, in the second section.

18. Robert Lowell, 'Night Sweat' and 'Water', in *For the Union Dead* (London: Faber, 1965), pp. 68 and 3.

19. Jamie McKendrick, *Ink Stone* (London: Faber, 2003), p. 25.
20. Eavan Boland, *Object Lessons* (Manchester: Carcanet, 1990), p. 11.
21. If we think about poetry as song, we might assume that what we hear are the notes of vowels; the swell or breath of a note. Not only may vowels sound 'pitched' – Gerard Manley Hopkins's vowelling-on and vowelling-off – but they seem to be the space through which a note sounds. Like the 'o' blooming and ballooning in its monosyllable, the word 'note' itself makes us think of the O written on the musical stave; of a circle to be filled with colour and timbre. Yet music is in fact notated by the *start* of each note – the strike, or puff – though this notation *includes* other information, such as pitch and duration. It's as if Western musical notation is, like the Hebrew alphabet, all consonants. For example, in Baroque-style string playing it's up to the string itself to keep the note vibrating after it's been sounded, to a much greater extent than in later schools of playing. Founded on the ability of modern instruments (differently strung, and with heavier bows) and techniques (legato bowing, vibrato) to sustain, these 'play through the note' to such an extent that the nineteenth century had to reintroduce the percussive element with new bowing techniques: *fouetté, staccato, spiccato, flying spiccato*.
    This suggests the possibility of a consonantal poetics. After all, speech is percussion – of tongue, lips and palate – as well as breath. The clatter of alliteration, so eagerly shed by poets the moment they leave the classroom, should at least alert us to the *audibility* of consonants. And in assonantal forms like Welsh *cynghanedd*, it's the consonants which draw the veil through which the vowels work: concealment once again also acting as a projective screen. Alliteration was part of the patterning of the Finnish traditional material which became the *Kalevala*, as indeed of the Estonian *Kaevipoeg*, Old Norse, Anglo-Saxon verse including *Beowulf* and even the Middle English prosody of *Pearl* and *Piers Plowman*. Indeed, to compare the burr of assonantal poetry with the click and chime of something led by the consonants, is to be aware of how deeply integrated consonantal alertness already is – as to the difference between those two articles, 'the' and 'a'. The former is thickened, softened and anonymised by that almost-pluralising *th*, while the latter arguably sounds baldly isolate.
22. St Cross House Day Centre, Newport, Isle of Wight, Isle of Wight District Health Authority, 1993.
23. Ibid.
24. *Solomon and Saturn* 420–2. My translation: for a more fluent version see Fiona Sampson, 'Two passages from *The Second Dialogue of Solomon and Saturn*' in Greg Delanty and Michael Matto (eds), *The Word Exchange: Anglo-Saxon Poems in Translation* (New York and London: Norton, 2011), pp. 247–57.

25. Robert Alter, *The Art of Biblical Poetry*, revised and updated edn (New York: Basic Books, 2011). He has a particularly useful summary on p. 32.

26. These verses are slightly varied in the seventeenth century by the *King James Bible*:

> 1. The LORD is my light and my salvation; whom shall I fear? the LORD is the strength of my life; of whom shall I be afraid? [...]
> 4. One thing have I desired of the LORD, that will I seek after; that I may dwell in the house of the LORD all the days of my life, to behold the beauty of the LORD, and to enquire in his temple.
> 5. For in the time of trouble he shall hide me in his pavilion: in the secret of his tabernacle shall he hide me; he shall set me up upon a rock.

Psalms 27:1–5 in *The King James Bible*, http://biblehub.com/psalms/27–1.htm to http://biblehub.com/psalms/27–5.htm. Retrieved 2/1/16.

27. Olivier Messiaen in conversation with Claude Samuel, *Music and Colour*, E. Thomas Glasow (trans.) (Portland: Amadeus Press, 1994), p. 69.

28. Edward Thomas, 'Adlestrop' in *The Annotated Collected Poems*, Edna Longley (ed.) (Tarset: Bloodaxe, 2008), p. 51.

29. Ibid. 'Cock-Crow', p. 96.

30. Douglas Dunn, 'A Removal from Terry Street' in *Terry Street* (London: Faber, 1969), p. 20. Douglas Dunn, *The Donkey's Ears* (London: Faber, 2000).

31. Philip Larkin, 'The Trees', 'The Whitsun Weddings', 'Wild Oats' in *Collected Poems*, Anthony Thwaite (ed.) (London: Faber and the Marvell Press, 1988), pp. 166, 114–16 and 143.

32. Christopher Marlowe, 'The Passionate Shepherd to his Love', http://www.poetryfoundation.org/poem/173941. Retrieved 27/12/15.

33. Philip Larkin, 'An Arundel Tomb' in *The Whitsun Weddings* (London: Faber, 1964), pp. 45–6.

34. John Burnside, *Waking Up in Toytown* (London: Cape, 2010), p. 147.

35. Jorie Graham, *Overlord* (Carcanet: Manchester, 2005), p. 86.

36. Charles Olson, *Collected Prose*, Donald Hall and Benjamin Friedlander (eds) (Berkeley and Los Angeles: University of California Press, 1997).

37. What then to make of Timothy Polashek's 'Babble' computer programme, which generates 'poems' by sound? http://muse.jhu.edu/journals/lmj/summary/v015/15.1polashek.html. Retrieved 27/1/16.

38. Hugo Ball, *Dada Manifesto*. Read at the first public Dada soirée, Zurich, 14 July 1916.

39. As in Heathcote Williams's polemic *Badshah Khan*, which tells an important story from Pashtun history in double-spaced lines of free verse. The effect is of being told a children's story, a point I made in a review in *The Independent* on 12/7/15. Heathcote Williams, *Badshah Khan* (London: Thin Man Press, 2015). Fiona Sampson, 'The Leader Who Was More Remarkable than Mahatma Gandhi' in *The Independent*, 12 July 2015. http://www.independ ent.co.uk/arts-entertainment/books/reviews/badshah-khan-by- heathcote-williams-book-review-the-leader-who-was-more- remarkable-than-mahatma-10383353.html. Retrieved 27/12/15

40. Lewis Carroll, *Alice's Adventures in Wonderland and Through the Looking Glass* (Harmondsworth: Puffin, 1962).

Chapter 4

Chromaticism

In 1879 Hubert Parry wrote, in *Grove's Musical Dictionary*, that: 'Secular music has long displayed the very free use of chromaticisms similar to the modern style of writing' (by which he meant musical composition). In turn, the *Oxford English Dictionary* has quoted this entry to demonstrate how the idea of 'chromaticism' is used: for *Grove's* is still, as it was when Parry contributed to it, the key reference encyclopaedia for British musicians.[1] Sure enough, thinking of tonal or harmonic variations in terms of colour – as *chromaticism* does – may have its literal origins in synaesthesia, but such thinking is now so much part of the language of Western Classical music that it's barely audible to musicians, even as metaphor.[2]

When he wrote his entry Parry was not yet the established composer, in particular of church music, who would so famously set William Blake's poem 'Jerusalem'. He was still the youthful protégé of the *Musical Dictionary*'s founder, George Grove, and was struggling to escape a career in business and as a Lloyds underwriter. Nevertheless, the more than one hundred entries he wrote as a *Groves* staffer would secure him the Professorship of Composition and Musical History at the Royal College of Music. They also influenced generations of British musicians. Among them was Edward Elgar; who told his old friend, the violinist William H. Reed, that he had found Parry's articles particularly helpful because of his own lack of formal musical training.[3]

Elgar himself was to evolve into the pre-eminent British chromaticist composer. His characteristically sensuous sound gains both its edge and its tendency to slipperiness from chromaticism's rapid movement between musical keys, and inclusion of notes from outside any given key. There is something touching about an establishment figure, such as Sir Edward became, characterising his musical education as ad hoc. It also implies a process cozily resembling traditional British pragmatism. Reed, who *had* undergone the usual formation (studying the violin at the Royal Academy of Music with Émile Sauret, among others), will have been aware of this. Nevertheless, it is apt and suggestive that a composer who went on to use the *feel* of harmony in new ways might have *felt* his way into professional musicianship: a process with echoes of the 'legitimate play' we saw at work in Chapter 2.

For another way to describe a chromaticist is to say that the composer uses pitch and modulation *because of what they sound like* rather than because of any formal, systematic relationships among them. We shouldn't get carried away by a notion of Elgar's technique as something folksily homemade, however. The ten-minute tone-poem Prelude that opens his *The Dream of Gerontius* Op. 38 was written in 1900, just over twenty years after Parry published that *Grove's* entry. Yet the sound world it creates is startlingly complete. Elgar's *leitmotifs*, present from the outset, are every bit as assimilated as Richard Wagner's in his *Ring Cycle* WWV 86 (which had been completed in 1878). The sustained, and sustaining, character of Gerontius's faith is portrayed, in the Prelude's first four bars, by clarinets and violas. Both are instruments characterised by a plangent tone, and here they inch along stepwise – then down a single minor third. They're followed – in bars five and six, the instrumentation now slightly augmented by the related timbres of cellos and cor anglais – by the upward-straining intervals that represent Gerontius's hope for transcendence. First a fifth, then a fourth (as if hope or expectation must always be reduced), the intervals of this leitmotif are also characteristically Elgarian, but here they appear without the striding ardour of the *Introduction and Allegro* for strings Op. 47, or even that late work, the Cello Concerto Op. 85. They subside immediately into a reprise of the faith as consistency theme by the original instruments, with the addition of French horn (and second violins) (see Fig. 4.1).[4]

Such fluency in the use of chromaticism is the result of much

Figure 4.1 Opening of the Prelude to Elgar's *The Dream of Gerontius*

more than simply two decades of consolidation by an individual, even one as exceptional as Elgar. Parry's *Dictionary* entry went on to point out how, for the last thousand years, Western art music has consistently used elements that are *not* strictly predicated by tonal harmonies, in order to produce particular sensations. Thus, around 1026, Guido of Arezzo's *Micrologus Guidonis de disciplina artis musicae* disallowed certain pitches which he called *musica ficta*, on the grounds that they disrupted the sacred order (*musica recta*) of Gregorian chant. Like many revisionists, Guido d'Arezzo claimed his discrimination followed a natural order of things:

> For me, to bring boys to music among their other studies is both the natural condition and an imitation of goodness it is generally useful to perform diligently. Eventually, aided by divine grace and through imitating the harmonies, our notes are trained by use until the unseen and unheard space of song is on one single plane of song [...] I do not know how whoever cannot do this dares call himself a musician or a singer.[5]

In response composers such as Josquin des Prez, in his four-part motet 'Ave Maria ... Virgo Serena', used *musica ficta* accidentals either as a kind of decoration, which sounds to our later ears like a passing note, or consciously to disrupt that sacred order.[6]

In nineteenth- and twentieth-century music, the role of diatonic chromaticism – that is, the inclusion of notes from outside the particular key in which a piece is set – scarcely differed.[7] Catherine Clément's feminist analysis of *Opera, or the Undoing of Women* looks at how often operas use chromaticism, which deviates from the norm of the harmonic given, to characterise female roles; echoing the way that, in the societies from which its composers come, masculinity is the prescribed norm from which women's roles and experiences deviate.[8] These kinds of insight have been familiar since Simone de Beauvoir's groundbreaking *The Second Sex*, published in 1949.[9] But the feminist musicologist Susan McClary goes further, in her book *Feminine Endings*, showing how this use of chromaticism doesn't simply 'wrong' characters by differentiating them from the kind of wholesome, foursquare tonality it reserves for the good, and the male. It also actively contributes to stereotypes of women characters as dangerously sexy, often exotic.[10]

We can hear this in the sliding semitones that introduce the heroine's *habanera* 'L'amour est un oiseau rebelle' in Act 1, Scene 5 of Georges Bizet's *Carmen* (see Fig. 4.2).[11] The habanero rhythm is initially sketched out lightly, even skittishly, by the cellos. It's a traditional dance form that entails the stylised acting out of heterosexuality: Bizet himself thought he was adapting a genuine folksong for this number.[12] The ostentatious

Figure 4.2 Habanera from Bizet's *Carmen*

timidity of that opening half-bar, and of the first phrases of the solo line, are a seduction narrative. Carmen advances – in fact she *descends* – slinkily, by chromatic semitones. The orchestra transforms this solo dance into something altogether more like an oompah street band when it introduces the masculine principle. Don José is added to the mixture for all the world as if this were a classic love duet (which, in a sense, is just what it is). The harmonically conventional *bel canto* descant (rising to F#5) with which Carmen responds to his advances is the sound of sexual confidence; but it is also the sound of her being

Figure 4.3 *Parsifal* leitmotif (a)

Figure 4.4 *Parsifal* leitmotif (b)

appropriated to her conventional role, as she fits herself into Don José's tonal world.

De Beauvoir was at work four decades earlier than either Clément or McClary, and the argument she makes is that this kind of cultural construction is much more than local to one particular cultural moment. Sure enough, while some Western composers link chromaticism to what Clément – in the striking translation by Betsy Wing of her comments on Wagner's *Tristan and Isolde* – calls 'feminine stink', they may also link it to *otherness* in general. Richard Wagner's notorious anti-semitism has laid him open to accusations that Klingsor, the sorcerer in *Parsifal*, is Jewish. The sliding colours of his Klingsor's sorcery theme are literally 'creepy' as they inch around the semitones (Fig. 4.3),[13] then slip, is if in some kind of confirmation of prejudice, into Klingsor's personal leitmotif (Fig. 4.4),[14] where chromaticism's use of messy accidentals visibly 'dirties' the score.

We take for granted this kind of error of judgement on the part of such a notorious figure. We take for granted, too, that the judgement call is intentional. As Theodor Adorno says, 'What specifically characterised Wagnerian expression is its intentionality: the *leitmotiv* is a sign that transmits a particle of congealed meaning.'[15]

We know these *leitmotifs* are attempts at characterisation, or at least the crystalisation of character into a symbol, because of the story that's told by the music they are part of. Yet we ignore the similar problem of estrangement that arises in, for example, the pantomime *Aladdin*, or when W. S. Gilbert and Arthur Sullivan's 1885 pantomimic light opera *The Mikado* gives its characters 'foreign' – that is, chromatically 'out of step' – music.[16] The problem is, of course, that Gilbert and Sullivan's denigratingly named love-interest Yum-Yum isn't foreign *to herself*.[17] As far as she is concerned, she dwells (I use that loaded Heideggerian verb deliberately) in her own context just as characters who enjoy what the composer might well think of as 'good tone' do. (Hollywood deals with 'foreign' characters in the same way when it has them speak *accented or broken* English among themselves. Our ignorance of their language is portrayed as their ignorance of ours.)

Claude Debussy's exploration of an Indonesian sound world in 'Pagodes', from the 1903 *Estampes* L100 for piano, poses a different problem.[18] We can't ignore the fact that this was written at the time when *chinoiserie* was all the rage among the artistic connoisseurs of salon Paris; where Debussy lived and worked, and where he had first heard gamelan music at the 1889 *Exposition Universelle*. Orientalism distanced Western observers and collectors from such fruits of empire, even while seeming to celebrate their artistic value. The American musicologist Richard Taruskin argues that, elsewhere, the orientalism of Russian composers who were in their prime when Debussy was a student and young man (think of Modest Mussorgsky's *Pictures at an Exhibition*, Alexander Borodin's *In the Steppes of Central Asia* and Nikolai Rimsky-Korsakov's *Scheherezade*, written in respectively 1874, 1880 and 1888) reveals Russian ambivalence about their non-European neighbours even within shared national borders, and is reductive as much as evocative of:

> not just the East, but the seductive East that emasculates, enslaves, renders passive. In a word, it signifies the promise of the experience of *nega*, a prime attribute of the orient as imagined by the Russians. [...] In opera and song, *nega* often simply denotes S-E-X *à la russe*, desired or achieved.[19]

Nevertheless 'Pagodes', like the wider appetite for *chinoiserie* that was its context, teeters between appropriation and a more generous principle of artistic curiosity. Chromaticism is necessary to Debussy's piece because Indonesian music naturally uses it *own* scales, which cut across Western circle of fifths tonality. A composer who, as here, tries to learn Balinese and Javanese scales, and sees them as artistic resources, is doing something more than and different from one who only hears this music as non-Western, and doesn't try to learn from what is new to him. Debussy's 'Pagodes' exhibits the artistic greed that is the other side of artistic curiosity; but it gestures towards diversity rather than seeking to establish a normative version of the world. (It is also very much of its time, making the characteristically Modernist gesture of trying to enlarge its own vocabulary by borrowing from other traditions. We see this equally in folksong collecting by Zoltán Kodály, Béla Bartók and Ralph Vaughan Williams; or in Pablo Picasso and George Braque's imitative fascination, in the summer of 1910, with the pre-Romanesque frescoes of the church of St Martin de Fenollar in the Eastern Pyrenees.)

Chromaticism, then, is far from innocent. It's guilty of revealing how porous the boundaries are between a work of art and the social conditions under which that work was produced. But it also reveals something about the musical project itself. Guido d'Arezzo's *Treatise* included the phrase, 'unius mensis spatium invisos et inauditos cantus': 'on a single plane the unseen and unheard space of song'. From the infinite polyphony of potential musics, in other words, the musician must create a single unified plane. D'Arezzo argued that this was essential for practical reasons: so that we can sing some *thing*, and also so that what we sing can have maximum *effect*. The composer's role is to reduce infinite possibility to what can be comprehended by both singers and audience, or congregation. Composition is a human-centred, *social* task, even if it is divinely ordained. Chromaticism – *musica ficta* – he went on to argue, trespasses upon this agreed way of going on.

In other words, it's a simple matter of rule-breaking. Not only Gregorian chant, but Western art music in general, experiences itself as governed by rules. The term 'Classical music' – strictly, applied only to composers working between the Baroque and Romantic eras – remains in much more general use today, arguably because it carries forward this sense of rule-structured music. The broken rule is the exception that proves the rule. Thus chromaticism was able to enjoy free play only while such (neo-)classical elements as sonata form remained active *within* musical Romanticism. Late Romantics like Richard Wagner and Gustav Mahler stretched the old diatonic framework as far as it would go, and early twentieth-century 'Classical' music found itself having to sustain such extremes of extension and ornamentation that the balance of harmonic power was changed, and with it the whole logic of musical progression. In fact chromaticism had been audibly pushing the boundaries of classical form since at least the late great Beethoven quartets, written from 1815 onwards. But by the early twentieth century chromatic music was being built from pitches and progressions which were not related through the cycle of fifths but appealed directly to the ear.

Chromaticism *presaged* atonality. In the surprising directions taken by Carl Neilsen's symphonies from the third, *Sinfonia Espansiva* Op. 27 (1910–11) onwards, or in the almost-dissonance harmonic density of Alexander Scriabin's later work – particularly the piano sonatas written between from 1907 and his death in 1915 – it almost seems as though tonality has already been thrown off completely in favour of a kind of *pitch expressionism*. But chromaticism also *precipitated* that atonality when the degree of variation it created simply became too much for an underlying tonality to sustain – or resist. We even see this shift happening *within* Scriabin's body of work. The abundant dominant thirteenth chords so characteristic of his earlier work become crowded: just some among so many dominant chords that their exceptional character is unmoored. Eventually, in the last sonatas, only the trace of a recurring dominant seventh connects the work to tonality at all.

The result is a swirl of sensation, sometimes dressed up as mysticism or the numinous, of the kind Virginia Woolf calls the 'halo of the unconscious'. Such 'halos' seem very much to chromaticism's point. The Australian art critic Robert Hughes, writing about a visual artist who, though briefly contemporary with both Neilsen and Scriabin, was several decades younger than both, says:

> One does not read Rothko's tiers and veils of paint primarily as form: they are vehicles for colour sensation [...] almost voluptuous in their wholehearted abandonment to feeling.[20]

Hughes is too intelligent to fall for what we can call the *emotional fallacy* in art: Mark Rothko is not simply 'expressing himself'. The 'feeling' this reading evokes isn't emotion but the non-denotative, sensual quality of musical 'colour sensation' within the rubric of Western art. Analogously, the 'expression' in musical *pitch expressionism* is illusory. Even when it's used to evoke a character or create a mood, chromaticism isn't expected to reveal a composer's 'true feelings'. Music is able generally to escape the trap that Confessionalism lays for poetry.

In fact, we might do better not to think of 'colour' as denotative at all, but purely as kinds of sensation. The English Natural Philosophers John Locke and George Berkeley were already framing colour itself not as a material thing but merely as a 'secondary quality' – a visual experience – of *coloured things* at the turn of the eighteenth century.[21] It's unarguable that chromaticism reveals and celebrates the *experiential* nature of the art-forms in which it makes an appearance: the *what goes on* in viewer, listener or reader that the art produces. Indeed, affirming the experiential nature of such art, the moment at which some Western art music allowed itself to be guided by these sensations – most particularly in work by that cluster of French composers including Gabriel Fauré (1845–1924) and (almost a musical generation younger) Claude Debussy (1862–1918) and Maurice Ravel (1875–1937) – is often called Impressionism (though the composers themselves resisted the term).

It was at the same moment, and also in France, that poetry made explicit its interest in chromaticism as both a topic – something to be observed and described – and a strategy. (The apparent coincidence is of course nothing of the sort. A famous example of mutual influence is Debussy's 1894 tone poem *Prélude à l'après-midi d'un faune* 86, which – in Debussy's key term – does not 'set' but 'illustrates' Stéphane Mallarmé's poem 'L'après-midi d'un faune'.[22]) For the cluster of French Symbolist poets, from Charles Baudelaire (1821–67) and Mallarmé (1842–98) to Arthur Rimbaud (1854–91) by way of Paul Verlaine (1844–96), sensory apprehension was primary material, on which their poetry focused attention. Descriptions of sensation rather than the argument of ideas structured their material. (Unlike their composer peers, though, they were also interested in exploring and evoking emotion.)

Rimbaud's precocious 'Voyelles' sonnet can be read as launching this movement. Written when he was seventeen, it spells out the synaesthetic colours vowels have for the poet-narrator; and creates an atmosphere of decadent fantasy as it does so:

> A black, E white, I red, U green, O blue, vowels
> One day I'll talk about your unknown origins;
> A, black plush corset of shiny flies
> Buzzing around the odours of cruelty,[23]

We saw in Chapter 2 how Baudelaire's *Fleurs de Mal* (1857) offered its contemporary readers an explosion of colour; as if the world had passed from black and white into the era of colour film. His synaesthetic use of colour to evoke mood is spelt out in another sonnet, 'Correspondences':

> There are perfumes fresh as children's bodies,
> Sweet like oboes, green as fields,
> – And others corrupt, rich and triumphant,[24]

Here too chromaticism is used as a sign of transgression: Verlaine identified himself, Mallarmé, Gérard de Nerval, Arthur Rimbaud and others as decadent *poètes maudits*, out of kilter with their own gifts, lives and times. The chromatic poetic strategies they adopted included an unusually frequent use of adjectives to modulate, or even occlude, the denotative work of nouns and verbs: in much the same way that the semitone modulations of chromatic notes adapt a pitch or harmony. They also developed particular ways of drawing attention to the poem's own texture, rather than simply what it tells; these include pacing its ideas, and changing the register it uses. It's no coincidence that all of this produces the kind of writing often dismissed with the synaesthetic epithet 'purple'.

In jazz, too, 'colour' describes an experience that is aesthetic, affective and meaningful, but not strictly denotative. 'Blue notes' are the tasty, disobedient sevenths, ninths and thirteenths that both expand, and seem to transgress, the harmonic series. Like those plangent unexpected flattenings called *fictional* in mediaeval *musica recta*, the Blues started as a dolorous music in which conventional harmonies were distorted by grief; a move that shows up in simplified form and far beyond that genre in Cole Porter's 'Every Time You Go Away' when the melody

– and the words – step sideways from the major into a minor key. The Blues are not the hymns that built the white midwest. The happy harmony of the four-part hymnal is what they subvert. Many great Blues are redemption songs – after all, the root of the Blues is in Spirituals – but 'singing the Blues' still denotes songs of sorrow and suffering. Yet in jazz, as in the rest of Western music, chromaticism has over time become associated with sexiness rather than grief. Each of these – grief, suffering and sex – could be viewed as a kind of misstep, a deviation from the ideal life. But it would also be fair to argue that this range of connotations suggests how arbitrary the connection is between chromaticism and what it 'represents'.

Besides, *every* piece of music has some (home key) pitch 'colour', and what chromaticism names is not just this but the specific experience of being *led* by the feel we call 'colour'. As the later French chromaticist Olivier Messiaen (1908–92) says, 'The classical chords have attractions and resolutions. My chords are colours. They engender intellectual colours which evolve along with them.'[25] But here too we have to pause and acknowledge that in fact *all* creativity is by its nature a deviation from the given, the product of individual choice, as we saw in Chapter 3. So the composition of music and poetry is *always* inherently chromatic.

So 'chromatic' can mean not merely what's formally *disobedient*, but more broadly whatever's put in the poem for *sensory*, rather than grammatical or denotative, reasons. Chromaticism represents a principle of 'give' – of flavour, or even of deviation – within poetic language, and this principle has a number of aspects. The first of these is *semiotic independence*. It's possible to hear the play of sound not as an unanchored quality of language itself, but as necessarily – or at least residually – denotative. (It's as if we can't really bear the medium's resistance to our own 'desire lines', the ways we want it to be useful *to us*; or else we have a utopian vision of how transparent language should be.) For the Scottish poet Don Paterson, for example, phonemes don't just differentiate but enact meanings:

> Consider, say, a mother's frustrated demand to her child, 'Put down the cup.' It's easy to separate out the four vowels | ʊ | aʊ | ɪ | ʌ | ('oo – ow –ih – uh') then imagine the first vowel pitched high to indicate urgency, the second dipping down an interval of a fifth or sixth to

reinforce the impression of sane control, the third pitched identically to the first to reinforce the imperative, and the last rising another fifth – and increased in loudness – to convey the non-negotiability and frustration of the demand. The emotional sense would be clear from such a performed sequence of tones, if not the literal sense; but the consonants *pt dn th cp* alone will give us a fair stab at the semantic content, if not the tonal shape.[26]

Yet, if we listen to what happens when sound does take the stage, it's impossible to ignore the way the semiotic – the element of pure sound in language – almost overpowers the semantic.

Verse plays out this struggle for their common territory. No matter how many times I listen to a recording of Les Murray reading his poem 'Bats' Ultrasound', I can't catch all the words. And I don't do much better when his heavily and inventively vowelled 'bat English' is on the page in front of me.[27] Compare a passage from David Harsent:

'The Duffel Bag'

God's blood beads on the tarmac and something rough is boiling up just this side of the vanishing-point, so it's probably time to get

off this stretch of blacktop and into the wayside bar, where every cup runneth over and you breast a thickening fret

of stogie-smoke to get to the dank back room where a high stakes game turns against you despite your trey of jacks, and soon enough

you're in way over your head with nothing and no one to blame but the luck you've been getting since first you threw your stuff

into a duffel-bag and hooked up with the halt and lame, with the grifters and drifters, the diehards, the masters of bluff,

the very bastards, in fact, who are lifting the last of your stash ...[28]

Of course, there's an *abab* end-rhyme across these couplets. But notice, also, how 'dank back ... stakes ... jack', chiming within the space of just two lines, make an affect accelerator; how the knotted assonance of the last two lines quoted here mimetically cross-stitches 'diehards ... bastards... // last of your stash' with 'grifters ... drifters ... // lifting' into a mutual inescapability; and how assonance and alliteration crowd close up and personal at 'lifting the last of your stash'. In other words, in deploying the semiotic alongside the semantic, Harsent stages a separation of language powers that's every bit as explicit as Murray's; and he does so in order to have them *reinforce* each other.

This striking, and paradoxical, reunification of the elements of verse suggests that the semiotic *can* convey meanings and feelings; and that these may differ from the ones language explicitly *denotes*. Under pressure, language stops its grammatical forward march and becomes a 'rolling English road' of repetition, hedging, phatic jumble, stumble and malapropism. For Julia Kristeva, as we saw in Chapter 2, this 'play', or give, in language represents an inadvertent, psychotic return to pre-linguistic infancy, in which the child's babble (*lalation*) doesn't *denote* anything but *is* pure experiential play.[29] In other words, we lapse away from signification into sound when under stress; and though this sound-play is *involuntary* it's not *accidental* or *insignificant*. Kristeva's notion of the *semiotic chora*, a sensual bubble of bondedness between mother and infant in which nothing is yet divided into the conceptual entities that are building-blocks of language, may be an idealised, theoretical picture. But it is empirically true both that children have problems learning to handle their own agency – the 'terrible twos' – and that noises like humming and bubble-blowing are non-denotative ways in which a baby occupies and pleases herself. We could imagine him or her producing a halo of sound; a kind of aural Ready-Brek, part insulation, part self-extension. This halo of *extra*-ness, this part leftover for pleasure, the *play* in language – and other things – is what the French sexily call *jouissance*.[30] It's also what essentialist feminists like Hélène Cixous and Luce Irigaray contrast with the 'phallogocentrism' of baldly denotative language, the singular viewpoint of a traditionally-unquestioned and unquestioning masculine authority.

And so we come full circle, to a reclamation of the sexiness of deviance. Here I proceed with care. Certainly, the *logos*, naming and policing the world, is foundational to the Abrahamic worldview, in which protagonists are largely male: think of the 'begats' with which Christianity's Good Book (in fact irrelevantly) opens St Matthew's Gospel.[31] But gender essentialism is tricky; its capacity for own goals pretty much limitless. After all, female librarians do catalogue, and male poets do play with sound. It's also true that semiotic play *need* not indicate a psychotic return to infancy. We often enjoy it as a sign of high spirits – and not only in children: Dylan Thomas's improvised rhymes were legendary in the pubs of West Wales.[32]

Becoming aware of sound as a disobedient, labile, linguistic bonus – a principle of give and take, of flexibility and local il/ logic within language – is clearly useful in thinking about poetry. So there are fruitful aspects to the idea of linguistic *jouissance*. And in fact sound has the generosity – the plenitude – of an element we can't come to the end of. It's the context within which everyone with hearing lives continuously: I can always *look away now*, but I can't *listen away*. So it's not surprising that we've developed sophisticated, purely aural forms of awareness, including the ability to respond to non-verbal, into- national prompts such as the supportive or disapproving 'um', or to the soothing effect of lullaby. This rich and continually renewed body of aural experience, secondly, may be the knowl- edge that allows us to 'get' much of what music – and poetry – does. Certainly, the ear has no trouble understanding how the alexandrine amplifying the line in Rimbaud's 'Bateau ivre' is like that poem's dreamt-of horizon, or the alliterative clatter and assonantal straight-talk of a Charles Causley ballad take the reader straight back to nursery rhyme and playground din.

As this suggests, a third and key facet of chromaticism is *affect*: not the expression, but an acknowledgement or descrip- tion, of (emotional) response; or of something that evokes such a response. This affect *seems* to be all the reader's; but this is something to which we'll return in Chapters 8 and 12. Fourthly, however, chromaticism can also operate like a palimpsest, as a 'vertical' intensification of sensory experience. We think of musical and poetic 'give' as lateral, or chronologic, but tumble 'vertically' into the unexpected plangency of a *tierce de Picardie*, or of an epithet that suddenly raises the stakes of a poem.

Fifthly, musical instrumentation can create an inflection that's both aural and symbolic – we feel *and* understand it – by means of what I call *iconic chromaticism*. For example, the flute J. S. Bach used in setting the *Crucifixus* of his *B Minor Mass* would have been made of bone, serving as a *memento mori* with which to 'play dead'. The purely mimetic tolling tubular bells of Hector Berlioz's 'March to the Scaffold' are upstaged by four brass bands in his *Grand Messe des Morts*: since brass instruments *represent* both martial music and the last trump.[33] In poetry, formal allusions offer similar symbolic opportunities. A sonnet always has some reference to love, even if to the potential loss of all that one loves (as in John Donne's 'Death be not Proud'). It may use that affective freight to add weight to a poem about, for example, place (in William Wordsworth's 'On Westminster Bridge') or politics (thus, Percy Bysshe Shelley's 'England in 1819'). These *iconic* functions of form, that are additional to their other, technical properties, function, like an iconostasis, to indicate *the direction of the gaze*. Just as the iconostasis represents what it conceals – the holy of holies, the 'business end' of the church – iconic form stands in for what we don't directly *hear*.

Musical key can also be used iconically: as when the names of notes spell out a message. The collaborative FAE Sonata for violin and piano, by Brahms, Schumann and Albert Dietrich, is built on the mnemonic for their Romantic motto, *Frei aber einsam (Free but alone)*. J. S. Bach used B-A-C-H (B♭ is H in North European musical nomenclature) in his late, unfinished *The Art of Fugue*, and this progression has since been used, as a homage, by composers as disparate as Schumann, Liszt, Rimsky-Korsakov, Webern and Pärt. Operating only within the music's *scoring*, and not its sound – since even if you have perfect pitch and can recognise the F, for example, you're simply *identifying* the customary name for a sound, not *hearing that name* itself – this kind of iconicity finds its best analogy in some kinds of concrete poetry. The line-breaks of George Herbert's 'Easter Wings' are both displayed *and* enacted – rhyme making their 'flight' of rise and fall, as well as the shape of their fanned wings, audible:

> Lord, Who createdst man in wealth and store,
> Though foolishly he lost the same,
> Decaying more and more,
> Till he became
> Most poore:
>
> With Thee
> O let me rise,
> As larks, harmoniously,
> And sing this day Thy victories:
> Then shall the fall further the flight in me.
> [...]34

On the other hand the 'sonnets' of performance poet Patience Agbabi's 'Problem Pages', fourteen-line blocks of justified text, are a form that exists purely in print.[35]

Iconic chromaticism and concrete poetry, both of which privilege the eye over the ear, make us question whether the score or book should have primacy over the aural experience of music and verse. Is the musical *ur-text* the autograph manuscript, that fragile, sometimes almost illegible, piece of paper; is it the 'definitive' performance by a Solti or a Karajan; or is it neither of these? When someone reads a signature poem without the poet's own characteristic inflections, is that the reader's failure, a failure of the poet's scoring – or no failure at all? And how does the poem's own scoring differ from the way that actors 'score' a text, working out the timings – the rhythm – of a performance that is entailed, but not determined, by the text? (It seems that, just as singing is willy-nilly out loud, so a poem, in becoming a language act, is inherently *communicative*. This is something we'll return to in Chapter 6.)

In David Harsent's 'The Duffel Bag', we saw assonance and internal rhyme form a cat's cradle of congruence to both contain and guide the reader or audience, and to produce the *sound of integration*. This integration is a technical matter of managing language material. But it is established through, and establishes, readerly complicity: as when rhyme prompts us to complete the famous couplet in Shelley's 'The Mask of Anarchy', we also complete – that is, at some level assent to – the poem's *sentiment* that 'I met Murder on the way – / He had a mask like Castlereagh.'[36] Sixthly, then, chromaticism creates complicity with the reader. Sometimes it builds on expectation; at others, disrupts it. The frisson of the unusual, particularly in loan-words and dialect, is another example of such pleasurable disruption. 'The Obligatory Dialect Poem' in Toby Martinez de las Rivas's pamphlet (*Faber New Poets 2*) is fair play on, for example, John Glenday's *Grain*, Robin Robertson's *The Wrecking Light*, Don Paterson's *Rain* or Fiona Benson's *Faber New Poets 1*.[37] This private, experiential and *direct* relationship between those consenting adults, the poem and its reader, offers a radical alternative to fashionably reductive reading by topic, which instructs audiences and students that the poem is just a sort of spreadsheet of ideas and, just possibly, technical poetic strategies.

Poetry's chromaticism works against the grain of this fashion to remind us how *only the poem itself* does *being* the poem. It draws the reader's experience into the dense texture of the poem itself, situating it alongside the audience's experience of music. I'll return to the importance of these experiences in my final chapter. Next, though, we plunge into that density itself.

Notes

1. Hubert Parry, 'Harmony' in *Grove's Dictionary of Music and Musicians* (Oxford: Oxford University Press, 1900), https://en.wikisource.org/wiki/A_Dictionary_of_Music_and_Musicians/Harmony.Retrieved29/6/15.

2. Samuel Taylor Coleridge used the term 'synaethesia' for literary tropes that 'unite unlike things'. For him, knowing meant knowing sensuously, by feel or 'tact'; while the senses provided knowledge which could only be decoded by metaphor. See for example David Ward, *Coleridge and the Nature of Imagination: Evolution, Engagement with the World, and Poetry* (London: Palgrave Macmillan, 2013), pp. 8–11.

3. W. H. Reed, *The Master Musicians: Elgar* (London: Dent, 1943), p. 11.

4. Edward Elgar, *The Dream of Gerontius* (London: Novello, 1902). Public domain: http://imslp.org/wiki/File:PMLP40537-Elgar_-_The_Dream_of_Gerontius,_Op._38_-_Part_I_(orch._score).pdf. Retrieved27/12/15.

5. 'Cum me et naturalis condition at bonarum imitation communis utilitatis diligenteum faceret, cepi inter alia studia musicam tradere pueris. Tandem adfuit mihi divina gratia, et quidam eorum imitation chordae, nostrarum notarum usu excercitati, ante unius mensis spatium invisos et inauditos cantus ita primo intuit indubitanter cantabant, ut maximum spectaculum plrumis praeberetur; quod tamen, qui non potest facere, nescio qua fronte se musicum vel cantorem audeat dicere.' https://ia902707.us.archive.org/11/items / micrologusguido00hermgoog / micrologusguido00hermgoog.pdf. Retrieved 14/4/15. Guido d'Arezzo, *Micrologus Guidonis de Disciplina Artis Musicae*, Mich. Hermesdorff (ed.), (Trieste: Commissions-verlag der J.B. Grach, 1876).

6. Josquin des Prez, 'Ave Maria . . . Virgo Serena', Charles H. Giffen (ed.), http://www3.cpdl.org/wiki/images/d/d3/Josquin-Ave_Maria_a_4.pdf. Retrieved 27/12/15.

7. Throughout this book, 'chromaticism' refers to diatonic chromaticism in music, unless I stipulate otherwise.

8. Catherine Clément, *Opera, or the Undoing of Women*, Betsy Wing (trans.) (Minneapolis: University of Minneapolis Press, 1988).

9. Simone de Beauvoir, *The Second Sex*, H. M. Parshley (trans. and ed.) (New York: Vintage, 1997).

10. Susan McClary, *Feminine Endings: Music, Gender and Sexuality*, reprint edn (Minneapolis: University of Minnesota Press, 2002).

11. http://www.free-scores.com/download-sheet-music. php?pdf=6925# Free and legal. Retrieved 27/12/15.

12. The tune turned out to have been composed by the Spaniard Sebastián Yradier. When Bizet realised this, he added an acknowledgement to the published score.

13. http://www.monsalvat.no/motiftop.htm. Retrieved 2/1/16.

14. Ibid.

15. Theodor Adorno, *In Search of Wagner*, Rodney Livingstone (trans.) (London: New Left Books, 1981), pp. 44–5.

16. Though the *story* of Aladdin seems to have come from an eighteenth-century Maronite Syrian, Youhenna Diab, via Antoine Galland, the archaeologist and linguist who first added it to his French translation of *A Thousand and One Nights*.

17. Revealingly, Gilbert himself said, 'I cannot give you a good reason for our … piece being laid in Japan. It … afforded scope for picturesque treatment, scenery and costume' in 'Workers and Their Work: Mr. W. S. Gilbert', *Daily News*, 21 January 1885. Reprinted at the Gilbert and Sullivan Archive, http://diamond. boisestate.edu/gas/gilbert/interviews/dlynws850121.html. Retrieved 29/6/15

18. See Wong Hui Min, 'Debussy and Bali: A cultural rendezvous', http://musicinvestigation.blogspot.co.uk. Retrieved 29/6/15

19. Richard Taruskin, *Defining Russia Musically* (Princeton: Princeton University Press, 1997), p. 165.

20. Robert Hughes, 'Mark Rothko in Babylon' in *Nothing If Not Critical: Selected Essays on Art and Artists* (London: Collins Harvill, 1990), p. 242.

21. John Locke, *An Essay Concerning Human Understanding*, Peter H. Nidditch (ed.) (Oxford: Oxford University Press, 1990), p. 1689. George Berkeley, *Principles of Human Knowledge and Three Dialogues*, Roger Woolhouse (ed.) (Harmondsworth: Penguin, 1988), p. 1710.

22. We return to the significance of this concept of music *illustrating* the poem in Chapter 6.

23. https://fr.wikipedia.org/wiki/Voyelles_(sonnet). Retrieved 25/1/16. My translation. First stanza.

24. Charles Baudelaire, 'Correspondances' lines 9–11, from *Fleurs du mal* in *Selected Verse,* Francis Scarfe (trans.) (Harmondsworth: Penguin, 1961), pp. 36–7 (parallel text). My translation.

25. Olivier Messiaen, *Music and Colour: Conversations with Claude Samuel*, E. Thomas Glasow (trans.) (Portland: Amadeus Press, 1994), p. 62.

26. Don Paterson, 'from The Lyric Principle Part 2: The Sound of

Sense' in Fiona Sampson (ed.), *A Century of Poetry Review* (Manchester: Carcanet, 2009), p. 337.

27. Les Murray, 'Bats' Ultrasound' in *Selected Poems* (Manchester: Carcanet, 1986), pp. 149–50.

28. David Harsent, 'The Duffel Bag' in *Night* (London: Faber, 2011), p. 24.

29. Julia Kristeva interviewed by Sue Sellers, 'A Question of Subjectivity' in *Women's Review* 12 (1982), pp. 19–21. Julia Kristeva, *Pouvoirs de l'horreur* (Paris: Editions du Seuil, 1980).

30. 'At the simplest level of meaning – metaphorical – woman's capacity for multiple orgasm indicates that she has the potential to attain something more than Total, something extra – abundance and waste (a cultural throwaway), Real and unrepresentable.' Betsy Wing, 'Jouissance' in 'Glossary' of Hélène Cixous and Catherine Clément, *The Newly-Born Woman* (Minnesota/Manchester: University of Minnesota/Manchester University Press, 1987), p. 165. For Luce Irigaray, it's not multiple orgasm but genital plurality that makes woman into a 'plural' 'sex' and entails the semiotic element she believes women's writing authentically privileges. Luce Irigaray, *Ce sexe qui n'en est pas un* (Paris: Minuit, 1977).

31. Matthew 1:2–17.

32. Dylan Thomas's pub poem 'Sooner than you can water milk or cry Amen' concludes the edition of his poems collected by his old friend the composer Daniel Jones. Dylan Thomas, *The Poems*, Daniel Jones (ed.) (London: J. M. Dent & Sons, 1971), p. 242.

33. Hector Berlioz, *Symphonie Fantastique*, Op. 14.

34. George Herbert, 'Easter-wings' in *George Herbert*, Jo Shapcott (ed.) (London: Faber, 2006), p. 7.

35. Patience Agbabi, *Bloodshot Monochrome* (Edinburgh: Canongate, 2008).

36. In conversation. *Percy Bysshe Shelley*, Fiona Sampson (ed.) (London: Faber, 2011), p. 23.

37. Toby Martinez de las Rivas, 'The Obligatory Dialect Poem' in *Faber New Poets 2* (London, Faber, 2009). John Glenday, *Grain* (London: Picador, 2009). Robin Robertson, *The Wrecking Light* (London: Picador, 2010). Don Paterson, *Rain* (London: Faber, 2009). Fiona Benson, *Faber New Poets 1* (London: Faber, 2009).

Chapter 5

Density

We probably shouldn't be surprised if visual artists think with greater sophistication than musicians and poets about the resources of the material world. After all, such resources are their artistic alphabet. The printmaker doesn't just enjoy the tones created by cross-hatched lines, he understands the effects of acid. The maker of bronzes knows how that metal behaves during the casting process.

The same resources are also their vocabulary: a colour study is *about* the colours it's made from. In *On Modern Art*, Paul Klee distinguishes between colour, weight and tone:

> Colour is primarily Quality. Secondly, it is also Weight, for it has not only colour value but also brilliance. Thirdly, it is Measure, for besides Quality and Weight, it has its limits, its area and extent, all of which may be measured.
>
> Tone value is primarily Weight, but in its extent and boundaries, it is also Measure.
>
> Line, however, is solely Measure.[1]

Enmeshed in this spatial materiality, visual art isn't precisely analogous with, so much as simply offering a series of metaphors *for*, elements within music and poetry. Even the term *chromaticism*, having crossed over the 'bridge' of metaphor to speak for music, seems to forget its origins in the visual.

But I'm not arguing for such an analogy between art and music – or even for one between music and poetry. As my subtitle points out, this book isn't a *comparative* study, but instead thinks about what poetry does as *an extension of* what music does. For such an approach to make sense, we need to see those aspects of poetry that it shares with music working in the same way as they do there. In the last chapter we looked at chromaticism as one example of how the non-denotative 'give' of elements in poetic language pull against conventional structures *in the same way* that musical elements pull against each other. Other elements that modify the *feel* of a poem or of a piece of music include semiotic play, affect, palimpsest, the degrees of integration of different kinds of material, and explicit complicity with the reader or listener. All of these share a *lateral* quality: that is, they modify sensation *as it goes along*.

As we saw in Chapter 1, temporal extension is key to a poem's identity. This *chrononomie* flowers in the verse novel form that, though sometimes dismissed as a hybrid, enjoyed a revival in Anglophone poetry of the 1980s and 1990s. In such works verse is doubly extended, becoming both a chronologic and a narrative form, and so offers us an ideal opportunity to see how apparently non-denotative elements 'thicken up' a poem. In particular, we can see how book-length structures help construct *meaning*: for example, the sonnets that make up Vikram Seth's *Golden Gate* (1986), a romantic comedy set in Los Angeles, repeatedly offer an elegant, anecdotal rounding-off gesture; while Anne Carson's study of jealousy and relationship breakdown in the thirteen 'Tangos' of *The Beauty of the Husband* (2001) gets to the attritional heart of conflict.[2]

But most poetry – and indeed most music – is shorter than such substantial works. And we can also think about the *vertical*, which is to say simultaneous, way in which non-denotative elements contribute to a piece or poem. It's this simultaneous quality, which I call *density*, that is the subject of this chapter.

As so often with abstract forms, density is more easily spotted in music than in verse. It's easy to believe there just *is* more going on at any one moment of a thickly orchestrated symphony than of a string trio: more diversity, even though not necessarily more in the way of musical ideas, and above all simply *more noise*. In the larger ensemble, even unison passages are facetted by numerous instrumental timbres: as in the famous passages of Jean Sibelius's Symphony no 2 in D major, Op. 43 (1902), with its *tutti* anthem and the scales that pass above and below it, between woodwind and strings, like organ voluntaries. Sibelius's strategy differs from the one Sergei Prokofiev uses in his Fifth Symphony Op. 100 (1944), where the martial one-bar figure repeated fifteen times consecutively on its final pages by an accumulating proportion of the orchestra seems to force the piece to a standstill. It's not so much that there's nothing left for the symphony to do, the growing unison seems to say, as that there's no instrument left with which to do it.[3] Nevertheless, in both symphonies the unison brings its own distinctive weight to bear on its material: creating what Klee could with justice term both 'brilliance' and 'measure'.

Instrumentation, then, is a ready example of musical density, adding colour as well as volume (for all the world like a high-end hair care product). Despite the qualitative differences between these compositional strategies, instrumentation (one glorious example is the exuberant efflorescence of tubular bells, triangle and brass of the 'Viennese Musical Clock' in Zoltán Kodály's *Háry János Suite* Op. 15) joins diatonic chromaticism – in other words 'accidentals', such as those used in Maurice Ravel's String Quartet in F (1903) – in creating colourist effects.[4]

Despite the tonal variation afforded by orchestration, however, a great deal can also go on at once in the slimly scored string quartet. For example, the Marxist American producer and writer Maynard Solomon says, of Ludwig van Beethoven's late works, that their use of 'aggressive dotted-rhythmic polyphonic textures [...] creates a simultaneous sense of irresistible motion and unbearable strain'.[5] The key word here is 'simultaneous': Solomon has identified a particular kind of push-me-pull-you. Something – forward momentum – is going on at the same time as something else: the braking motion of the dotted rhythm, which as it were *withholds* each semiquaver. The effect is of both movement and resistance to movement; of weight and counterweight.

I remember how when performing these pieces one experiences this as an almost physical exhaustion. The bridge passage that leads into the 'Grosse Fugue' of Beethoven's String Quartet Op. 133 (1825), for example, always brought with it a huge sense of embarkation. Yet the piece is not exceptionally 'difficult'. The technical instrumental demands it makes are not in the same league as those of chamber music being composed less than 150 years later, such as Witold Lutosławski's String

Quartet of 1964, or Olivier Messiaen's clarinet-led *Quartet for the End of Time* (1941). Running for roughly sixteen unbroken minutes, the 'Grosse Fugue' is regarded as long; yet the sheer stamina it requires is as nothing compared to an orchestral violin part in a Richard Wagner, or indeed a Philip Glass, opera.[6] It is, though, hard to sustain interpretively. This is partly because it remains in a state of continual deferral. Unlike the sonata form, the fugue has no essential 'story arc' but holds itself a continuous present. All fugues do this to a greater or lesser extent, but the Grosse Fugue's structural complexity stretches the possibilities of such holding back to the utmost. For fugal form *can* create an arc. In Handel's *Messiah* HWV 56, the upbeat chorus 'For unto us a Child is given' is a fugue that joyfully intermingles 'is born' and 'is given' and leads on into the unison epithets 'Glorious', 'Wonderful', that form a prelude to the 'Hallelujah Chorus'. The 'Grosse Fugue' holds itself back from the good cheer of such a resolution.

These kinds of countervailing pressures are familiar to musicians but less so to poets and their readers. Perhaps this is because the denotative elements of language work to disguise such processes. Mainstream Western culture certainly has some resistances to the notion that the multiple meanings and actions of language might be deliberately deployed. The generations of student writers who studied Sir Ernest Gowers's *Plain Words*, for example, learnt that linguistic complexity is a problem to be solved. Sir Ernest's guide, written for the Civil Service in 1948 but still on A-level syllabuses in the 1980s, instructed us to 'Be short, be simple, be human': although it's arguable whether the third of these qualities follows from the first two.[7]

Psychoanalytic theory, however, sees the complex layers of meaning that etymology and association have laid down within a word as all *too* human; indeed as engaged in what almost amounts to a struggle against communicative *intention*. It seems to envisage this as operating on a single plane, for all the world like Guido of Arezzo's *musica recta*. In Chapter 2 we saw Julia Kristeva's work on (regressive) elements of pure sound that creep into language when something painful is being talked about. Sigmund Freud made parapraxis, the 'Freudian slip' in which the unconscious mind says what the conscious doesn't wish to, into a famous example of this struggle with communicative intention. (Not necessarily letting slip repressed information, parapraxis always expresses more than the speaker's conscious intention. Freud's example, in *The Psychopathology of Everyday Life*, of his own Signorelli parapraxis is singularly innocent. In trying to remember the name of that Renaissance painter, the Doctor produced instead the names Botticelli and Boltraffio via, he argued, a complex set of associations with places where he himself had recently travelled and stayed: in other words, through supplementary, apparently irrelevant, information.[8]) As we'll see again in Chapter 8, Jacques Lacan, in some ways Freud's ultimate successor, claimed that a text is inherently unstable; and that it is destabilised by these and the innumerable other ramifications which are part of every speaker's own private prehistory with language. The difficulty, he argued, doesn't arise in the same way with spoken language, which benefits from the context *and the doing* of speech, both of which act upon language and highlight what it 'means' to say, as if carrying speech and so communication through or past language. Notoriously, and inadvertently, Lacan illustrated this distinction in his own practice as a charismatic and persuasive *lecturer*, whose *writings* are exceptionally rebarbative.[9]

So meaning doesn't always manage to keep pace entirely with the other elements of language. In 'Crystal', a poem about the changes of consciousness that crystal meth produces, the New York poet Mark Doty beautifully evokes the sense of meaning rushing past mere words:

> I can't stop speaking, though I'm saying nothing:
> the words want to come flying, habit and vestige.
> No time now for speech, and isn't this
>
> what my whole life's wanted, to go flying
> past the words
> [...]? So that I might arrive on the far bank
>
> > of what could be said [...][10]

At other times meaning seems to pucker into *scrunches* of intensity which, whether they form part of a communicative trajectory or acting as isolated 'hits' to contradict it, are part of what we might think of as the vertical *meaning* of a work. When meaning thickens up like this it can open up poetry's polymorphous perversity; from, say, the *double entendre* of Robin Robertson's boozy whore who 'drank [him] under the table' to the Metaphysical sting in George Herbert's 'Love'.[11] Such scrunches are often belied by the prosody's elegant surface. The ferocious final couplet of William Shakespeare's 'Sonnet 18' – 'So long as men can breathe, or eyes can see, / So long lives this, and this gives life to thee[12]' – sounds blandly proverbial. But it is definitive in *both* senses; at once naming and delimiting the sonnet's object and project. The masculine ending of the 'see'/ 'thee' rhyme *speaks over* the traditionally feminine-gendered values of 'lives'/ 'gives life', whose own chime is rendered relatively inaudible by being set on feminine, unstressed syllables. These line-endings also appropriate the corroborative work of the alliterative 'l's leading up to the masculine stress on 'life'. This key word is also the lightly misogynist sonnet's key claim, as it wrestles the ability to 'give life' away from the feminine and arrogates it to the masculine, stressed syllables.

Emily Dickinson's signature tension between an undemanding grammatical structure and a sophisticated metaphysical idea perfectly illustrates the principle of vertical density:

> I cannot dance opon my toes—
> No Man instructed me—
> But oftentimes, among my mind,
> A glee possesseth me [13]

The hymnal metre, plain as Shaker weatherboarding, is conspicuous for its constraint, and this intensifies the subversive shock of Dickinson's double meanings. Her capitalised – Idealised – 'Man' is just as much individual masculine suitor as he is the possibility of the divine, defined by the figure of mere humanity. The metre lifts the very first foot into contention – opposing 'I can' to 'No Man' with nice immodesty – and highlighting, thus, the paradoxical, metrical ghost of 'I can' within '*I can*not'. These apparently meek, obedient iambs are in fact anything but: the poet does indeed 'dance', at least 'among [her] mind'. In the rest of this poem's five stanzas (it is relatively expansive for a Dickinson lyric) she puns ('I was out of sight, in sound, / The House encore me so'), gently mocks 'Ballet Knowledge' ('Nor hopped for Audiences—like Birds— / One Claw upon the air—'), and enjambs across both line and stanza breaks. In short, she leads the reader a merry dance.

Dickinson's virtuoso play with metrical conservatism is exceptional. But it also suggests a *principle* of poetic density: according to which the more complex a poem's ideas are, the less baroque its versification may be. It seems a kind of balancing act. It is as if there's only so much material, or attention, a poem can sustain before it collapses into something else – jingle, rant, prose poem, polemic or memoir – rather in the way that, as we saw in the last chapter, an 'excess' of chromaticism collapses tonal forms. If combined with expansive versification, highly ambitious thought seems to place poetry under strain, as it does in Ezra Pound's *Pisan Cantos*, with their ever-present risk of hubris, or in Geoffrey Hill's *Canaan* and other late collections, where the attempt to bring the sensibility of the King James Bible to bear on the contemporary State of the Nation places the poem's own diction under such pressure that it moves out of reach of many readers.[14]

Complex metaphysical poetry, however, seems to be distilled and clarified by tight form. As Gerard Manley Hopkins demonstrates, in the Terrible Sonnets he wrote in the 1880s, sonnet's tangy paradox and Janus-faced extended metaphors are suggestive not only of complexity but of the dual nature of meta/physical experience. But this form is also predictable and short. Free verse finds other ways to articulate the complexities of faith. The Welsh priest-poet R. S. Thomas's late great work uses a tightly reined-in free form whose skeletal diction, short lines and emotive register slow and focus the reading eye. 'Le Dormeur du Val' opens, 'In the beginning / the word. Will the word / be at the end?'[15] Pauline Stainer's hair's-breadth perfection produces such clarity that her meditations on such unfashionable topics as incarnation can be read and understood even by a largely secular contemporary audience:

'Madonna lilies'

Their fluted whites
should rebuke all fever

but they thirst, they thirst,
tongues urgent as pollen

for the angel's transaction,
the accidents of bread and wine.[16]

Sometimes complexity enters poems and pieces as an absence. This is no tidy theoretical paradox but a poetic strategy that particularly characterises certain traditions. Understatement asks the reader to supply or work out its emotional punchlines. For example, the elegiac strand in the British lyric tradition – which Thomas Hardy made his own but which continues today in the work of Andrew Motion, Carol Ann Duffy and others – adopts the opposite strategy to that of the Anglo-American Confessional poets led by Robert Lowell in the mid-twentieth century.[17] While the Confessionals, including Anne Sexton and Sylvia Plath, used heightened imagery and extravagantly line-ated free verse to portray emotional responses to circumstance, elegiac British verse states the circumstantial fact such as a par-ticular death but, with what is almost a modesty, does not articulate any emotional responses *to* it. 'The Death of Harry Patch', Andrew Motion's elegy for the last British survivor of the First World War trenches, never names the fact of Patch's death, but simply imagines him running late to parade to take his place among the dead:

> When he has taken his place, and the whole company
> are settled at last, their padre appears out of nowhere,
> pausing a moment in front of each and every one
> to slip a wafer of dry mud onto their tongues.[18]

The imagery is heightened – this is a resurrection scene, after all – but *at the same time* uses the dowdiness of mud to deprecate itself. Such understatement omits the fiercer emotions. What is not said is used as an intensifier. It's a strategy frankly borrowed from Motion's mentor (and first biographical subject) Philip Larkin.[19] In Larkin's poem 'Mr Bleaney', the view from – and then of – the lodger's room is the hand Larkin deals him to measure his life by: 'Bed, upright chair, sixty-watt bulb, no hook // Behind the door, no room for books or bag.'[20] The poem may be 'about' existential despair, but the closest it approaches it is to detail the *circumstances* of that despair.

At the other end of the formal seesaw, the more expansive versifiers tend to be less semantically compacted. A capacious poem like Allen Ginsberg's 'America' is a variety act bringing together multivalent elements, from food politics to queer theory. Yet its conscious compendiousness produces what in *formal* terms is not much different from a simple list poem. The verse-novel, too, applies an easy-running motor of narrative to the heft of extended verse. This is perhaps best exemplified by Derek Walcott's *Omeros* – with its *terza rima* in iambic sestrameter – or, as we've already seen, Vikram Seth's George Meredith-inspired sonnets in *Golden Gate*.[21] Like Les Murray's *Fredy Neptune*, with its 252 pages of octets, these volumes *keep metrical step* with themselves. The fate of four verse novels all published within three years of each other is telling. The easy-reading successes of John Haynes's *Letter to Patience* and Adam Foulds's *The Broken Word* contrast with the extent to which Ciaran Carson's exquisite, palindromic *For All We Know*, and Glyn Maxwell's multi-narrator *The Sugar Mile*, a series of persona poems which put 9/11 in the context of the Blitz, were overlooked.[22]

Doubtless the principle of poetic density could be reduced to an equation: say, $D = CV$ (density = content × versification). After all, it's the contention of this book that, in music and poetry, abstraction *is* what can be counted. But density's resistance or 'difficulty' itself remains one of the most difficult-to-quantify elements of both music and poetry. For whom, after all, is a piece or poem 'difficult': performers, listeners, readers or authors? Is that difficulty technical, practical, intellectual or even emotional? Does it have to do with execution, or with comprehension? If the latter, what does *comprehension* mean, anyway? And – not least of all – who says so?

This leads us to question whether poetry is shaped by the fuzzy surface of readerly apprehension itself.[23] In 1960s America, reader-response theory informed much university teaching of English Studies. Its radical 'who says?' argued that a text *was* what the reader made of it.[24] Not for nothing is a key summative text from 1980, by Stanley Fish, titled *Is There a Text in This Class? The Authority of Interpretive Communities*. In Chapter 8 we'll look at the figure of the Ideal Reader. Unlike this structuring Ideal, Fish's actual, individual readers have no necessary relationship with the text: which means that it can't control their responses. The discriminatory role of the critic underlines this freedom. As we see in Chapters 10 and 11, rival poetics often resist each other. The authority who 'says' is often taken (or takes itself) as the keeper of a True Faith. The influence of such figures (like the late twentieth-century British poet-editor Ian Hamilton, founder-editor of *The Review* (1962–72) and *The New Review* (1974–9), not to mention a critic at the *Times Literary Supplement* and on BBC TV's *Bookmark*), is as much emotional as argued for.[25]

My *principle* of density is just a notion, more thought experiment than technical device, to be dismantled once its work is done. But it does allow us to glimpse poetic structures that aren't dependent upon, but instead *produce*, conventions of versification. Density's push-me-pull-you throws up both familiar poetic forms, such as stanza breaks, and the *shapes* meaning takes in verse. My final example in this chapter is poetry of extended semantic challenge: which brings us full circle, to the verse novel. In the 1980s Gwyneth Lewis, later to be the first National Poet of Wales, studied creative writing in the US, at Harvard University and the Graduate Writing Division of Columbia University in the City of New York. It's not surprising to hear behind her diction the flattened, intelligent chatter of much late twentieth-century American poetry, from James Merrill to Amy Clampitt and from Linda Gregerson to Don Share. In the following extract from her fictionalised memoir, *A Hospital Odyssey*, we pick up its characters and action *in medias res*. Maris's husband has life-threatening cancer, and in Book 2 the couple encounter the New Age mood police:

> Maris rushed forward, found she was held
> by green-robed minions, 'Are you mad?
> Why are those frightening nurses veiled?
> Why shouldn't a man be furious, then sad,
> about his illness?' 'I forbid,' thundered the druid,
>
> 'negativity.' He made to plunge
> his sword into the heart. 'He must vibrate
> to higher frequencies.' Then Maris lunged
> at the doctor, scattering initiates.
> 'Kill me, then,' she screamed, 'because I hate
>
> his cancer. And you're a bunch of fakes
> and charlatans.' She overturned a tray
> of instruments. 'You're nothing like
> a real doctor. This isn't *Peace*, it's a fantasy
> of mind over matter. I want reality,

not props and magic.' 'Take him away!'
commanded the druid, then mocked, 'Go ahead!
The evil inside you will have its day.
Your husband, bitch, is as good as dead.'
Maris charged at him. He fled.[26]

This is a highly disobedient cancer poem, its diction coloured by the explicit stakes – 'frightening', 'furious', 'sad', 'illness', 'evil', 'dead' – which inform not only the vocabulary but its choice, not of image but of metaphorical device. That 'druid' could have stepped out of the sci-fi scenario an earlier passage makes of the contemporary hospital in which much of the book is set. But Lewis is a *Welsh* poet, for whom the druid also represents irrational social authority, and is a figure dreamt up not by a thousand hippies but by a sometimes punitively traditional national culture.[27] Yet this intensity is carried along on an understated, loping metre – fundamentally iambic, its irregular numbers of feet bound together by strict *ababb* rhyme – that doesn't intrude but instead allows her story to build momentum over the long haul (at 150 pages, the book is double the length of most single collections).

Another, roughly contemporary, poem that 'does length' is Alice Oswald's pamphlet-long *A Sleepwalk on the Severn*. In one palimpsest:

all you crabs in the dark alleys of the wall
all you mudswarms ranging up and down
I notice you are very alert and worn out
skulking about and grabbing what you can

listen this is not the ordinary surface river
this is not river at all this is something
like a huge repeating mechanism
banging and banging the jetty

very hard to define, most close in kind
to the mighty angels of purgatory
who come solar-powered into darkness
using no other sails than their shining wings[28]

Unbroken by the kind of conventional punctuation which, as the American poet W. S. Merwin has it, risks 'stapling' a poem to the page, this muscles onward, piling presence on presence ('crabs ... wall ... mudswarms').[29] But Oswald also renders the felt, personal movement of an individual pedestrian, through a metre whose feet vary in both number and form. Monosyllables and significant words carry the stresses: 'to the míghty ángels of púrgatory', or 'I nótice yóu are véry alért and wórn out'. (Listen to how that spondee 'worn out' applies its mimetic brake to the dactyl that 'very a-' leads the ear to expect.) Like every concatenation of sound and sense, this fixes the lines and makes them seem unassailable; while at the same time expressing a to-and-fro of inflection, a kind of hesitation, that mimes the very processes of discovery and reflection the poem describes.

Oswald's assonantal vocabulary, in which her *a*s, 'banging and banging ... angels of purgatory .... solar ... darkness ... sails than', push repeatedly, like the estuarial tide, against the clipped silhouettes of the ascenders and descenders – 'jetty ... define ... kind ... mighty ... using ... their shining wings' – recalls the honest-Joe diction of the later Ted Hughes, whom Oswald acknowledges as an influence.[30] Here the Australian fellow-environmentalist poet John Kinsella goes one further than Oswald. He writes about assonance itself as a *sfumato* representational technique, something that blurs and drags the sounds of the words into each other.[31] Sound becomes part of how the natural world is *denoted*.

Density, then, changes abstraction's relationship to the denotative work of poetry. It's where number and proportion overlap with, and play a part in, what the poem is *about*. That we have some shared understanding of this relationship between the *content* of an idea and its *measure* is apparent in turns of phrase like 'a balanced account' or 'keeping it in proportion'. We all know that by spending longer with one idea than another, or giving it the additional emphasis of a higher register, texts of any kind – from movie scripts to political speeches – argue *for* that idea. Poetry, like music, uses this familiar apprehension to create sensory experiences which are pleasurable but can also be denotative. With this interaction between denotation and the other elements of language in position, we can turn to look at 'meaning' in poetry and music.

Notes

1. All the same, there's something uneasy about this project. As he attempts to systematise elements he himself uses with apparent spontaneity, Klee sounds more like a quantity surveyor than an artist. Paul Klee, *On Modern Art* (London: Faber, 1948), p. 23.
2. Vikram Seth, *Golden Gate* (New York: Random House, 1986). Anne Carson, *The Beauty of the Husband* (New York: Vintage, 2001).
3. See for example Leonard Bernstein's score from the New York Philharmonic's archives: http://archives.nyphil.org/index.php/arti fact/444c461b-80f7-4b4d-8e95-ffc46bdfaa20/fullview#page/208/ mode/2up. Retrieved 12/6/15.
4. Musicians tend to use the term 'colour' for both harmonic and tonal play and the effects of instrumentation, but reserve the term 'chromaticism' for the former.
5. Maynard Solomon, *Beethoven Essays* (Cambridge, MA: Harvard University Press, 1988), p. 296.
6. Wagner's *Ring* cycle runs for fifteen–sixteen hours. Philip Glass's *Einstein on the Beach* lasts around five hours.
7. Sir Ernest Gower, *Plain English: A Guide to the Use of English* [1958], Rebecca Gowers (ed.) (Harmondsworth: Penguin, 2015).
8. Sigmund Freud, *The Psychopathology of Everyday Life*, Anthea Bell (trans.) (Harmondsworth: Penguin, 2003).
9. I'll return to this in Chapter 8. *Jacques Lacan Parle: un film de Françoise Wolff*, https://www.youtube.com/watch?v=31iQQTPY-kA. Retrieved 30/6/15. In the film Lacan speaks at the University of Louvain in 1972.
10. Mark Doty, *Deep Lane* (London: Cape, 2015), pp. 9–10.
11. Robin Robertson, 'Wonderland' in *The Wrecking Light* (London: Picador, 2010), p. 13.
12. William Shakespeare, 'Sonnet 18' in *The Complete Works*, Peter Alexander (ed.) (London and Glasgow: Collins, 1971), p. 1311.
13. 'opon': *sic*. #381 in *The Poems of Emily Dickinson*, R. W. Franklin (ed.) (Cambridge, MA: Belknap/Harvard University Press, 2005), p. 175.
14. Ezra Pound, *The Cantos* (New York: New Directions, 1999). Geoffrey Hill, *Canaan* (Harmondsworth: Penguin, 1996).
15. R. S. Thomas, *No Truce with the Furies* (Tarset: Bloodaxe, 1995), p. 74.
16. Pauline Stainer, *Crossing the Snowline* (Tarset: Bloodaxe, 2008), p. 40.
17. I've written about the British elegiac tradition elsewhere. Fiona Sampson, 'The Oxford Elegists' in *Beyond the Lyric: A Map of Contemporary British Poetry* (London: Chatto & Windus, 2012), pp. 57–74.

18. Andrew Motion, *The Customs House* (London: Faber, 2012), p. 11.
19. Andrew Motion, *Philip Larkin: A Writer's Life* (London: Faber, 1993).
20. Philip Larkin, *Collected Poems*, Anthony Thwaite (ed.) (London: Faber, 1988), pp. 102–3.
21. Derek Walcott, *Omeros* (New York: Farrar, Straus and Giroux, 1990).
22. Les Murray, *Fredy Neptune* (Manchester: Carcanet, 1999). John Haynes, *Letter to Patience* (Bridgend: Seren, 2006). Adam Foulds, *The Broken Word* (London: Cape, 2008). Glyn Maxwell, *The Sugar Mile* (London: Picador, 2005). Ciaran Carson, *For All We Know* (Dublin: Gallery, 2008).
23. There are analogies, of course, with the actions of fuzzy logic.
24. Stanley Fish, *Is There a Text in This Class? The Authority of Interpretive Communities* (Cambridge, MA: Harvard University Press, 1980).
25. We'll return in Chapter 12 to how this links with our emotional investment in music and poetry themselves.
26. Gwyneth Lewis, *A Hospital Odyssey*, Book 2 (Newcastle: Bloodaxe, 2010), pp. 29–30.
27. One that has sometimes been inhospitable to this *woman* poet who brought 'foreign' (English) forms into the language.
28. Alice Oswald, 'Prologue' in *A Sleepwalk on the Severn* (London: Faber, 2009), p. 3.
29. W. S. Merwin, 'Preface' in *The Second Four Books of Poems* (Port Townsend, WA: Copper Canyon Press, 1993), p. 1.
30. Oswald gave the 2005 Ted Hughes Memorial Lecture, and has edited a Ted Hughes anthology. Alice Oswald (ed.), *A Ted Hughes Bestiary* (London: Faber, 2014).
31. In an email to the author, 4/5/10.

Chapter 6

The Meaning of 'Meaning'

We resist new forms of meaning. We're even resistant to the *idea* of them. It simply *is* difficult to conceptualise ways of understanding that we haven't thought through before, or that differ from our usual ways of thinking. This is something we have to *work* at: as all school pupils can attest. To 'get your head round' something: even the cliché conveys a sense of effortful rearrangement. From such practical difficulty flow the many religious, philosophical or 'commonsensical' beliefs – some of them notorious – which in turn reinforce these resistances.[1]

Our own resistances are hardest of all to spot. So what about 'us', the 'you' and 'I' this text posits – and posits as cultural and conceptually located in ways roughly similar to each other? Our thinking seems to start with language; and language seems irrevocably embroiled in denotation. We even have terms of pure denotation, like the English 'thingummy', 'whodyamaflick' and 'doovalacky', that are entirely about the *gesture of indicating* an object, and not at all concerned with the qualities of the object in itself.

But language *also* has a semiotic element: a 'musical', rhythmic ebb and flow, as independent of logic as a 'hum' by A. A. Milne's Winnie the Pooh, and related to a stream of consciousness like the one that James Joyce gives Molly Bloom in *Ulysses*.[2] 'Stream of consciousness' is a *literary* trope, of course; and semiotic ways of going on do receive special attention in literary contexts – not least poetry. At first glance they seem to be of less use when something needs to be imparted: although recent educational research shows the semiotic supporting the semantic, for example when music helps children learn to read.[3]

Still, in the main, when we catch ourselves thinking like Molly Bloom we say we're being 'absent minded'. Even in fiction, the semiotic is frequently used to represent a character daydreaming or ruminating. Novelist Niall Griffiths often uses first-person stream of consciousness narration. In *Stump* (2004), he disrupts grammar, and omits both conjunctions and the rhythmic order imposed by conventional sentence structures, to orchestrate a semiotic blur. Shortcutting denotation like this evokes a filmic fast-forward through a landscape there's no time to notice properly:

> Deeper, further into this country, lakes the same slaty shade as the clouds above and the mountains granite-spurred and serrated on the flanks as if gnawed by some massive maw and the alleys between them sucking the eye through the deep troughs to where other swellings equal destabilize greyly the horizon, ripple and peak and spike and sawtooth the grey horizon and beyond that still and always the same sight repeated, repeated to the abrupt escarpment of the sea at which this laboring car and the two inside it are aimed.[4]

Pausing to name each moment and experience would have slowed this passage down and made us feel as though we were on a bicycle or on foot rather than in a speeding car.

A distinctive characteristic of the semantic in language is the *syntactic* relationship it makes with the objects of experience; and it's this relationship Griffiths's unconventional syntax elides. These objects of experience may be concrete or imagined – the actual oranges on the kitchen table don't function differently, in my mental syntax, from the as yet-virtual ones I'd like to buy – so the semantic doesn't have a special relationship with the world of the senses. But it *is* allied with 'making sense'. It maintains a syntactic distance we might almost call 'orderly' between the object of a thought and the person thinking about it: the grammatical agent who used, in the period from the rise of German Idealism to the rise of postmodernism, to be called a Subject.

This orderly sense-making turns out to be the engine of denotation. And it's the very element of language that my previous chapters haven't explored. We've seen how abstract formal elements such as texture and formal proportion can supplement literal, denotative meaning. We've also seen how a richer sense of 'meaning', and richer *meanings*, can be found in discourses such as poetry, which try to harness the semiotic elements in language, than in those such as instruction manuals, that do not.

Now, though, I want to look at whether we can think of these semiotic or 'musical' elements in language, particularly in poetry, as *meaning-laden* in their own terms. But to do that we need to ask how *music* itself 'means'? This question brings us back to the human resistance to unfamiliar forms of meaning-making. Non-musicians, in particular, tend to search for where, in music, they can situate the kinds of meaning-making they *are* familiar with. For example, the cultural critic Edward Said argues that it's a *problem* that Western art music thinks of itself in its own terms:

> because music's autonomy from the social world has been taken for granted for at least a century, and because the technical requirements imposed by musical analysis are so separate and severe, there is a putative, or ascribed, fullness to self-sufficient musicological work that *is now much less justified than ever before.* [My italics.][5]

Traditionally commissioned by the ruling classes as part of a display of wealth and power, Classical music is even now associated with high ticket prices and other marks of privilege (something we'll return to in Chapter 8, when we come to look at opera). Said's vision of it as one discourse among the many that construct social meaning is acute and convincing. Even the public 'doing good' of Antonio Vivaldi's music composed for the orphans of the Convent of Ospedale della Pièta, Venice, or George Frideric Handel's donation of the proceeds of his *Messiah* to the Foundling Hospital in London's Coram Fields (both charitable enterprises from the first half of the eighteenth century) arguably reinforced this discursive role; just as, today, a Charity Dinner serves to underline the wealth of those who donate. There are exceptions, of course. The youthful musicians of the Venezuelan El Sistema have played themselves out of the favelas and into a salaried, vocational future. The post-war Education Act of 1944 allowed free musical instrument lessons to British state school pupils with aptitude; some of these pupils, too, went on to study music and enter the music profession.[6]

Still, Said's analysis of the social meaning of music is itself partial. He writes, of J. S. Bach's *B Minor Mass* BWV 232, that 'music quite literally fills a social space, and it does so by elaborating the ideas of authority and social hierarchy directly connected to a dominant establishment imagined as actually presiding over the work.'[7] In doing so he conflates Bach's God with the Elector of Saxony. Like all religious organisations, the Lutheran church for which Bach frequently worked was a source of patronage and worldly power. This does not mean that all its employees automatically lacked religious faith, or understood its 'authority and [...] hierarchy' as *entirely* worldly. Bach would have been quite capable of imagining – and worshipping – a divine hierarchy and authority even if *at the same time* he knew that it was the Elector's money that allowed him to do so in musical terms. Besides, the music of a Mass is doubly instrumental. It is used to set a text; and the finished piece is 'used' in the rite of religious service. Context thus permeates these works in a particular, exceptional way: while, in Said's argument, the context-dependence of the *B Minor Mass* is simply on a continuum with that of any other piece of music.

All the same, there *is* a level at which the performing context defines what all music means. As we'll see in Chapter 8, the Ideal Reader is a way of conceptualising the essentially communicative function of a novel or poem, and is built into its very structure. Music's equivalent of the Ideal Reader is surely an Ideal Auditor; which is to say, a personification of the possibility of the piece's taking place. This is no actual individual but a Platonic Ideal, entailed by the work predicated upon him or her as reader, performer or listener. Like the Ideal Reader, the Ideal Auditor may vary tremendously in the detail of 'his' attributes according to the work in question; but 'he' always represents a level of attentiveness and knowledge sufficient for that work.

Closely related to this is another, more complicated version of the Ideal. Karl-Heinz Stockhausen's *Helikopter-Streichquartett*, with its performing space in the eponymous quartet of helicopters, reminds us that the Ideal Occasion is always written into the score along with the Ideal Auditor. In another string quartet – say, Josef Haydn's Op. 76 No. 3 – this Occasion is that four sufficiently able string players be gathered together in one room. But this is so familiar to us that we simply forget that the 'chamber' of 'chamber music' is part of that work's structure.

Within the limits of practice – human fallibility and creative limitation among them – a piece must be true to itself. Authenticity to itself is involved in any creative act, from icing a cake to composing a symphony. The work must more or less fulfil the project it has set itself: classical sonata form, for example, must complete what it started with a development and recapitulation of both subjects, or themes; or else become either something else or a sonata whose formal transgression is musically significant. So it's not as Said claims because the 'technical requirements imposed by musical analysis are so separate and severe' that Western art music thinks of itself in its own terms; but rather because it is simply being itself. However, musical terms are a special case in one respect: which is the *untranslatability* of the experience of music itself. Experience can't be paraphrased: which is why sports commentaries are so florid. In 1958, Michael Polanyi coined the term 'tacit knowledge' to designate certain kinds of experiential knowledge. This concept collapses on examination because the 'tacit', what cannot be put into words, can nevertheless be communicated, not only by example but by, say, physical manipulation of the learner's body (in yoga, or violin lessons), or by performance.[8] A better term for 'tacit knowledge' would therefore be 'practical knowledge'.

However, there is a kernel of insight lodged within Polanyi's notion. While I can convey *what I know* as a result of having an experience, my experience *itself* is by definition mine alone, since *having* it is part of what locates the boundaries of *me*. While Said is partly right about the meanings of music's social context, then, music is also 'about' the actual sounds it makes. Not for nothing is the classical form that develops purely musical material called '*sonata*': *that which is sounded*. Sound – musical content – leads this form, with its integrative movement 'out', working over and 'return' to musical material. (Charles Rosen's idea of the 'sonata principle', expounded in his 1971 study *The Classical Style*, usefully captures the notion of a *working* approximation to sonata form, one which retains the 'feel' of it, or elements of this process.[9])And this double meaning is what we must bear in mind if we are truly to understand the musical project. Even the composer and music professor Ernest Bloch (1880–1959), who writes about music's 'self-language, its *humanly absolute poetry a se*', can also state that:

Social trends themselves have been reflected and expressed in the sound-material, far beyond the unchanging physical facts and also far beyond a merely romantic *espressivo*. No other art is conditioned by social factors as much as the purportedly self-acting, even mechanically self-sufficient art of music; historical materialism, with the accent on 'historical', abounds here.[10]

This is somewhat problematic: after all, the visual arts, literature and music are all equally saturated by 'professional' demands, and by the artistic and intellectual fashions of their day. 'Sound-material', to use Bloch's helpful term, is shaped by contemporary musical movements among the composer's peers as much as by commissioners.[11] It's no coincidence that Ernst Bloch was a Marxist, though of a particular kind, and so thought through music's *material* context. Still, even Bloch doesn't dispense with the *experience* that 'sound-material' imparts. So musical meaning is a problem that only seems to arise when we stop to think about the people who use and produce music. (And this is surely tautological. What would music *be* without people producing and using it?[12])

Meaning in poetry seems easier to understand. Surely a poem means what it says? 'Common sense' ascribes good faith in meaning to language and hence to poetry; better faith than it does to musical 'meaning'. Language engages with denotation, and the grammar and vocabulary of language are common knowledge in way that the 'separate and severe' technical repertoire of Western art music is not. Yet poetry is also sometimes accused of constructing particular, occult meanings. When someone says, 'I don't understand this poem,' they usually mean not, *I don't speak much English* but, *I don't like this*. Similar comments about contemporary art music mean not, *I'm deaf* but, *I can't make sense of this*. But where to locate this difficult or occult 'meaning' that isn't what the poem or piece of music *does*? For there *is* no text beyond the text – as we saw in Chapter 2. A codified political or even existential meaning that's in the poem is still in *its* words. Likewise, *in itself*, a piece of music can only mean itself: however it gets *used*.

My sense is that one of the reasons contemporary philosophers of music, like Peter Kivy, run into difficulties when they think about musical meaning is that they assume that meaning is semantic, and that whatever's *semantic* must be *narrative*.[13] But

– as we've spent five chapters observing – even if meaning *were* only whatever can be done by *language*, it need not be purely semantic. And even if we concentrate on the semantic elements within language, poetry – in common with other familiar forms, such as the shopping list, or Rules and Regulations – offers many models as well as simple storytelling. (Kivy is looking in a different place from Said, but like him is trying to see 'beyond' music itself to kinds of meaning with which he's more familiar.) Moreover, as we've seen, even denotation can be slant: the meaning of a poem – as of a piece of music – can be the feeling or atmosphere it *evokes*. Poetic language can gesture *to* itself: in rhyme or 'purple' passages or by deploying a form, such as the sonnet, with a particular set of literary–historical resonances. So at least one *meaning* of a poem might be 'the way it tells it': that particularity of *these* words in *this* order which, apparently, gets lost in translation.

Despite all the resources of language, music is not language, and does not create linguisitic meaning. It makes meaning *in its own terms*: and this meaning is *musical*. For if its meaning were something external to itself, that music had to indicate or mimic, all 'abstract' music – including everything that's purely instrumental, apart from film scores and progamme music – would be 'meaningless'. Yet that's not our experience. We experience it as meaning*ful*, even when it's *not* evoking a particular emotion: as something that is non-arbitrary, that coheres in a recognisable form, creating patterns and pleasurable sensation.

Recognising this restores a kind of agency to music; so much so that we can begin to speculate how musical form might entail the textual, rather than necessarily the other way around. That turns out to be a working assumption in ethnomusicology. In the 1970s, the Hungarian musicologist János Maróthy was able to reconstruct how 'variative' song – a single, unmetrical musical phrase repeated with variation – was used in European tribal society for the recitation of epics; and its further occurrence in metrical, strophic form was evidence of the way that, in more recent, feudal times, epic was translated into ballad. Among the many examples of musical meaning producing, or reproducing if not a language element then certainly a semantic one, the choric strophe and antistrophe choreographed both the *narrative* motion of Classical Greek drama and the *onstage* movements of the chorus. (This relationship of mutual suggestion between poetry and music is one to which I'll return.)

Elsewhere, music seems to 'undo' or 'redo' a text. Twentieth- and twenty-first-century art music often sets texts without reference to traditional verse metre. Instead, these non-arbitrary settings identify other *aural* tropes, as well as *semantic* stresses and releases, within the language. One of the pieces Benjamin Britten sets in his *Serenade for Tenor, Horn and Strings* of 1943 is Tennyson's 'The Splendour Falls' (as we'll see when we look at song in Chapter 7). The poem's opening couplet is not Lord Alfred's finest hour: 'The splendour falls on castle walls / And snowy summits old in glory.' You don't have to be a student of Gerard Manley Hopkins to hear the depressive effect of vowelling-on from the *e-our* of 'splendour' down to the *a-e* of 'castle' and the *o*s that dominate the second line. The tangle of abstraction ('old in glory') isn't exactly vivid. But Britten lifts up the *e*s of 'splen-' and '-tle' towards a glowing 'old' as he explodes this phrase from its metrical limits.

Part of what the music seems to do here is to illustrate what the text is doing. In effect, it's ekphrastic. A useful side-effect of thinking about musical setting like this, as something carried out *alongside* the poem rather than completing it in some way, is that it solves the problem of why one would set poetry to music when it already has its *own* aural, semiotic life. *Why illustrate a poem?* is a different kind of question from, *Why make it sound a certain way?* because it implies no lack. (*The Lindisfarne Gospels* weren't produced in the belief that the biblical texts were in some way lacking: but resoundingly the reverse. Children love pictures in the books that we read to them.)

What happens if we do after all shift the stakes for musical meaning itself to denotation? When the celebrant of a religious rite lifts his voice from speech to chant, he performs a speech-act concerned with heightening, privileging or demarking the occult in discourse. There are traces of music as speech act in our consensual use of pitch. I match my 'tone' to yours when we meet, whether across the interview desk or at the water-cooler. This kind of matching is cultural as well as interpersonal. We all know what Shakespeare means by 'that phrase again, it had a dying fall' when Duke Orsino wallows in lover's melancholy: I know of no culture in which an upward flourish is a gesture of *tristesse*. It's no coincidence that car alarms and *nee-nawing* ambulance sirens appropriate the dolorous descending minor third of children's calls: *Coming, Coo-ee, Mummee*.

This human tendency to match words to tunes – which also suggests how melody can imply language – is at work not only in Hungarian musical history but today. When bored musicians or football fans improvise obscenity to fit anything from Tchaikovsky's Fifth Symphony to *Jesus Christ Superstar*, it feels as if these lyrics have been implied or even produced by the music; as if we can go beyond Chapter 3's notion of a grammatical music and see melody *generating* meaning, in ways that are akin to grammar.[14] (As we'll see in Chapter 7, not all *a posteriori* lyrics are scatological. Frederick Chopin's Prelude Op. 28 No. 20 was set by Barry Manilow as 'Could It Be Magic' (1975); J. S. Bach's Air on the G String, from the second movement of his Orchestral Suite No. 3 in D major, BWV 1068, reappears in Procul Harum's 'A Whiter Shade of Pale' (1967).)

When grammar and melody move towards such coincidence, they seem to do so through the phrasal logic of a breath: its rise and fall and deployable extent. Breath is, to say the least, human-centred. In Chapter 3 we saw how its dimensions are built into music and poetry. We also saw how *impersonal* those dimensions are. But music also shows us how *impersonality* can be the whole basis of form, because the terms in which it's organised, being self-generated, are in a way hermetic.

Could this impersonality also apply to poems? After all, they too use the phrasal breath; and they too are organised in their own terms. To try and answer this, let's go back to where this book started, with the experience – familiar enough to any poet – of giving a poetry reading on automatic pilot. Probably you're tired, the train was late, you rushed to the venue. And now, you don't quite know how, you're on stage and halfway through an old standby. You give the thing its usual shape – the familiar pauses and intonation – but you just aren't quite 'there'. Your poem has *a* voice, but it's not *your* voice. Instead, you find yourself putting the form 'out there' as a sequence of phrasal gestures and timings. The *text* is communicating, but you, in some ways, are not.

This experience of impersonal detachment strikingly resembles my experiences as a performing musician. Musical performance is 'impersonal' in a sense much like T. S. Eliot's:

> [...] the poet has, not a 'personality' to express, but a particular medium, which is only a medium and not a personality, in which impressions and experiences combine in peculiar and unexpected ways.[15]

For, however exploratory the rehearsal, in concert a fine interpretation floats free of self-consciousness. In fact, the task of performance is to remove the self that – as we'll see in Chapter 12 – can create a barrier between audience and music. This is despite at the same time continuing to make conscious stylistic choices and to be alert to cues from fellow performers. The 'self' is both absent – and involved.

Surprisingly, the closely related scenario in which you perform a highly autobiographical poem without *feeling* confessional holds true even in the clinical context. When I worked in psychiatric hospital units, I found service users readily 'shared' poems detailing all sorts of abuses or emotions that they would never 'tell' the group. Psychoanalytic art therapy calls this depersonalising, distancing capacity for symbol formation – 'symbol' here means *both* the use of such literary tropes as metaphor *and* the actual making of a version on paper – a 'scapegoat transference'.[16] The *text* takes the blame. If challenged, the writer can say, 'It's only a poem', screw up the paper and throw it in the bin. And many a 'professional' poet has used the same line to gloss an indiscretion of the kind U. A. Fanthorpe snaps in her portrait of 'The Poet's Companion', who 'Must sustain with grace / [...] camera's curious peeping / When the Poet is reading a particularly // Randy poem about her, or (worse) about someone else'.[17]

Yet this *experience* of impersonality, by both composer and performer, is curiously overlooked by those readers, or critics, who like to identify poet with poem in an old-fashioned, pre-Barthesian way; who, like Émile Zola, want to *chercher l'homme*.[18] Confessional poets are made particularly vulnerable by the way this kind of reception shrinks poetics to personhood. What we might call the Confessor School of Reader-response holds that whatever a poem says expresses what its author is feeling. Leaving aside the paucity of this picture of both literary craft and language, it's a strangely innocent position to adopt. Have these readers never found themselves telling a lie?[19] But non-poets do tend in general to read register in literal ways: to *believe* it, as it were. Sylvia Plath's verse trails its notorious comet's tail of reception, by psychoanalytic critics like Susan Kavaler-Adler as well as literary critics who should know better, as symptomology rather than brilliantly crafted poetics.[20] Anne Stevenson recently accused fellow American Anne Sexton of using writing as therapeutic dirt-digging.[21] Yet another leading American poet, Sharon Olds, celebrated for poetic explorations of child abuse, refused until recently to acknowledge that her source material might be autobiographical, precisely in order to continue to be read for her *literary* strengths.

As all this suggests, despite the impersonality of the poetic process, a key facet of poetic meaning is *affect*: not the expression, but the acknowledgement, description or evocation of a response, often emotional; or of something that evokes such a response. A famous example of this is the 'dreamy divagation' of Elizabeth Bishop's old couple chatting on the bus before they see 'The Moose':

> 'Yes …' that peculiar
> affirmative. 'Yes …'
> A sharp, indrawn breath,
> half groan, half acceptance,
> that means 'Life's like that.
> We know *it* (also death).'[22]

This passage establishes complicity with the reader by portraying both our ability to *understand* such cues and – as Bishop goes on to imagine 'down in the kitchen, the dog / tucked in her shawl' – their *associations* for us. We understand the poem by understanding how conversations such as the one in this poem work. We ourselves are prompted by the conversation's phatic prompts. But Bishop's interlocking *ssss* sounds are also semiotic. They *feel drowsy*. The poem uses the reader's susceptibility as an element of textual capacity. In Billy Collins's 'Books', which starts with a 'library humming in the night, / a choir of authors murmuring inside their books / […] together forming a low, gigantic chord of language', the undulating *mmm*s work on us in the same way.[23]

And there's a fine aesthetic line between effect and manipulation. Leonard Cohen's cheerful cynicism about how this works, in his famous song 'Hallelujah', makes us smile in part because lyrics and setting are so 'perfectly pitched' to each other as the words sing about what the tune is doing.[24] U. A. Fanthorpe is perceptive on the true usefulness of sentimental manipulation in 'Patience Strong': 'And *See*, he said, *this is what keeps me going.*'[25] You don't need the emotional intelligence of either Fanthorpe or Cohen, though, to notice the tendency of a poet like Mary Oliver to tread the boundary between fine, riskily metaphysical poetry and occasionally – in a poem like 'Love Sorrow', whose very title should sound a warning note – slack-jawed homily.[26] Though Oliver often sounds closer to late, great Czeslaw Milosz, there's something ersatz about passages which race towards a sentiment they don't seem patient enough to evoke. Like Desiderata on a tea-towel, or Shaker 'style' in fitted kitchens, they 'miss the meaning', and in so doing forfeit the thing itself.

But not all deliberately conjured affect is manipulative. Poetic register is both intrinsic and important. Each word of a late Plath poem like 'Lesbos' seems to be hair-raisingly on stilts. Blank verse lends Sean O'Brien's work a steadying, and historically grounded, air of authority that prevents it from sounding like special pleading, whether for communities saddled with Thatcher's post-industrial legacy or – in elegies such as those for Barry MacSweeney, Thom Gunn or Peter Porter – individual emotion.

So affect – the *having* of the experience of a poem – is a key part of the poem's meaning. It isn't a simple matter of emotion, but something more complex and thoroughgoing: a kind of reaction, or even reassembly. Since it's in and of the poem's *own* meaning (and isn't, say, *my* memory of being read that poem by a boyfriend, and *my* resulting emotions), affect must be impersonal: that's to say, available to all. It is, in effect, the Ideal Reader who 'has' it. As we've seen, a poem's affect is often conjured by its non-denotative elements. In just the same way, affect is part of music's meaning, and is conjured by *musical* elements, which are by definition non-denotative. Meaning is something the poem or piece of music does. Yet it goes on at the fuzzy border between an artwork and the occasion on which we encounter it. This experiential quality of both artforms is what we're nostalgic for when we call poetry musical, or music poetic.

This highlights a paradox in the nature of musical scores. Between the seventeenth and nineteenth centuries, these moved from recording information about how to perform a piece – the figured bass – to a transcription of how each part should sound in performance. Poetry's analogous journey leads from orality to non-lineated Classical and Anglo-Saxon inscriptions in abbreviated (even runic) script, and on to fully-laid-out – that is, scored – print: and today's preoccupation with forms of reproduction, both digital and live, which dispense with written text altogether. These changes echo their context in the historical shift from elite expertise to the point where general literacy means everyone can read a poem.

And they produce an overlap, or tension, between *score and performance*. When the poem on the page, like a musical part, scores the whole sound of a poem, *the way it goes*, there's no longer any space in which the poem exists *as distinct from* how it sounds. Even its meaning can't sustain an existence independent of that sound: for what would that *mean*? What's left open is interpretation; the *particular*, rather than Ideal, occasion on which a poem is read or a piece of music 'run through'. It's to these occasions that we'll return in Chapter 12.

Notes

1. The consequences of such resistances have been written into world history by extremists from Savonarola to Senator McCarthy.
2. James Joyce, *Ulysses* (Harmondsworth: Penguin Modern Classics, 2000). A. A. Milne, *Winnie the Pooh* (London: Egmont, 2013).
3. J. H. Towell, *The Reading Teacher*, 53:4 (1999), pp. 284–7.
4. Niall Griffiths, *Stump* (London: Vintage, 2004), p. 73.
5. Edward W. Said, *Musical Elaborations* (London: Chatto & Windus, 1991), p. xii.
6. It would be wrong to dismiss these and other examples as no more than paternalistic interventions by an educationally privileged class. That would be to argue that the goods to which wealthier social groups have access can never be redistributed. It's more useful to see such examples as incremental changes in the way Western Classical music situates itself.
7. Said, *Musical Elaborations*, pp. 64–5.
8. Michael Polanyi, *Personal Knowledge: Towards a Post-Critical Philosophy* (Chicago: University of Chicago Press, 1958). Enlarged in Michael Polanyi, *The Tacit Dimension* (Chicago: University of

Chicago Press, 1966). Polanyi's work is expanded by Harry Collins. He identifies three forms of the tacit: what is insufficiently explained, knowledge which must be processed by the body and not the mind, and collective knowledge such as the rules for language use. Harry Collins, *Tacit and Explicit Knowledge* (Chicago: University of Chicago Press, 2010).

9. Charles Rosen, *The Classical Style: Haydn, Beethoven, Mozart* (London: Faber, 2005). Peter Kivy, for example, uses the term about the Finale of Act 2 of Mozart's *The Marriage of Figaro*. Peter Kivy, *Introduction to a Philosophy of Music* (Oxford: Oxford University Press, 2002), p. 175.

10. Ernst Bloch, *Essays on the Philosophy of Music*, Peter Palmer (trans.) (Cambridge: Cambridge University Press, 1985), pp. 126 and 200.

11. Bloch would gain immediate practical knowledge of such discriminations through a bittersweet combination of North American exile and professional success. The first Musical Director of the Cleveland Institute of Music, he was later also Director of the San Francisco Conservatory.

12. We saw in Chapter 3 how structures like the breath-length phrase build human dimension into these forms.

13. Peter Kivy, *Osmin's Rage: Philosophical Reflections on Opera, Drama and Text* (Princeton: Princeton University Press, 1988).

14. Noam Chomsky's notion of a generative grammar has been discredited as too narrowly culture-specific, but it remains an interesting thought experiment even if it isn't 'true', in the sense we puzzled over in Chapter 4. Noam Chomsky, *Aspects of the Theory of Syntax* (Cambridge, MA: MIT Press, 1965).

15. T. S. Eliot, 'Tradition and the Individual Talent' in *Selected Essays* (London: Faber, 1999), pp. 13–22.

16. Joy Schaverien, 'Chapter 2: The Scapegoat Transference' in *The Revealing Image: Analytical Art Psychotherapy in Theory and Practice* (London: Jessica Kingsley, 1992), pp. 30–61.

17. U. A. Fanthorpe, *Neck Verse* (Cornwall: Peterloo, 1992). It's no coincidence that some commentators see *writing* poetry as a kind of translation. According to the American poet and writer Jay Parini, for example, 'poets translate from silence itself, finding a language adequate to their experience, moving yet another fragment of the unsaid into "said" territory.' Jay Parini, 'Hard, Beautiful Truths', *Poetry Review* 96:4 (December 2006), pp. 82–5.

18. In 'The Death of the Author', published in 1968, Barthes showed how authors were no longer seen as people who had made a textual object, but as textual 'brands'. Roland Barthes, 'The Death of the Author' in *Image-Music-Text*, Stephen Heath (trans.) (New York: Hill & Wang, 1977), pp. 142–8.

19. A question Marlon Brando also asks in relation to acting. Interviewed on the Dick Cavett Show, 12 June 1973. https://www.youtube.com/watch?v=yfy-T3R9Ju0. Retrieved 21/1/16.
20. Susan Kavaler-Adler, *The Compulsion to Create: A Psychoanalytic Study of Women Artists* (London: Routledge, 1993).
21. Anne Stevenson interviewed by Charlotte Austin, 'Anne Sexton Forty Years On', *Poetry Review* 99:4 (December 2009), p. 59.
22. Elizabeth Bishop, 'The Moose' in *Complete Poems* (London: Chatto & Windus, 1991), pp. 169–73.
23. Billy Collins, 'Books' in *Taking off Emily Dickinson's Clothes* (London: Picador, 2000), pp. 11–12.
24. Leonard Cohen, 'Hallelujah' in *Various Positions*, John Lissauer (prod.) (New York: Columbia Records, 1984).
25. U. A. Fanthorpe, 'Patience Strong' in *Selected Poems* (Harmondsworth: Penguin, 1986), p. 16.
26. Mary Oliver, *Red Bird* (Newcastle upon Tyne: Bloodaxe, 2008), p. 64.

PART II

Chapter 7

Song

While I've been working on this book I've frequently found myself explaining that I'm not writing a study of song. Yet music and poetry do *meet* in song. What we know of human prehistory suggests that they share an overlapping origin, in live performance, as material that was improvised and memorised, and that relied on traditions of collective transmission. But I'm no archaeologist, and specialists – like those working on the bone flutes of the early Neolithic site at Jiahu in Henan Province, China for example, or in the Acoustics and Music of British Prehistory Research Network – are articulating this field far more fully than I ever could.[1] Their detailed findings belong beyond the scope of my project. However, song is also of special interest for this book because forms such as metre and stanza appear in it simultaneously: they form both the lyrics and melody *together*.

Of course these forms also occur elsewhere in each medium: in poetry not set to music and in music without words. Among the best known 'Songs Without Words' are Felix Mendelssohn's eight volumes of pieces for solo piano, published in the years from 1829 to 1845; in 2012 the contemporary Greek Cypriot/Nederland composer Yannis Kyriakides responded to these with a 'Words and Song without Words' for solo cello, sound and video.[2] Rare examples for voice include the famous opening section of the first movement 'Ária' in Heitor Villa-Lobos's *Bachianas Brasileiras No. 5* for soprano and cello ensemble (1938–45). Villa-Lobos said of himself, 'I don't use folklore, I *am* the folklore' and like the heroine's *habanera* in Bizet's *Carmen*, this 'Cantilena' uses a traditional musical form as what is unmistakably a seduction 'line'.[3] When this happens, each reminds us of the other art. And because 'being reminded' isn't always conscious, these formal references create a vague sense of a continuity between the genres. As we've seen repeatedly, Classical instrumental music employs melodies which could also serve – and sometimes have – as song tunes. Franz Schubert's 'Death and the Maiden' *lied* D531 reappears in his Quartet No. 14 in D minor D810, for example.

In fact simple mechanisms, rather than occult affinities, are at work. Ballad form lets us see them clearly. Its iambic quatrains alternate four-stress with three-stress lines. This is highly recognisable, and what makes ballad more recognisable still are the ways in which what its lyrics 'say' also refer to the form's roots in oral transmission.[4] For ballad is a dramatic form. It tells stories that have universal resonance, that are suited to the widest possible range of listeners – as stories which traditionally entertain an entire community must be. It's also fabular: the bearer of morals, whether political or ethical, which aren't usually spelt out. The implication is that the moral of the ballad doesn't *need* spelling out; it has an audience who can supply it.

In asking the audience to do so, ballad welcomes them *into* its own performance. Occasionally, however, it also addresses those listeners directly – usually in the closing lines. At sixty-one stanzas 'Chevy Chase' is almost an epic by ballad standards. It tells of a borderers' dispute over hunting rights, and ends:

> God save our King, and bless this land
>   With plenty, joy and peace:
> And grant henceforth that foul debate
>   Twixt noblemen may cease.[5]

In his at the time widely read 1920 anthology of *English Ballads* (in which, somewhat cheekily, he includes two of his own compositions), Sir Henry Newbolt tells us that 'Sir Philip Sidney in his *Apologie for Poetry* remarks of [this ballad]: "I never heard the old song of Percy and Douglas that I found not my heart moved more than with a trumpet."'[6] Sidney's famous remark, his 'I found not my heart moved', goes to the heart of ballad: whose fabular, moral-bearing and yet not instructive role implies an *equality* of moral understanding between singer and listener. Ballad relies on, and reinforces, a *shared* system of values that is either already in place or in the process of being constructed. The occasion of performance is thus a way to share communal values: in other word, it implies a community.

From the sixteenth century onward, newly composed ballads circulated as broadsides, single printed sheets sold by chapmen and hawkers at fairs and in streets and pubs. In the second half of that century alone, more than two thousand new ballads were registered with the Stationers' Company, then the national publishing licensing body.[7] By the seventeenth century, this trend collided with the pamphleteering dissemination of political views in a genre that was ideal for the expression of political dissent. It's a tradition that has never fully died out. During the seventeenth-century English Civil War, the poet John Milton was among the most active Republican pamphleteers. Most of his tracts were written as prose, but in 1694 his *Letters of State* contained 'Sonnet 16', in praise of Oliver Cromwell, 'who [...] Guided by faith and matchless fortitude [...] Hast rear'd God's trophies'.[8] However ballads, because of the way they could be sung – and sung to familiar, existing tunes – could be more readily memorised than either prose or such occasional verse, and their reach was correspondingly greater. Their already-familiar form fitted music the singers and listeners already knew to such an extent that they were – and still are – often published without music. The sense of familiarity, of 'belonging to' everybody, that this creates can be potent in establishing new political and social ideas.

Twentieth-century US protest songs include Bob Dylan's 'A Hard Rain's A-Gonna Fall', which is based on the Scottish Border Ballad 'Lord Randall' and protests against the Cold War; and 'Which Side Are You On?', written by Florence Reece, the wife of a Union organiser during the 1931 Miners' Strike in Harlan County, and based on the earlier ballad 'Jack Munro', also though to be British in origin.[9] UK protest ballads have been a little less widely disseminated; except by specialists, such as Charles Parker of the BBC in Birmingham.[10] But examples from the 1980s and 1990s, engaging with topics such as the Miners' Strike and the Poll Tax Riots, are still widely performed on the folk music scene.[11]

Contemporary poets exploit similar feelings of familiarity when they compose ballads. Almost like the key that has been

agreed beforehand between singer and fiddler, there remains a
sense of a prior agreement about what the ballad *is*; a sense that
we 'know the tune'.[12] W. H. Auden starts his 1937 ballad 'As I
Walked out One Evening' with familiar, rural images, as if he's
tuning up and agreeing the key with his precursors:

> As I walked out one evening,
>   Walking down Bristol Street,
> The crowds upon the pavement
>   Were fields of harvest wheat.[13]

The ballad darkens, as ballads will, and turns into a reflection
on the tragedy of our mortality. This is, after all, a poem written
fewer than twenty years after the First World War, during
the tragedy of the Spanish Civil War and in the approaching
shadow of World War II. It's a related impulse that has the
poet and memoirist Laurie Lee entitle the 1969 volume of his
autobiography, in which he busks round Thirties Spain as the
clouds of civil war gather, *As I Walked Out One Midsummer
Morning*.[14] Unlike the static 'Once upon a time' or 'There was,
and there was not', which traditionally introduce a story, the
balladic 'As I walked out ...' gives us a narrative and a narrator
already in motion. Its way into storytelling dovetails satisfyingly
with the perpetual *and then ... and then* of music and poetry
themselves.

These resonances work across contexts. 'Early One Morning',
the 1962 piece by British sculptor Anthony Caro, is held to be
the first to introduce *and then ... and then* into sculpture by
combining rather than integrating a series of forms. His title,
taken from a narrative folksong which is not quite a ballad –
'Early one morning / Just as the sun was rising' – is another
version of 'As I walked out'.[15] Charles Causley's 'Ballad of the
Bread Man' (which, adapting Henry Newbolt's editorial policy,
he includes in his own *Modern Folk Ballads* of 1966) even *ends*
on foot. Its protagonist, the resurrected Christ, walks among
those who disowned him in life:

> Through the town he went walking.
> He showed them the holes in his head.
> Now do you want any loaves? he cried.
> Not today, they said.[16]

As we saw in Chapter 3, walking draws an *and then ... and then* line through both space and time. On Martin Heidegger's *Holzwege*, his forest paths, we follow a line of thought with a walker-philosopher who believes that 'Way and weighing [...] // On a single walk are found.'[17] The twentieth-century landscape artist Richard Long's key 1967 piece *A Line Made by Walking* sets out from a from this same cultural origin.[18] In his 2015 essay for radio, *On Songs and Laughter*, John Berger expands on this *and then ... and then* relationship between song and time. He says that songs bring the past into the present through the intrinsically oral nature of their transmission. They have been by being heard on a previous occasion. They also 'lean forward' into the future as they hope to be passed on again and again. Traditional songs carry not only the 'not-here, not-now' of storytelling but also a longing for a posterity.[19]

Song also links music and poetry by the obvious means of making them collaborate directly with each other. But this is also where tensions between the two forms are most marked. Precisely because they must work most closely together, we see here the ways they struggle with each other: for example, in ongoing debate about the status of song lyrics. Famously, the North American literary critic Christopher Ricks argues that Bob Dylan's lyrics are poems, and analyses them as such in *Dylan's Visions of Sin* (2001).[20] Ricks's argument seems to turn on the dual notion that because Dylan's lyrics can be technically adroit and indulge in wordplay he is a poet; and that because he is a famous singer-songwriter, if he's a poet he must be a great one – in short, the 'halo effect'.[21] Poets tend to disagree with Ricks, but Dylan has been nominated for the Nobel Prize for Literature with depressing regularity. (However, neither side can be said to argue from the artist's own intentions since, confusingly, Dylan himself has said both, 'I think of myself as a poet first and a musician second', and, 'I think of myself more as a song-and-dance man.'[22])

As well as such arguments *about* songs, makerly tensions exist *within* them, as music and words struggle for priority, and force each other into compromises. As we saw in Chapter 6, a classic example of such compromise is when an existing tune is put to a new use, and words are written to fit it. The protest ballad is presumably such a successful exception because the pre-existing form is a *poetic* as well as a musical genre. Sometimes, even other song forms manage to 'trade up' to better words. The lamentable lyrics of the British National Anthem are not excused by the music's later life as '*Heil Prinz, dir!*', the Prussian State Anthem, whose lyrics, though similar in sentiment, are at least a little less repetitive:

> Heil dir im Siegerkranz,
> Gerrscher des Leipzig!
> Heil, Prinz, dir!
> Fühl in des Thrones Glanz
> Die hohe Wonne ganz
> Liebling des Volks zu sein!
> Heil, Prinz, dir!

Musical 'translation' need not be clumsy, as the story of another national anthem, the *Deutschlandlied*, confirms. Its melody famously appears in Josef Haydn's String Quartet Op. 76 No. 3, 'The Emperor'. In 1848, roughly fifty years after it was composed, Hoffmann von Fallersleben wrote the words of '*Lied der Deutschen*' to fit this tune.[23] However, Haydn had *originally* composed the music in 1797 as the setting of yet another other poem, '*Gott erhalte Franz den Kaiser*' ('God save Franz the Emperor'), written by Lorenz Leopold Haschka as an anthem to Emperor Francis II.

What this to-and-fro does illustrate is the pull that exists between music and language. We saw in the last chapter how familiar orchestral musicians are with the way tunes seem to attract or evoke words. The eponymous 'Surprise' theme of Haydn's Symphony No. 94 in G has long acquired an innocent rhyme – 'Papa Haydn's dead and gone / But his memory lingers on' – while the waltzing third movement of Tchaikovsky's Fifth Symphony, Opus 64 in E minor, has acquired the less decent 'Once I was a virgin / Now I am no more, / Once I did it never, / Now I do it more and more and more and ...'

In part these are just games played in boring rehearsals. But in part they represent a peculiarly pertinent solution to the recurring Anglo-Saxon problem of how to sing a musical interpretation. For most European musicians this question never arises. They simply use *solfège*; each note is sung to the name its role within a key gives it. For the Anglo-American musician, product of a more happenstance harmonic training, this option isn't readily to hand – or mouth. He simply doesn't know what sounds to utter in order to utter music.

And yet that utterance is at the heart of musical practice. Musicians *sing* passages in rehearsal, and when teaching, to convey what they mean: precisely because, as we saw in Chapter 6, the way a piece 'goes' is unparaphraseable. So Anglo-Saxons substitute sound-words for the *do-re-mi* of *solfège*, clothing their wordless singing with 'Tah-te' or 'Dah-de-dah-de-dah-aa'. For rehearsals in the large spaces of an actual concert hall, the orchestral conductor's enunciation carries best – and retains its precision – when he sings rather than whistles or hums. But in the smaller rehearsal room or teaching studio this isn't the case; yet musicians still *sing*. Some non-acoustic imperative imposes, or shapes, these vocalisations. It's as if we experience music, or at least the uttering breath, as *calling for* speech. As if, in other words, something in the experience of the musical phrase suggests the spoken – the *verbal* – phrase.

We came close to what this 'something' might be in our discussion of the phrasal grammar of breath in Chapter 3. Riffing jazz singers replace the disciplinary 'Taka-taka' of the orchestral conductor with sound-words like those that gave Doo-wop and Bebop their names. In these improvisations too, utterance seems to imply uttering *language*. But jazz musicians go further than classical performers, *composing* music as quasi-verbal structures. The pressure on the musical phrase to *be* language that this underlines is apparent not only in song, nor simply when we think about the infant's shift into language, as we did in Chapter 2, but also when we observe such related phenomena as 'speaking in tongues'. The Pentecostal babble of some fundamentalist Christian worshippers is, they believe, the human approximation to pure testimony, an Edenic speech beyond speech. We'll return to this intuition in Chapter 9, when we look at the possibility that melody itself is semantic.

When a composer sets an already existing poem, all of this happens in reverse. The sensory 'surplus' that, as we saw in Chapters 5 and 6, is part of the poem's identity, is put at risk, limited, or even lost. Even singer-songwriters can recognise that a poem is a complete *aural* work of its own kind. When Leonard Cohen published his ninth book of poems, *The Book of*

Longing, in 2006, he didn't just collect together some lyrics he hadn't bothered to write the music for.[24] He was taking the term 'poetry' to name some particular formal *attribute* (perhaps, for example, related to the role of poems as a 'high stakes' way of using language). Pertinently, Cohen was a poet before he was a songwriter. His first collection, 1956's *Let Us Compare Mythologies*, inaugurated the McGill Poetry Series. In the Sixties, before his musical career took off, three further collections were published by McClelland & Stewart, another distinguished literary imprint.[25]

Poet-librettists make an analogous distinction from the other direction. Two leading contemporary British librettists, David Harsent and Michael Symmons Roberts, both make a distinction between poetry 'proper' and the verse libretti they compose *for* music. Both are distinguished as poets, and each collaborates primarily with a single composer: Roberts with James McMillan and Harsent with Sir Harrison Birtwistle. Roberts has talked about how McMillan asks for libretti written in much looser language than his characteristically compact lyric verse: in other words, with a less overdetermined musical character of their own. Harsent says that, 'Writing for the opera stage involves writing for voices. A poem – at the point of composition – is written for the *inner* voice' (my italics).[26]

Such distinctions are built around the way poetry distances itself from everyday speech. The role of poetry as *not quite being* other, related ways of going on, such as music or prose, is one it traditionally self-declares through register, theme, form and occasion. Possibly one reason for the fierce struggles between alternative schools of poetic form, such as those between the New York and Black Mountain Schools in 1970s North America, or between postmodernists and the lyric-modernist mainstream in the UK today, is that poetic form isn't secondary to, but an intimate part of, the life of a poem. Even its more understated registers – such as irony or quiet elegy – which at first glance seem 'natural' or 'debunking', are far from conversational. Their very consistency is the first sign that their use, in a poem like Robert Frost's 'Home Burial', is anything but simple reportage. Frost's use of direct speech, colloquialism and that apparently laconic mode with which country dwellers preserve both privacy and dignity, was revolutionary at the time this poem was first published, in 1914. But look how they are transformed by the containing note of blank verse:

> He saw her from the bottom of the stairs
> Before she saw him. She was starting down,
> Looking back over her shoulder at some fear.[27]

In its bleak immediacy, the poem isn't simply trying to record the ebb and flow of actual speech; it goes beyond mere dramatic monologue. Reviewing *North of Boston*, the collection from which it comes, in *The New Republic*, Amy Lowell observed that Frost 'writes in classic metres, and uses inversions and clichés whenever he pleases, those devices so abhorred by the newest generation. He goes his own way, regardless of anyone else's rules, and the result is a book of unusual power and sincerity.'[28] 'Home Burial' uses realism to shock but at the same time, and even *within and through* this strategy, its diction is heightened. Indeed, poetry often offers itself *as* the heightened speech we need in order to address big themes, such as love and death. In 1997, the death of Princess Diana produced an outpouring of verse, on florists' cards and soft toy labels at impromptu shrines as well as in public condolence books, that had nothing to do with literary renaissance and everything to do with the search for an apt form for Big Feelings. Even in twenty-first-century Britain it's not unusual for it to be a poem that is read at a wedding or civil partnership ceremony, funeral or christening; secular substitutes, perhaps, for the liturgies that as we have seen are often in verse form.

Whatever school it emerges from, then, poetry *declares* that it has been made. The traditional argument for full rhyme, that it makes a poem memorable, implies not only portability but durability. Poetic form is what tells us that the poem isn't ephemeral in the same way as conversation – or even journalism, for example.[29] Despite all this, poets don't automatically or necessarily resist the idea that their work might be set to music. In *Schubert's Winter Journey*, the singer Ian Bostridge quotes Wilhelm Müller, the author of the poems Franz Schubert sets as *Winterreise* D911. Müller clearly longed for someone to recognise, and so release, the musicality of his poems. This is from the diary entry on his twenty-first birthday:

> I can neither play nor sing, yet when I write verses, I sing and play after all. If I could produce the melodies, my songs would be more pleasing than they are. now. But courage! Perhaps there is a kindred spirit somewhere who will hear the tunes behind the words and give them back to me.

Seven years later, he wrote to thank the composer Bernhard Josef Klein for setting six of his poems:

> For indeed my songs lead but half a life, a paper existence of black-and-white, until music breathes life into them, or at least calls it forth and awakens it if it is already dormant in them.[30]

Yet anxieties remain. Questions of priority, duplication and mutual cancellation seem to cast a shadow across what happens when a poem is set to music. Like most musical settings – Gilbert and Sullivan, Brecht and Weill are conspicuous *because* they're exceptions – art songs are officially credited as the *musician*'s work. Their *opus* numbers locate them within the composer's corpus: we simply don't say 'Franz Schubert and Wilhelm Müller's *Die Winterreise*'. In the familiar anecdote, this is the point made by admirers of lyricist Oscar Hammerstein – or possibly by his wife – when the composer Jerome Kern is congratulated on the solo success of 'his' Broadway show *Showboat*.[31]

Lieder are arranged for voice and piano. Art music settings of songs for other ensembles do exist: they include Franz Schubert's *The Shepherd on the Rock* D965, for soprano, violin or clarinet and piano; Ralph Vaughan-Williams's *On Wenlock Edge* (1909) for tenor, piano and string quartet; or indeed Sally Beamish's *Tree Carols* (2014) for baritone and string quartet. But these are exceptions. In the conventional *lieder* ensemble the pianist is called the 'accompanist', which makes it sounds as if words have conceptual primacy. But in fact, it is *melody*, not language, that has primacy over the harmonies of the piano part. The singer is carrying not just the words but the *tune* which shapes our experience of them.

Primacy isn't the same as chronological priority, but the two aren't unrelated. We've seen how words tend to be written before, or at the same time as, the music of a song. (Exceptions are most often from the world of popular music: where, arguably, music is more formulaic and words do less complex semantic work. When Shirley Bassey sings her 1950s hit 'Kiss Me Honey Honey', the lines work perfectly and not only as a camp classic, because they rise to their cheerful occasion and no further. Paul McCartney's 1965 'Yesterday' started life as a wordless tune; a running joke for several months, until he came up with the lyrics, it was sung to the words, 'Scrambled eggs / Oh my baby how I love your legs': not as bad as the lyrics of the National Anthem, but not far off.[32]) Yet much 'serious' poetry *is* written in particular forms; implying that it could be composed even *for* the particular constraints set by a piece of existing art music.[33]

Three aspects of art song make this relatively difficult to pull off. One has to do with the character of the musical setting itself. A *lied* tends to be a through-composed conceptual whole, with much greater development of musical material over its course than is the case in traditional or popular song. The second has to do with poetry's own forms. Even strict poetic form is elective; 'specially' chosen. (For example, the contemporary Anglophone poet finds iambic pentameter, which can contain relatively sustained passages of thought but sounds a serious, almost impersonal note, harder to use in confessional or lyric verse than for political or metaphysical thought. Free verse can seem too loose and woolly for intellection.) Moreover, every original poem represents a whole series of small technical formal decisions – such as breaking up a series of weighty monosyllables, or patterning assonance – each of which changes the poem's meaning, even if only at the level of register.

Thirdly, it's difficult to obey particular *sound* forms without making semantic compromises.[34] Indeed the sound and sense of poetry are so intimately connected at the level of meaning that this connection might be poetry's defining characteristic. The Russian Futurist poet and theorist Osip Brik first published his work on 'Sound Repetitions' in a 1917 essay of that name. As Maria Enzensberger summarises it:

> Brik's discovery and classification of the repetitions of consonantal groups in Russian verse was used to demonstrate the innermost ties between sound and meaning in poetry, i.e. the role of euphony in the creation of figures of speech, the interaction of phonic and semantic devices. Sound orchestration, Brik argued, is not an extrinsic device applied to poetic creation. Very often the poet starts from a

consonant word prompted by the ear and works towards its logical justification.[35]

In other words, most poets disagree with Wilhelm Müller's belief that their poems lead 'a paper existence of black-and-white'. A poem *sounds*, and it does so in the way it's scored to sound *by its layout on the page*. We saw in Chapter 3 how line-breaks, even in free verse, map phrases and also units of thought in a way that separates verse from prose. W. S. Merwin's unpunctuated poems use the to and fro of line-breaks to mimic the to and fro of reflection; at the same time, they have an unusual momentum because they are couched in a single sentence.[36] John Burnside's signature stepped lines propel and inflect his work and create a unique, underdetermined music for his unusually evocative, suggestive poems. These sounds can be lost in the competing soundscape of song.[37]

Worse, a musical setting can make a poem's *sense* disappear. It can be hard even to hear the words. The challenges of matching a human voice to a grand piano are considerable; those a soloist encounters when singing against full orchestra are greater still. Words set in ways that differ from conventional speech rhythms are particularly hard to catch. This isn't to say that poems are play-scripts. But each language has normative sound patterns, that stress significant words such as verbs and subjects rather than prepositions, that use stress and pitch to underline a key concept, and that deploy repetition, phatic tropes or clichés to match their rhythm to the music. Poetry knows and plays with these semiotic conventions; and so, at its best, does song. The chorus of the Shetland folksong, 'When I Was a Little Boy', which ends each stanza of hyperbolic boasting, 'With my tooral laddy, whack fol laddy, tooral looral ling', is a glorious example of *phatic hyperbole* – and of language at play.[38]

Pitch and key sometimes capture affect – when the key word is at the top of a singer's range, for example – but can equally disrupt the ear's intuitive grasp of 'what's going on'. I wrote in Chapter 6 about Benjamin Britten's setting, in *Serenade for Tenor, Horn and Strings*, Op. 31, of Tennyson's 'The splendour falls on castle walls'. The composer's emphasis, 'The *splen*dour falls on castle *walls*' absolutely disrupts the spoken rhythm, 'The splendour *falls* on *cas*tle walls', as well as the metrical shell imposed on it, 'The splendour *falls* on castle *walls*.' This brings out the down-dale and up-hill arpeggiated sense of the singer's line; with its mimicry of fortifications. Britten's unexpected emphasis on '*splen*dour' also suggests the sudden striking of sunlight, or of reflection. The composer knows the voice he's writing for so well – after all, it belongs to his partner, Peter Pears – that he is able to contain his instrumental ensemble, a string chamber orchestra as well as the French horn, *with* the tenor line; leaving space for the 'echoing' horn to chase the voice that has 'Set the wild echoes flying'. Pulsing string chords create an opening in which the tenor sounds out as clearly as Tennyson's 'bugle'.

We gather much less than this level of textual detail when we listen to *lieder* in a language we don't know. We may have a rough sense, at least from its title, that a song is 'about' trout, or a girl spinning. But this tells us nothing *about* that 'about': what its treatment reveals in terms of emotional or philosophical insight, linguistic pleasure or characterisation. The narrowing principle of the canon, with the repetition and familiarity that brings, does at least allow us to plot in outline the story famous songs 'tell'. We know that 'The Erl-King' is about a child stolen away by Death, despite a desperate night-ride in which the father tries to outstrip the pursuer. But do those of us without German know *how* the words tell this story; what each line actually *says*? (Apart, that is, from the child's cries, 'My father, my father ...', held up by Schubert at the climax of each stanza: 'Mein Vater, mein Vater', is *so* conveniently close to English.) In a recent panel discussion, Ian Bostridge says, 'It matters *that* the song is saying something, not *what* it is saying.'[39] True enough: what we hear is the attempt at – the gestures of – communication. *Poetry* is replaced by *utterance*.

Poets worry that their work will be 'lost in translation' not only by the composer, but by musicians' performances. Sure enough, in the modern concert hall *lieder* can seem far from home, their unknown language making the singer appear like someone seen beyond glass, mouthing words we can't hear. Yet song reminds us that our human dimensions are pretty much the same as the singer's. Without special training the singing human voice simply doesn't reach very far. We're used to the idea of hearing folksong in a pub; traditionally, songs were also sung at home and in the workplace, where even the farm labourer worked within earshot of his teammates.

So singing implies being in the *same* space: it implies face-to-face communication. The *lieder* form is written for the 'kammer' which in German means, as *chamber* does in English, a space both formal and intimate. In German it's also used as a prefix in the formal title 'Kammersänger', a distinction conferred by various institutions on exceptional Classical musical singers. This institutionalised chamber is a room intimate with power, its affinities to the Cabinet or Star Chamber as much as to any mere salon. This implies that the audience are distinguished participants in a musical occasion; for all the world like the commissioning princes of past centuries. At the heart of chamber music is a gesture of recognition: of parity and involvement not so different from the one we saw ballad create. This has to do with proximity and scale. Compared to today's undifferentiated audience in the concert hall or listening to a broadcast; the people in the 'chamber' are individuals.[40]

And so song is as much an individuating as it is a communal form. The Australian twentieth-century composer Percy Grainger killed this speaking intimacy in the folksongs he collected. His settings, like 'Country Gardens' or 'Shallow Brown', over-control how they are performed, obsessionally scoring every detail with exact dynamics and tempo markings. Grainger claimed that he was honouring the folksingers from whom he collected material by recording them on wax cylinders, rather than noting the tunes down on paper as contemporaries Béla Bartók and Vaughan Williams did. If the technology of his time had allowed these recordings to be circulated and the singers to become well known, this would have been the case. As it did not, his subsequent attempts to capture their *performances* in scores merely broke up folksong's traditional transmission: through being 'picked up' by singers and 'made their own'.

History shows us that musical setting has often put the words at risk. In his *Introduction to a Philosophy of Music*, Peter Kivy prefaces a discussion of the relationship between song's words and music – tellingly titled, 'First the words; then the music' – with an historical exegesis.[41] During the Counter-Reformation, church composers were censured by the Council of Trent (1554–63) for writing 'luxurious' music that made the texts they were setting unintelligible to congregations. (A pleasure of this judgment, for today's poet, is its notion of music's mere utility.) One way in which musical settings can be useful is by *adding* something to a text, such as beauty or memorability: the principle of illustration, as we saw in Chapter 6. Another is not by adding elements but by underscoring textual material. Sixteenth-century polyphony, the music the Council was censoring, was highly developed. Faithful to principles of praise song, Italian composers like Orlando de Lassus and Giovanni Pierluigi da Palestrina were creating superstructures of beauty to inspire and move believers. Works fit for a king, they were by metonymic extension tributes to a divinity. Sixteenth-century Roman Catholic liturgy was in Latin, not the demotic; so, arguably, the reverent and moving atmosphere of music might be more important for supporting the faith of an uneducated congregation than words they couldn't understand. But polyphony occluded the texts it set rather than underscoring them, and the Council of Trent ruled that it was important to hear, even if not to understand, their liturgical content.

At the same time, opera was beginning its development in the hands of the Florentine Camerata. Members of the Camerata – intellectuals and humanists as well as poets and composers, all of whom met under the patronage of Count Giovanni de' Bardi – were also concerned that highly developed polyphony had come to mean music for its own sake. They felt this obstructed the emotive power of the texts being performed. Eventually, both the Camerata and the Council of Trent settled for a compromised polyphony that was nevertheless text-driven, and which tried to come close to the patterns of speech. In other words, both the sacred and the secular powers of the time believed that texts, not music, supply meaning in song; and both chose *duplication* – underlining these words *with* the music – as a remedy against losing that meaning.

The Camerata's proto-operatic form was modelled on their belief that Greek tragedies – and comedies – were sung. The *stile rappresentativo*, later more famously used by Claudio Monteverdi, for example in *Orfeo* (1607), *The Coronation of Poppea* (1642) and the lesser-known *The Return of Ulysses to his Homeland* (1641), followed human speech pattern and, in order to do so, abandoned abstract formal elements, such as the stanza form, that would already have been familiar to both the Camerata and Monteverdi from folksong and medieval carol. We know now that their stylistic innovations *were* in fact faithful to Greek tradition: even though they had had to rely on readings of Aristotle's *Poetics* to work out what that could be. Recent archaeologists have discovered a number of Greek lyric verses annotated with a kind of musical scoring. Decoded, this turns out to be a pitch notation that tracks the rising and falling pitches of speech; duration isn't noted because the *texts* are already metrical.[42]

Speech-pitch setting was never wholly abandoned, even in Classical and Romantic music. In 'The Erl-King', the child's cry, 'Mein Vater, mein Vater' stands out starkly with its shivering semitone rise and fall. But his father's major-pitched oh-so-reasonable denials – 'It's just the wind in the reeds, son' – are just as accurately recorded. The writing is mimetic but also expressive; a doubling which prevents 'empty' duplication by the music of the words. Exaggerating, or otherwise distorting, speech pitch is another way to avoid duplication. The late twentieth-century jazz/outsider musician Moondog builds up noodling melodies, and eventually harmonies, from phrases that he sings at exaggerated speech pitch. In songs like 1997's 'New Amsterdam', Moondog's diction becomes as swooping and dramatic as a camp aristocrat or a circus entertainer.

But speech-pitch settings don't sacrifice abstract formal strategies. Moondog uses repetition to create structure; the Greek lyricists employed strict formal metres. 'The Erl King' uses stanza form and the tightening effect of strict metre (both formal elements that Johann Wolfgang von Goethe's original *poem* supplies) to create its containing formal integrity. When folksong uses stanza form and repetition to break down the story of betrayal in 'O Waly Waly' or 'The Foggy Foggy Dew' into a stepwise, quasi-ritualistic progression, it makes it feel more inevitable and universal – this is what young men do to young women – and shifts the song from mere confession to tragedy.[43] In each of these examples it's the *words* that restore abstract formal qualities to song.

So what happens when music and poetry achieve the fullest possible integration in song? Perhaps the case of Ivor Gurney, a poet and composer who achieved canonical distinction in both genres, can suggest some answers. Through the happy accident of being born near Gloucester, at the height of the Three Choirs Festival's influence on British contemporary music, Gurney – who as a boy secured an apprenticeship to the Cathedral organist – won a scholarship to the Royal College of Music and became a composer.

The English Musical Renaissance he was part of all his life is arguably the most enduring manifestation of Modernism in Britain. As an adult, Gurney would apply its techniques to his verse, borrowing old-fashioned locutions, and traditional forms such as ballad, and juxtaposing them with suddenly conversational style and leaps of thought, whose nearest analogy is the *sui generis* harmonic progressions of chromatic, Modernist music. His own music, on the other hand, feels continuously integrated; each gesture is assured and confident, as if gaining structure and certainty from its dialogue with the Classical-Romantic tradition that, in the poem 'Schubert', he called the 'ordinary good-health technique / of Beethoven'. For though Gurney's musical education was excellent from an early age, the rest of his schooling – he was a tailor's son, in class-ridden Edwardian society – was undistinguished. It was only as an adult composer, in *setting* Shakespeare, Fletcher *et al.* for *Five Elizabethan Songs*, that he became interested in verse. He went on to publish two collections, *Severn and Somme* (1917) and *War's Embers* (1919), both written from the trenches.[44]

All his life Gurney was preoccupied by walking, the chronologic 'line' that, as we saw in Chapter 3, is characteristic of both music and poetry. He boasted that he had been 'a night-walker from age sixteen'; his walks are a dominant theme of both the poems and the songs. 'Roads are sometimes the true symbolical / Representations of movement in the fate of man', he wrote in 'Roads – Those Roads'. In 'The Companions':

> On upland bleak and bare to wind
> Beneath a maze of stars I strode;
> Phantoms of fear haunted the road,
> Dogging my footsteps close behind.

Though this is walking as narrative, not as a Heideggerian line of thought, in both Gurney's rhythmic verse and the lack of polyphony within his music, we hear the aesthetic of this 'walking line'.

It's as if his forms borrow from each other. Gurney's verse, with its abrupt changes of direction, motet-like 'crisscross' rhythms or grammatical deferments of meaning, is unusually rhythmic, even dance-like. He often uses the triplet stresses of the trochee and anapest, moving between them to create a sense of spontaneity. In the stylish setting of 'Early Spring Dawn', the repetition of 'light' and 'leaping', and the sounding together of thin/line/faint/lessen/lighten, make the lines bounce. This aural crisscross mimics the poem's 'leaping' light: 'Long shines the thin light of the day to the north-east, / The line of blue faint known and the leaping to white'. These rhythms, unusual in verse, would be easily notated in music. Yet he wrote *both* the words and music of relatively few songs. 'Severn Meadows', possibly his most famous work, is the glorious exception that proves this rule. Gurney, who had famously poor mental health, spent the last years of his life in asylums.[45] His life, and its difficulties with integration, stands as a kind of strange testament to the intractable difficulty with integration which is at the heart of song.

Notes

1. 'The authors of the paper describing the Jiahu findings are Juzhong Zhang, from the Institute of Cultural Relics and Archaeology of Henan Province, Zhengzhou, China, and the Archaeometry Laboratory at the University of Science and Technology of China; Changsui Wang, also from the Archaeometry Laboratory; Zhaochen Kong, from the Paleobotany Laboratory, Academia Sinica, Beijing, China; and Garman Harbottle from Brookhaven.' https://www.bnl.gov/bnlweb/pubaf/pr/1999/bnlpr092299.html. Retrieved 16/11/15.

   The Acoustics and Music of British Prehistory Research Network, part of the AHRC/EPSRC Science and Heritage Programme. https://ambpnetwork.wordpress.com Retrieved 16/11/15.

2. http://www.kyriakides.com/words_and_song_without_words. html. Retrieved 28/12/15.

3. Manuel Negwer, *Villa-Lobos: Der Aufbruch der brasilianischen Musik* (Mainz: Schott Music, 2008), p. 8. The cellos are of course pitched like the *male* speaking voice.

4. Vladimir Propp is best known for his Structuralist analysis of the *morphology of* – the elements common to – folktales. But he also published work on Russian epic and lyric songs: for example in his 1958 study of Russian Heroic Epic. Vladimir Propp, *Russkij gero-iceskij epos* (Moscow: Gosudarstvennoe izdatel'stvo xudozestven-noj literatury, 1958).

5. Newbolt's note comments that, 'The version here printed belongs to the period of James I of England. This later version, which excels the earlier in language and feeling, is not perhaps its equal in dignity and rugged strength [...]. Both versions appear in Dr Percy's *Reliques of Ancient English Poetry.* The original manu-script reposes in the Bodleian Library at Oxford.' 'Chevy Chase' in Henry Newbolt (ed.), *English Ballads* (London: Edward Arnold, 1920), pp. 14–23.

6. Ibid.

7. To say nothing of the unlicensed ballads. https://stationers.org/the-hall-heritage/library-archives/24-the-hall-heritage.html. Retrieved 15/1/16.

8. John Milton, 'Sonnet 16', in *Complete Shorter Poems*, Stella P. Revard (ed.) (Oxford: Wiley-Blackwell, 2009), p. 360.

9. Though Dianne Dugaw notes a version 'on an 1830s Boston broadside in American Antiquarian Society, Uncatalogued Ballads.' Dianne Dugaw, *Warrior Women and Popular Balladry, 1650–1850*, reissued with new Preface (Chicago: University of Chicago Press, 1996), pp. 101–3.

10. Archived at the Library of Birmingham: http://www.libraryofbir-mingham.com/article/charlesparker/charlesparkerarchive. Retrieved 16/11/15.

11. And included in anthologies marking particular industrial dis-putes, such as: David Betteridge (ed.), *A Rose Loupt Out: Poetry and Song Celebrating the UCS Work-In* (Middlesborough: Smokestack Publications, 2011).

12. I've written elsewhere about how elegy, being a familiar form, allows the expression of socially awkward emotion. Fiona Sampson, *Beyond the Lyric* (London: Chatto & Windus, 2012), pp. 58–9.

13. W. H. Auden, 'As I Walked Out One Evening' in *Collected Poems*, revised edn, Edward Mendelson (ed.) (London: Faber, 2007), pp. 134–5.

14. Laurie Lee, *As I Walked Out One Midsummer Morning* (London: André Deutsch, 1969).

15 Michael Fried, writing in *Art and Objecthood*, describes his defin-ing 1961 encounter with Caro's sculptures *Midday* and *Sculpture Seven*. Quoted in Ian Barker, *Anthony Caro: Quest for the New Sculpture* (Aldershot: Lund Humphries, 2004), p. 102. Of course, Caro *wasn't* entirely innovative, as anyone who has looked at the Parthenon 'Elgin' Marbles, or indeed walked around the

fifth-century BCE Parthenon itself, will recognise. The *and then ...
and then* principle of a sculptural frieze is older even than these: at
least as old as the Assyrian Lachish Relief, carved at the start of the
seventh century BCE, currently in the next room of the British
Museum.

16. Causley uses a three-stress line throughout. Charles Causley,
    'Ballad of the Bread Man' in Charles Causley (ed.), *Modern Folk
    Ballads* (London: Studio Vista, 1966), pp. 13–15.

17. Martin Heidegger, 'The Thinker as Poet' in *Poetry, Language,
    Thought*, Albert Hofstadter (trans.) (San Francisco: Harper &
    Row, 1975), p. 3. Some of the essays in this collection had indeed
    originally appeared in Heidegger's *Holzwege* (1950).

18. Richard Long's photographic record of the line he made by
    walking in a Wiltshire field is in the Tate collection. http://www.
    tate.org.uk/art/artworks/long-a-line-made-by-walking-p07149.
    Retrieved 16/11/15.

19. John Berger, 'About Song and Laughter', Sukhdev Sandhu (intro.),
    Tim Dee (prod.), BBC Radio 3, 3/5/15.

20. Christopher Ricks, *Dylan's Visions of Sin* (Edinburgh: Canongate,
    2001).

21. The term coined by American psychologist Edward Thorndike
    and first used by him in a 1920 article on assessment, where he
    identifies how excellence in one area (in particular including good
    looks) produces in assessors – or, later, other observers – an
    assumption of excellence in all others too. E. L. Thorndike, 'A
    Constant Error in Psychological Ratings', *Journal of Applied
    Psychology* 4:1 (1920), pp. 25–9. http://dx.doi.org/10.1037/
    h0071663. Retrieved 27/1/16.

22. According to the Academy of American Poets: https://www.poets.
    org/poetsorg/text/bob-dylan-im-poet-and-i-know-it.   Retrieved
    2/2/16.

23. Since the Nazi era, only the third stanza of the *Deutschlandlied* is
    sung as the national anthem. In 1848, these lyrics were seen as
    liberal and revolutionary; but since the Nazi era, only the third
    stanza is sung as the national anthem:

    > Einigkeit und Recht und Freiheit
    > Für das deutsche Vaterland!
    > Danach lasst uns alle streben
    > Brüderlich mit Herz und Hand!
    > Einigkeit und Recht und Freiheit
    > Sind des Glückes Unterpfand;
    > Blüh' im Glanze dieses Glückes,
    > Blühe, deutsches Vaterland!
    > Blüh' im Glanze dieses Glückes,
    > Blühe, deutsches Vaterland!
    >
    > (Unity and justice and freedom
    > For the German fatherland!

> Let us all strive for this purpose
> Brotherly with heart and hand!
> Unity and justice and freedom
> Are the pledge of happiness;
> Bloom in the glow of happiness,
> Bloom, German fatherland!
> Bloom in the glow of happiness,
> Bloom, German fatherland!'

24. Leonard Cohen, *Book of Longing* (London/New York/Toronto: Penguin/Ecco/McClelland & Stewart, 2006).
25. Cohen published his next volumes of poetry in 1978, 1984 and 1993. It may be relevant that other singer-songwriters who have also published books of poetry, like Dylan or Nick Cave, are also known for relatively serious and sophisticated song lyrics. There may be some link between going as far as they feel they can with language in lyrics, and now need the resources of an autonomous linguistic form.
26. David Harsent, in an email to the author, 14/7/15.
27. Robert Frost, 'Home Burial' in *Selected Poems*, Ian Hamilton (ed.) (Harmondsworth: Penguin, 1973), pp. 59–63.
28. Amy Lowell, *Tendencies in Modern American Poetry* (London: Macmillan, 1917).
29. Even when the poem is written for a particular occasions such as an epithalamium or public art commission
30. Ian Bostridge, *Schubert's Winter Journey: Anatomy of an Obsession* (London: Faber, 2014), pp. 11–12. It is an irony that Müller had died by the time of Schubert's settings in *Winterreise*.
31. 'In 1960 Leonard Lyons revisited the tale, and interestingly, Dorothy Hammerstein was credited with the response extolling her husband's contribution. It was possible that both Oscar and Dorothy made similar remarks:

> Mrs. Hammerstein, of course, always has been a determined spokeswoman for the importance of the lyric. When she heard a guest at a party say that Jerome Kern wrote "Ol' Man River," she dissented: "Mr. Kern did not write 'Ol' Man River.' Oscar wrote 'Ol' Man River.'" Then she hummed the melody: "What Mr. Kern wrote was 'La-La-Dumdum, La-La-Dumdum.'"

Also in 1960 the syndicated columnist Robert C. Ruark presented the anecdote:

> And while you can't knock the composers for their tunes, Dorothy Hammerstein had it right when she said "Jerome Kern wrote the dum-dum-dums, but Oscar Hammerstein wrote 'Show Boat'" And so he did.

'Lyricist versus Composer: The Song 'Ol Man River'. http://quoteinvestigator.com/2015/09/14/lyricist/#return-note-11996-3. Retrieved 16/11/15.

32. *The Telegraph*, 18 June 2015. http://www.telegraph.co.uk/culture/ music/the-beatles/11680415/Yesterday-the-song-that-started-as-Scrambled-Eggs.html. Retrieved 27/1/16.

33. This is, after all, how many songwriters produce *subsequent* verses of a song for which they work out the music and lyrics of the opening stanza together.

34. This same problem is often rehearsed in debates about poetry translation, where the formal experience of an original simply cannot be reproduced, and attempts to do so additionally compromise a poem's semantic content. As Vladimir Nabokov said, of translating Pushkin, '"Rhyme" rhymes with "crime", when Homer or *Hamlet* are rhymed. [...] The clumsiest literal translation is a thousand times more useful than the prettiest paraphrase.' He also said that 'To translate an *Onegin* stanza does not mean to rig up fourteen lines with alternate beats and affix to them seven jingle rhymes starting with pleasure-love-leisure-dove.' Vladimir Nabokov, 'Problems of Translation: "Onegin" in English' in Lawrence Venuti (ed.), *The Translation Studies Reader* (London: Routledge, 2000), pp. 71 and 83.

35. In *Sborniki po teorii poeticheskogo yazyka*, II, 1917, St Petersburg. Quoted by Maria Enzensberger, 'Introduction' in *Osip Brik: Selected Writings* (Oxford: Oxford Journals, 1974) *Screen* magazine online archive p. 39. http://monoskop.org/images/f/ff/Brik_ Osip_1974_Selected_Writings_Introduction.pdf. Retrieved 16/11/ 15.

36. W. S. Merwin, *Migration: New and Selected Poems* (Port Townsend, WA: Copper Canyon Press, 2005).

37. John Burnside, *Selected Poems* (London: Cape, 2006).

38. 'When I Was a Little Boy' 'sung by John Stickle, Baltasound, Unst, Shetland in 1947' in Ralph Vaughan Williams and A. L. Lloyd (eds), *The Penguin Book of English Folk Songs* (Harmondsworth: Penguin, 1959), p. 101.

39. In a panel with Richard Bronk, Armand D'Angour and Fiona Sampson at the London School of Economics Festival Literary Festival, 17/2/14, 6.30pm. Podcast http://www.lse.ac.uk/news AndMedia / videoAndAudio / channels / publicLecturesAndEvents / player.aspx?id=2931. Retrieved 29/8/15.

40. Sometimes, the pianists and singers in a room are not even performing at all, but are simply going through the music for their own pleasure; sight-reading perhaps.

41. Peter Kivy, *Introduction to a Philosophy of Music* (Oxford: Oxford University Press, 2002), pp. 160–81.

42. Armand D'Angour's British Academy-funded research into the music of Ancient Greek verse is introduced on his website: http://www. armand-dangour.com/2014/03/song-sirens/. Retrieved 29/8/ 15.

43. For example, in the first two stanzas of 'I wish, I wish', a song collected in the Midlands:

I wish, I wish, but it's all in vain,
I wish I were a maid again;
But a maid again I never shall be
Till apples grow on an orange tree.

I wish my baby it was born,
And smiling on its papa's knee,
And I to be in yon churchyard
With long green grass growing over me.

'Sung by Mrs C Costelo, Birmingham, (M.S. and P. S-S., 1951)' in Ralph Vaughan Williams and A. L. Lloyd (eds), *The Penguin Book of English Folk Songs* (Harmondsworth: Penguin, 1959), p. 53.

44. Gurney saw action in some of the most notorious battles of the Western Front, where he was shot and gassed. As a result his recurring mental distress was diagnosed in 1917 as shell shock.

45. In December 1922, Gurney was moved to the huge Victorian Stone House Asylum at Dartford in Kent. He was never released, and died there of TB in 1937. The hospital notebooks are full of poems, particularly up to 1926, and there was a burst of fifty songs in 1925. Thereafter, however, production tailed off.

Chapter 8

And Story Came Too: From Epic to Opera

Unlike song, opera is a highly specialised form; one that's frequently portrayed, by both admirers and critics, as having at least as much cultural significance off-stage as on-. It's at the opera that Anton Chekhov's 'The Lady with the Dog' is reunited with her lover. Their key scene takes place 'On the narrow, gloomy staircase over which was written "Entrance to Circle"'.[1] In today's Kyiv, the contemporary Ukrainian poet Yuri Burjak has a remarkably similar encounter 'At the Rear of the Circle':

> Just in front of me
> at the rear of the Circle
> I saw your eyes, as they are since
> we've said goodbye: unearthly,
>
> their earthy beauty
> hidden as ever.
> I turned left. The semicircular maze
> would bring me, I knew,
>
> to just where I saw you
> but you weren't there, you seemed
> to have melted away.[2]

This view of opera as a primarily social occasion seems paradigmatic of Edward Said's analysis of the social role of Classical music, which we looked at in Chapter 2.[3] But it's worth remembering that, in Chekhov's story, *The Geisha* opens not in Moscow but in the provinces: 'As in all provincial theatres, there was a haze above the chandelier, the gallery was noisy and restless [...] to the sounds of that atrocious orchestra, of those wretched screeching violins, he thought how lovely she was.'[4] In nineteenth-century Russia, opera may indeed serve as a relative signifier of wealth, but its exclusivity comes from the price of the tickets, not as a result of being artistically abstruse, metropolitan, or cutting-edge. In this context, opera isn't something 'difficult', or remote from the culture that surrounds it. On the contrary, that culture has successfully incorporated it.

Still, with its costumed cast of singers and its professional orchestra (unlike, say, the simple church choir and organ that liturgical music requires), and indeed the large spaces it needs to work with such forces, opera is inevitably expensive to stage.[5] By the nineteenth century it had swollen to the four- and five-act monsters, demanding huge performing resources, that we call Grand Opera. The nineteenth century even saw live elephants regularly exploited for Guiseppe Verdi's *Aida*. In a similar vein, since the 1980s, impresario Raymond Gubbay has staged 'Classical Spectacular' operas at the Royal Albert Hall.

Traditionally 'grand' in every sense, opera was earlier commissioned and patronised by the royal courts of Europe. The librettist Lorenzo Da Ponte's *Memoirs* (published in 1823) give us an insight into this world of court intrigues, royal pardons, and patronage bestowed – and the powers of manipulation required to deal with it. As he writes about the death in 1790 of one patron, the Holy Roman Emperor Joseph II and the accession of another, Leopold II:

> Shortly afterwards, Leopold arrived in Vienna. For his advent to the throne I composed an ode, wherein, with tears for the death of Joseph, I sang the virtues of Leopold. Sincere my sorrow, equally sincere my praise of this Sovereign, whom a thousand fatal eventualities were later to render unfavoring towards me.[6]

Once made, this association with privilege and power is hard to break: since social power, as the Marxist philosopher Antonio Gramsci pointed out, is inherently conservative.[7] Gramsci showed how power normalises its own values. 'A night at the opera' becomes a compulsory luxury, in the same way that (since thoroughbred horses are more expensive than greyhounds) Royal Ascot associates itself with the aristocracy, while a night out at the Swindon dog-track does not.

But we could also think of this very particular cultural practice as just one variant of song within the European Classical music tradition. For all the world like the parents in Philip Larkin's notorious 'This Be The Verse', opera contains all the paradoxes and potential for strain the last chapter found at work between music and verse in song – and adds to these the problem of narrative.[8] Yet a third approach would be to think of the form as on a continuum with the roots of human performance. As Burjak and Chekhov remind us, the *occasion* of opera is overwhelmingly theatrical and thus, like drama, the form has its roots in some of the earliest musical and poetic practices of which we have any knowledge. Indeed, since opera shares with theatre the key element of narrative, these roots offer a useful way in to thinking about how opera manages to combine its three constituent elements: music, poetry and story.

The epics that remain to us were not the first human expressive practice, but early examples date back more than four millennia. They offer surprising insights into opera, which is in certain ways their successor: both forms grapple to combine the same trio of constituents. Though occuring across centuries and cultures, all epics have in common a public storytelling role that relies on both linguistic and 'musical' – that is, at least pitched or incanted – tropes to make it more absorbing for its audience, and memorisable for the performer. *The Epic of Gilgamesh*, from Mesopotamia, dates from around the year 2100 BCE. The *Odyssey* and the *Iliad* are both thought to have been composed in the second half of the eighth century BCE, in Greek Anatolia. The Serbian folk epics, traditionally performed with the stringed *gusla* and collected in the nineteenth century, the Irish *Táin* which first appears in a manuscript form in the eleventh or twelfth century CE and includes oral material dating from the seventh century, the Anglo-Saxon *Beowulf*, composed in England sometime between the eighth and eleventh centuries, and the Finnish *Kalevala*, constructed in the nineteenth century from oral material which may in parts be three thousand years old, are additionally examples of the form's continuing significance, in Europe at least, as founding texts for national cultures. Ismail Kadare's novel *The File on H* explores how related practices are at work in parts of the Balkans, including Albania, even today.[9]

As in opera, in epic the three elements of music, verse and story are interdependent. Verse tells the story, using formal poetic tropes such as the 'underlining' kenning: Homer's famous 'wine-dark sea' is surely among the best known of these.[10] The story carries the verse, giving it content and length. The epic's music and verse – and therefore its story too – are coterminous. Music unifies an often lengthy narrative, and frames or highlights its lines: for example, as something different from speech. However, the coterminous interdependence of poetry and music in epic is no ideal solution to the problem of combining these forms, but a particular formal equation, with limits to what it can do. Nothing in the 17,000 verses of the Albanian *Lahuta e Malcís*, for example, is spoken 'unsung', and there are no wordless vocal riffs or instrumental cadenzas. There's no variation in texture; no dramatic dialogue or prose exegesis. Epic's narrative and verse also lock step. There are no reflective asides in the *Táin*. Epic keeps description to the minimum the story requires; when, for example, we *need* to 'see' how impressive an army is. Classicists like the American translator Peter Green reveal how this is an explanatory, not a metaphorical, mechanism. In Book III, lines 1–7 of the *Iliad*, for example:

> When both sides had been marshaled, with their leaders,
> the Trojans advanced with clamor and loud cries, like birds,
> like the clamor of cranes that goes up high to heaven
> when they're escaping winter storms and endless rain,
> and, calling, fly through the streams of Ocean,
> to Pygmy warriors bringing death and destruction
> down through the air, an offer of grim conflict.[11]

The migrating cry of cranes is evocative of aptly autumnal weather; but it's also a particular noise with the uncanny capacity to sound as though it's coming from all sides, and is used here as an exact synonym.

So we could say that epic poetry underexploits music, harnessing it directly to language as the performer *chants* the words. This chanting ranges from singing the words as a repeated two-line tune – in the Finnish *Kalevala*, for example – to the pitched recitation of Classical Greek poetry we noted in the last chapter. Archaeological evidence implies that such pitched recitation in strict metre may have been closer to *sprechgesang* than to recitative.[12] In other words, to our ears it would have been musically *rather dull*.

This anachronistic aesthetic judgement puts a finger on a key difficulty with the relationship that epic creates between music and poetry: which is that the music is *circumscribed*. To some degree, epic also circumscribes verse, which has to adopt formal aspects (such as consistency) that the music requires of it. But these constraints are not profoundly limiting. Though highly metrical, Classical Greek verse isn't confined, for example, to what can be said with just four phonemes: arguably an analogy with the extreme constraint on its musical elements. Besides, even today Western poetry, though performed without music and often non-narrative, continues to obey formal constraints, for example of register or metre. Literary verse has absorbed the principle of formal restraint as one among the many elements of linguistic complexity it exhibits. A good example of this is rhyme and how, particularly in a language with diverse, unmatched roots like those of English, it weighs on what the text 'says'. Indeed a degree of formal organisation *is* – in at least one definition – what separates verse from prose or speech.

The case is completely different for Western Classical music, indeed Western music of all kinds, which – though it uses a kaleidoscope of formal tropes of its own – has in recent centuries exploded, in both variety and scale, out of any restraints equivalent to those in epic form. We glimpse this explosion if we try to compare, say, Anton Bruckner's Symphony no. 8 in C minor WAB108 (composed between 1884 and 1892), or *Intégrales*, written by Edgar Varèse in 1924–5, with epic's two-phrase univocal chant. (Bruckner's opulent orchestration and love of chromaticism, and Varèse's apparently risky veering across the tonal and pitch palette of contemporary instrumentation, suggest that music might be a field of vast, if not infinite, possibility. This engagement with what, as we saw in Chapter 4, Guido of Arezzo called the 'unseen and unheard space' of potential music almost functions as a riposte to his *Micrologus de disciplina artis musicae*.) The difference between such works and the role of chant in epic is so marked that to compare them seems like a category error.

But to be freestanding in this way, art music must give itself form. (It is *not* a child's noodlings at the keyboard.) Such form must be both *discernible*, even if not always at first hearing, and somehow *determining*. It's not merely a recognisable element, such as a leitmotif, *within* a piece. But here I must go carefully. Recognisability and discernability are qualities of musical form, not roles carried out by a listener or a performer. Music can't depend upon a listener's acuity or taste or a performer's understanding to *exist*; any more than I could abolish the pieces I learnt as a child, however badly I played them (though some truly awful performances come close: YouTube is rich with postings of 'the worst school band ever').[13] The history of music has too many examples of hindsight revising the initial assessment of a work, to say nothing of divergencies within contemporary taste. Here for example is the Austrian composer Wilhelm Kienzl, recording reactions to the first performance of (three movements from) Gustav Mahler's Second Symphony in C minor:

> [in] one obstinately dissonant *fortissimo* passage in the brass [...] [Richard] Strauss, sitting on my left, turned to me wide-eyed with enthusiasm: '*Believe me, there are no limits to musical expression!*' At the same time Muck, on my right, twisted is face into an *unmistakable* expression of horror, and the single word '*Frightful!*' escaped through his clenched teeth. I, the 'man in the middle', thus had a good opportunity to observe the opposite effects of art on differently endowed natures, and the paramount subjectivity of all appreciation of art.[14]

In my final chapter, I'll look again at how music, like poetry, has to *occur*. (Because it takes place through time, it has to take place *in* time, as we saw in Chapter 1.) We'll examine how this necessary *taking place* means that music is in some ways dependent upon those who make it happen, not only in performances but, on other occasions, simply by reading a score or remembering a tune. Yet that dependence only has to do with each *particular* occurrence. Existentially – in the nature of its existence – music has to satisfy not tastes but formal criteria. These must (at least within the remit of this book) have some relationship to criteria for Western art music. Yet such criteria, too, are fashion-led – and so historicist. And they can also be used to assess 'quality': that is, the *success* of a piece in achieving its ideal form. The criteria for musical identity per se aren't quite the same as the techniques used in a particular piece, but they come close. When I was a student, like everyone else I was taught that it is a *fact* that certain moves within four-part harmony (such as the 'blare' of parallel fifths and octaves) are 'grammatical' *mistakes*. Yet a marking plan for student exercises is not a conceptual framework into which the whole of music, from all times and places, can be fitted. It simply wouldn't be accurate to measure the nineteenth-century symphony, Orthodox liturgical chant and gamelan music by a single set of criteria. As Said reminds us, music is a culturally located practice, not a one-size-fits-all essence. So the delicate matter of what music is when it's not combined with other artforms – and thus of *what* opera attempts to combine with poetry and narrative – is to be found somewhere between any *particular* trope and the *principle* of tropes and traditions.

How does this work in poetry? As we saw briefly in Chapter 5, the French psychoanalytic philosopher Jacques Lacan distinguished between language and discourse. For him, language is the tool of our communicative and reflective trades: its words, and their personal and shared meanings and resonances. Discourse is what we do *with* language: talk, think, establish rapport, confess or explain. The process of composition, which not only fixes language but takes longer than conversation to *do*, seemed to implicate Lacan in what is intractable about language – indeed he spoke of every word as being full of the 'traps' of its multiple, inadvertent meanings – which the communicative context of speech (such as the many seminars he gave without notes) seemed to carry him and his listeners past. (Communication, in this account, eliminates an excess of stray meanings: just as Guido d'Arezzo's *musica recta* was communicable because it eliminated the stray possibilities of *musica ficta*.) One of the problems language presented him with, then, was the possibility of its being 'taken out of context' (as politicians complain). This anxiety produced the gnarled, defensive complexity of his '*écrits*', with their notorious neo-algebraic formulae and graphs: such as those illustrating his 1960 lecture on 'The Subversion of the Subject and the Dialectic of Desire in the Freudian Unconscious'.[15]

Poetry, too, suffers from a confusion between what we might call its language-aspect and its discourse-aspect. As we saw Brenda Hillman point out in Chapter 2, the words (its language) both are and are not what the poem does (its discourse). A poem doesn't need to be *interpreted* – paradoxically, an attempt to separate its 'self' from the words themselves – in order to do these things. On the contrary, it does what it does willy-nilly, whether or not we notice it doing so.

A discourse is its own discursive occasion. And discourse rests in a different place for the pre-composed poem than in a seminar given by Lacan: which *is* the moment of language-choice, that's to say composition. As with music, the artform itself – rather than my or your reading of an individual poem – is the discursive occasion on which the poet is using language. As with music, poetry is a form that happens to have a strong historical relationship to performance: as well as the implicit, ongoing one we see at work in its 'scoring', and in the use of sound patterning.

But one of our key resistances to recognising the close kinship between the temporal, performative nature of poetry and that of music is that we feel we should exempt poetry from the demands of public performance. With near-universal literacy in the West has come a new kind of poetic occasion: reading a poem to oneself. Many poets and committed readers believe this is the ideal way to experience the poem. There's certainly no shortage of convincing arguments in its favour. Readings are held in centres of population or anyway, for example in the case of festivals, in centres where audiences gather; they can be costly to attend. They rarely include more than the dozen or so poems that make up a forty-minute set: hardly representative of a poet's entire oeuvre. Reading to oneself offers the pleasures of concentration, undistracted by such public occasions. The page allows the individual reader to *go at his own speed*. He can revisit a particular passage, pause – look something up, reflect on something he's reminded of – or go back to the beginning, all before going on to the end of the poem. Yet such readings also seem to break up the *and then … and then* of the complete poem: just as film, that story made out of light and time, can now be watched on personal devices, with pauses, fast-forwards and rewinds. (In 2004, the British TV series *Green Wing* played with this development, speeding up the 'boring bits' that get characters from A to B, and slowing down other sections.[16]) It takes an effort to remember that poetry *itself* remains chronologic.

In reminding us of the oral and theatrical nature of the first poetry, epic adjusts our relationship with this paradigm of reading to oneself. The shift from purely oral to written forms of transmission was protracted; its starting point long predates universal literacy. Early, semi-mythologised 'poets' – like Homer, David of the *Psalms*, or even the Welsh Taliesin – were each perhaps part living author, part symbolic mouthpiece of a particular oral tradition. Such records as we have of their work speak of oral transmission, yet paradoxically come down to us through their intersection with literacy, as later transcriptions. By the fourteenth century, we find Geoffrey Chaucer managing the lengthy and sophisticated *narrative* forms of his *The Canterbury Tales* or *Troilus and Criseyde* by writing them down. Like a masonic handshake, his authorship 'signs' that he belongs to the small, privileged group of readers and writers. This educated minority get to enjoy his importation of the Petrarchan sonnet, while the limits of literacy mean that the majority of the British population carry on reciting – or singing – ballads, folksongs, carols and rhymes. (It will take a long time for the 'uses of literacy' to become widespread.[17] Even two centuries later the first novel, Miguel de Cervantes's *Don Quixote*, published in 1605–15, will satirise the reader as someone whose head has been turned by too many courtly romances.[18])

Epic also shows us that operas are not *sui generis*. Their transmission of narrative verse *libretti* through theatrical performance overlaps – even though it doesn't perfectly coincide – with related aspects of forms including the epic and medieval romance, as well as song. Like the baddie in any number of thrilling railway movies, this tradition of public performance seems about to throw the reader off the poetry train. Perhaps the one we first encountered ambling through Transylvania in Chapter 1 ...?

Luckily, it turns out that the Ideal Reader is at hand to rescue the bookish, *human* reader. A key Structuralist concept but not monopolised by that theoretical school, this figure is anonymous in the way of all true heroes. The Ideal Reader is posited by the text, and is Ideal *first* because 'he' is imagined, and only *second* because as a consequence of this 'he' is perfect for the task. In short, the Ideal Reader is no human individual, but part of how the poem itself works. Ideal Readers are posited by writing in all the genres where a reading *experience* is being created: a legal document or a handbook articulates the necessary information but, notoriously, can be less concerned to make sure this information is *conveyed*.[19] The Ideal Reader represents the open, but at the same time intimate, orientation of *wanting whatever the text wants* to do. It isn't a character but a principle of understanding, designating the *possibility* of apt and adept attention posited by a text. (The Ideal Reader is the reason certain textual games don't form part of the genres of poetry or fiction. By his own admission, a conceptual 'poet' like Kenneth Goldsmith, who says his works are 'better thought about than read. They're insanely dull and unreadable [...] In fact, I say that I don't have a readership, I have a *thinkership*,' is simply engaging in another discourse.[20]) But not all Ideal Readers 'read' in the same way. The Ideal Reader of genre writing wants only one *particular* kind of story. Poetry's Ideal Reader is also an Ideal Auditor (though, as we've seen, this doesn't mean that a poem is written for performance. A poem isn't a script). The Ideal Audition is located *within* the poem or piece of music (something we looked at in Chapter 6).[21]

In other words, the qualities that music and poetry share, and that in each case are what allow them to work as freestanding forms, are the very ones that make it hard for them to collaborate – and to collaborate with narrative – in opera and related forms. As we saw in the last chapter, we can date opera's development to the Camerata of sixteenth-century Florence. The form's blowsy generosity – its costly theatricality – is the product of a push-me-pull-you of contending elements. Since the epic, music has broken free of language, and the price of that freedom, whenever the forms are reunited, is a new compromise. As we saw in the last chapter, where we looked at song, it is now poetry that compromises itself in order to collaborate with music.

But these tensions between the elements of opera have long been explicit. In 1671, the poet and librettist Pierre Perrin was the founding Director of the French *Académie des operas*, now the *Académie nationale de la musique*. Within a year his position had been usurped by the composer Jean-Baptiste Lully, 'who obtained the king's *privilège* and in 1673, after the death of Molière, established his *Académie royale de la musique* in the hall of the Palais-Royale'.[22] It was part of the shift towards defining opera as a musical, rather than a literary, form. Since then, opera's music has developed its alliance with storytelling rather than with verse. That alliance quickens and becomes more direct in the nineteenth century, when Romanticism opens the space of *expression* in music. (Thus, in his Prelude to the 1800 edition of the *Lyrical Ballads*, William Wordsworth, famously defines the source of poetry as a 'spontaneous overflow of powerful feelings'.[23]) Music now aims to create a shared experience of being moved, and in doing so aligns itself with catharsis, that oldest of dramatic processes.[24] This is the era of Gaetano Donizetti's *Lucia di Lammermoor*; the century of Giuseppe Verdi's *Aida* and of Giacomo Puccini's *La Bohème*: operas whose tragic heroines express the grievous unattainability of ideal love.

But opera isn't all denouement. It both enlarges, and disperses, storytelling's ability to move the listener beyond single-pointed catharsis. Mozart's *Don Giovanni* (K527) makes us laugh; Bizet's 1875 masterpiece *Carmen* is provocatively sexy; Wagner's *Parsifal* (WWV 111) makes us examine our own beliefs as we puzzle over what it symbolises. Opera can change its audience's emotional direction: in Alban Berg's *Woyzeck* (1922), we become party to the suffering of both the man and his girl; in Pyotr Ilyich Tchaikovsky's *Eugene Onegin* Op. 22 (1878) we change our mind about the eponymous Onegin after he dismisses the young Tatyana's indiscreet letter declaring love for him. Western art music has developed an immensely sophisticated repertoire of techniques and strategies.[25] Opera doesn't need poetry to tell its story: the music can reach straight past verse to the narrative. We don't have to read Alexander Pushkin's verse-novel, or the libretto Konstantin Shilovsky put together from it, to be moved by Tchaikovsky's opera version of *Eugene Onegin*. For while characters need to 'talk' (sing) in order to act upon each other, and us, in effect the *music* they sing often *is* what they have to say. As we saw in the last chapter, frequently the words simply can't be heard but are lost to the sheer volume of even conventional orchestration, to counter-intuitive musical setting, and to all the business of performance, from stagecraft to interpretation. The resistance of some musicians and critics to sur-titles – which project the libretto above the opera stage – isn't simply snobbery.[26] Instead the 'distraction' they complain of is poetry *intervening to prevent* music from acting directly in concert with narrative.

Opera's special capacity for narrative welcomes a much wider audience than exists for poetry. Edward Elgar's *The Dream of Gerontius* Op. 38 illustrates this by counterexample. A large-scale work for singers and orchestra, it is contemplative to an exquisite degree. Its world – the spiritual revelations experienced by a dying saint – is purely internal and immaterial, and so would be tricky to stage. There is in effect no narrative, but only a single extended tableau: Gerontius knows he's dying. And Elgar is at liberty to have this take more than an hour and a half to happen, because *Gerontius* is an oratorio, not an opera.

Sure enough, even minimalist composers have resisted the urge to break with narrative when they come to write opera. John Adams's 1987 *Nixon in China*, arguably minimalist despite its palimpsest use of quotation styles, is a Peter Sellars commission with libretto by poet Alice Goodman. Far from rejecting story, it examines storytelling itself, and how myth – here, modern political myth – is made.[27] As Sellars says, 'One of the most important reasons to do these operas was to say precisely that we *aren't* getting the actual history of our times. [...] Opera is able to [...] find what was not in the news, what was *missing* from the news.'

Indeed, opera has difficulty managing its *non*-narrative elements. For example, the 'Masque of the Seasons' has often been cut from Harrison Birtwistle's *Gawain* since its premiere in 1991. Yet there are many precedents for the masque as dramatic tableau. William Shakespeare uses it to narrative effect to resolve his comedies, as in the mass-marriages of *As You Like It* and *A Midsummer Night's Dream*. In *Romeo and Juliet*, the masque in Act I, Scene 5 is where Romeo falls for Juliet. Masque also has long traditions both as performance spectacle and within court life: the *Gawain* masque belongs to both. The form's origins were in entertainments both by and for aristocratic and royal courts, in medieval Burgundy and Tudor English *guisings*. Eventually it fell out of favour, but it informed English late seventeenth-century semi-opera (for example John Dryden and Henry Purcell's five-act *King Arthur* in 1691). The nineteenth century's interludes of spectacle, such as those elephants in Verdi's *Aida*, are another after-echo.

In *Gawain* the 'Masque of the Seasons' is a device to show time passing. In other words, it's a *narrative* device that exists to solve a narrative problem. The passage of time poses a technical problem for narrative representation, because it must simultaneously create a fast-forward – 'nothing happens here' – and, paradoxically, allow us to feel the lengthiness of that 'nothing'. One of the best-known solutions to this problem is the central section of Virginia Woolf's *To the Lighthouse*. The seaside house that is the novel's setting stands empty during the war years. Woolf makes this time 'pass' by means of 'still life':

> Nothing stirred in the drawing-room or in the dining-room or on the staircase. Only through the rusty hinges and swollen sea-moistened woodwork certain airs, detached from the body of the wind (the house was ramshackle after all) crept round corners and ventured indoors.[28]

The American novelist William Maxwell uses the same ingenious variation on the pathetic fallacy to set the openings of several of his mid-century novels, before his characters wake and so 'come on stage'.[29] *Gawain*'s masque tries to achieve theatrical balance by *taking time* – yet retaining the audience's interest through verse, music and dance.[30]

So time remains an important element of opera. Something has to *happen next*: in the music, in the libretto *and* in the narrative. Yet paradoxically the element of narrative, which can be paraphrased, makes the form less chronologic than music or poetry are. This triple yoke of music, poetry *and narrative* creates a problem of coordination. It also poses a problem that we might call *collective responsibility*. Which element matters most; which *drives* opera's *and then … and then*? This brings us back to the autonomous nature of its constituent elements. We can tell the opera's story without using its words and music. To do so is a cultural commonplace, from programme notes to children's music lessons. We can also appreciate its music without knowing the words, or even really the plot. The musicians in the orchestra pit are never shown the libretto, yet they're expected to interpret the work. Moreover, an opera's musical material regularly gets separated entirely from narrative context and textual content. The opera overture, a purely orchestral prelude, is – particularly in its nineteenth-century incarnation – the composer's medley of 'coming attractions': yet many have been divorced from their operas altogether to become staples of the concert repertoire. Beethoven's Overture to *Egmont* Op. 84 is frequently performed, but the rest of his music for Goethe's play, about a Dutch nobleman bravely resisting oppression, is a rarely heard curiosity. Bedřich Smetana's Overture to *The Bartered Bride* (1866–70) has a dreadful familiarity, for concertgoers and orchestral players, that substantially exceeds that of the opera itself. The same – and more – could be said of Gioachino Rossini's Overture to *William Tell* (1829).

Reading a libretto, however, tells us the opera's story, but is much more unusual than knowing only the work's music, or its story. We simply *do* have a set of expectations or practices that seem less concerned with the opera's verse than with its music and storytelling. This is slightly surprising, because not only do the finest poets of their day often write libretti – as W. H. Auden composed *Paul Bunyan* for what became Benjamin Britten's Op. 17, and Tony Harrison wrote the words for Birtwistle's 1984 *Yan Tan Tethera* – they also translate them. Anthony Burgess (admittedly a part-time poet) translated the libretto of Bizet's *Carmen* and wrote a new libretto for Carl Maria von Weber's *Oberon*; J. D. McClatchy's translations of the libretto of the Mozart operas have been published in a handsome volume by W. W. Norton.[31] And yet the thought of reading a libretto implies a certain austerity; some lack of spontaneous pleasure. A pleasurable 'flow' of connectedness unites the music, poetry and narrative in opera. But poetry is also made of denotative language. This language interposes grammatical logic, locates the experiencing self, and burdens the listener with inessential, non-narrative material. Not coincidentally, reading a libretto 'on the page' reminds us of the disruptive effect, during a performance, of reading its words as surtitles.

Opera's use of the 'trump' of narrative, its theatricality, and its collaborative nature, all reveal ways in which poetry and music remain chronologic where they occur. But it also shows us how this chronologic nature *is* each form 'doing itself' on its own terms. Opera reveals both the similarities between its constituent poetry and music: and their similarly uncompromising natures.

Notes

1. Anton Chekhov trans. Constance Garnett, 'The Lady with the Dog' in Anton Chekhov, *Short Stories*, Gordon McVay (ed.) (London: Folio, 2001), p. 416.
2. Yuri Burjak trans. Fiona Sampson, in *Poem* 3:1 (Spring 2015), p. 13.
3. After all, Burjak's 'Circles' are also Dantesque: the hell, or at least the purgatory, reserved for the 'lost souls' of unmatched or illicit lovers.
4. Chekhov, *Short Stories*, p. 415.
5. From the Salzburg Festival to London's Royal Opera House, scandals routinely surround opera ticket prices; although at the time of writing a degree of public subsidy imposes on the latter house the obligation to provide some cheap tickets for standing or 'in the gods'. See for example: http://www.telegraph.co.uk/culture/music/classicalmusic/8450660/Scandal-at-Salzburg-Easter-Festival.html. Retrieved 29/12/15. http://www.bloomberg.com/news/articles/2011-04-03/scandal-probe-at-salzburg-festival-drags-on-director-says. Retrieved 29/12/15.
6. Lorenzo da Ponte, *Memoirs*, Elisabeth Abbott (trans.), Arthur Livingstone (ed.) (New York: New York Review of Books, 2000), p. 168.
7. Gramsci's critique of cultural hegemony in his prison writings is sometimes diffuse, as a result of having to obscure what he was actually saying. But it is frequently summed up as: 'Common sense is the sense of the ruling classes.' Antonio Gramsci, *Selections from the Prison Notebooks of Antonio Gramsci* [written 1929–35], Quintin Hoare and Geoffrey Nowell Smith (eds and trans.) (London: Lawrence and Wishart, 1971).
8. Philip Larkin, 'This be the Verse' in *Collected Poems*, Anthony Thwaite (ed.) (London: Faber, 1988), p. 180.
9. Ismail Kadare, *The File on H*, Jusuf Vrioni and David Bellos (trans.) (London: Vintage, 2006).
10. For example in *The Odyssey* V, 132. Homer, *The Odyssey*, Edward McCrorie (trans.) (Baltimore: Johns Hopkins University Press, 2004), p. 70.
11. Although in this example – something for which there should be a discreet rhetorical term – the metaphor 'lands' at both ends, since the birds are also, in effect, like Trojans. Homer, *Iliad*, Peter Green (trans.) (Oakland: University of California Press, 2015), p. 66.
12. See the work of Dr Armand D'Angour, so far summarised in the British Academy award of a Mid-Career Fellowship: http://www.britac.ac.uk/funding/awards/Mid-Career-Fellowships-Awards-2013.cfm. Retrieved 29/12/15.
13. Surely some of these are revenge postings. For example: https://

www.youtube.com/watch?v=SR2NNV0qAEI. Retrieved 20/11/
15. Nor can they make any other kind of artifact *into* music. A
saucepan may become a musical instrument, if someone turns it
upside down and drums on the base, but it's what's improvised
that *is* music.

14. Wilhelm Keinzl, *Meine Lebenswanderung* (Stuttgart: Engelhorn,
1926), p. 143. Excerpted in Kurt Blaukopf and Herta Blaukopf
(eds), *Mahler: His Life, Work and World* (Paul Baker, Susanne
Flatauer, P. R. J. Ford, Daisy Loman, Geoffrey Watkins and Karen
Williams, trans.) (London: Thames and Hudson, 1991), p. 108.

15. Jacques Lacan, *Écrits: A Selection*, Alan Sheridan (trans. and ed.)
(London: Tavistock Publications, 1977), pp. 292–325.

16. *Green Wing*, Channel 4, 2004. http://www.channel4.com/pro-
grammes/green-wing. Retrieved 9/1/16.

17. Richard Hoggart, *The Uses of Literacy: Aspects of Working-Class
Life* [1957] (Harmondsworth: Penguin, 2009). This isn't just an
idle pun. As Hoggart's subtitle makes clear, his groundbreaking
book is a study of who makes a culture. At the time of its first
publication commercial and media mass culture was overtaking
the self-made cultures of the British urban working class.

18. Miguel De Cervantes Saavedra, *Don Quixote*, P. A. Motteux
(trans.), Stephen Boyd (ed.) (Knoxville: Wordsworth Classics,
1992).

19. Anyone who has tried to follow the manufacturer's instructions
while building flat-pack furniture knows that giving information is
not the same as helping one to understand it.

20. Kenneth Goldsmith, interviewed by David Mandl, *The Believer*
website http://www.believermag.com/issues/201110/?read=inter-
view_goldsmith. Retrieved 5/1/16.

21. The auditory occasion *is* part of what the music contains: otherwise the score would merely be a series of markings that record
arithmetical relations.

22. Of course, personal power politics played their part in this. Sir
Paul Harvey and J. E. Heseltine (eds), *The Oxford Companion to
French Literature* (Oxford: Oxford University Press, 1969), p. 4.

23. William Wordsworth, 'Prelude to Second Edition' of the *Lyrical
Ballads*, p. xiv. http://www.bl.uk/collection-items/lyrical-ballads-
1800-edition. Retrieved 9/1/16.

24. As used by Aristotle in *Poetics* (1449b, 21–8), 'It represents men in
action and does not use narrative, and through pity and fear it
effects relief to these and similar emotions.' Aristotle. *Aristotle in
23 Volumes*, vol. 23, W. H. Fyfe (trans.) (Cambridge, MA/
London: Harvard University Press/William Heinemann, 1932).
http://www.perseus.tufts.edu/hopper/text?doc=Perseus%3Atext
%3A1999.01.0056%3Asection%3D1449b Retrieved 9/1/16

25. Opera reveals how this can be reduced to 'moving' an audience.
Something related goes on in programme music, but there what is

being literally 'orchestrated' isn't necessarily emotion, but may be the visual or narrative imagination.

26. Such as the suggestion that everyone should already know an opera, and any foreign language in which it's being sung.

27. Peter Sellars, 'Creating Contexts: Peter Sellars on Working with Adams' in Thomas May (ed.), *The John Adams Reader* (Pompton Plains, NJ: Amadeus Press, 2006), pp. 241–2.

28. Virginia Woolf, *To the Lighthouse* (Ware: Wordsworth Classics, 1994), p. 91.

29. William Maxwell, *The Chateau* (London: Harvill, 2000), p. 3.

30. A decision to cut it is often seen as having to do with *Gawain*'s overall length since, uncut, it lasts for more than two and a half hours – without intervals. (Giacomo Puccini's *La Bohème*, for example, lasts for about an hour and three-quarters.) But in fact *much* of the libretto of *Gawain* is commentary or reflection rather than action, and the whole otherwise mighty piece is hard to 'keep moving', both on the stage and in time.

31. J. D. McClatchy, *Seven Mozart Librettos: A Verse Translation* (New York: W. W. Norton, 2010). W. H. Auden, *Paul Bunyan* (London: Faber, 1988).

Chapter 9

Closer Still: The Total Artwork

Richard Wagner's operas are often characterised by his own expression, *Gesamtkunstwerk*, which English musicologists translate as 'total artwork'. But Wagner himself only ever used the term in two essays, both published in 1849. 'Art and Revolution' and 'The Artwork of the Future' were both written from political exile; the first in Paris and the second in Zürich. The still young-ish Wagner (he was born in 1813) had supported the revolutions of 1848 and was an active, if not especially important, participant in the 1849 May Revolution in Dresden. As a result, he was to spend almost a decade in exile in Switzerland, followed by a further three years in Paris and, briefly, Venice. Revolutionary zeal meant real actions with real consequences. In any case, we may suspect Wagner was not especially interested in *ideas*: a suspicion borne out by the calibre of his notorious, anti-Semitic 'Jewishness in Music', which he had published just one year earlier.

All three essays – 'Art and Revolution', 'The Artwork of the Future' and 'Jewishness in Music' – were published in Leipzig. Together they drew a line under the composer's middle-period operas, with which he had enjoyed success in the Dresden of the 1840s: *The Flying Dutchman* (premiered in 1843), *Tannhäuser* (1845) and *Lohengrin* (performed in Weimar in the composer's absence in 1850). Wagner's other works contemporary with these essays were the libretti for the *Ring* cycle. (A libretto for a free-standing opera, *Siegfried's Death*, was completed in 1848.) Not surprisingly, these represented his first attempts to put *Gesamtkunstwerk* into action.

But what exactly did the term mean to him? Not simple

grandiosity: though it's easy to imagine the composer intervening, perhaps beyond his abilities, as producer, director and stage
designer. Fittingly for its political context, *Gesamtkunstwerk*
was a revolutionary principle; but Wagner did not name it
himself. He did not even spell it correctly, or at least in the conventional way. Wagner's version rolls its *m*s, if such a thing is
possible – *Gesammtkunstwerk* – as if to underline the togetherness, the *zusammen*, of *gesamt*, totality. The neologism itself
was coined in 1827, by the religious philosopher K. F. E.
Trahndorff. Trahndorff, himself the son of a musician, used it in
his study of *Aesthetic or Theory of Ideology and Art* to argue:
'that the four arts, [...] the art of the sound of the word, music,
mimic art, and dance, bear the possibility of coalescing to
become a single production'.[1]

Since the late twentieth century '*Gesamtkunstwerk*' has
been applied to other artforms, particularly architecture,
which like opera can unite a number of elements. (Architecture,
for example, marries engineering, landscaping and interior
decoration, among others.[2]) But its origins are in the late
eighteenth-century notion that all the arts could be unified in
poetry.[3] Trahndorff may have thought up the term, but the
case for both the possibility and the necessity that all artforms
be combined in one Ideal art was first made by the German
Idealist philosopher Friedrich Wilhelm Joseph Schelling (1775–
1854).

Schelling did not argue, from Romanticism's tendency to
exceed given limits, for a monumental artwork that could
produce monumental experience. *Gesamtkunstwerk* was not
simply an artistic equivalent of the mountainscapes beloved of
Casper David Friedrich, whose iconic paintings include the tail-
coated, cane-toting *Wanderer above the Sea of Fog* (1818), or of
Percy Bysshe Shelley, for whom:

> The wilderness has a mysterious tongue
> Which teaches awful doubt, or faith so mild,
> So solemn, so serene, that man may be
> But for such faith with nature reconciled;
> Thou hast a voice, great Mountain, to repeal
> Large codes of fraud and woe; not understood
> By all, but which the wise, and great, and good
> Interpret, or make felt, or deeply feel.[4]

Nor did Schelling propose breaking down boundaries between artforms for the sake of doing so; although the dream of 'making new' fed the revolutionary fervour of the time: to quote Shelley again, 'Nought may endure but Mutability.'[5] Instead, the philosopher made an argument about forms of knowledge. This influenced the English Romantic poets by way of its adherent Samuel Taylor Coleridge, who reproduced much of Schelling's argument in principle and even wholesale in his 1817 *Biographia Literaria*.[6] Coleridge's source was chiefly the *System of Transcendental Idealism* of 1800.[7]

As a school-friend of Friedrich Hölderlin and an early mentor, later rival, of Georg Wilhelm Friedrich Hegel, Schelling was well positioned to synthesise Romantic art and ideas. His argument, that art is important because it totalises all forms of knowledge, seems to make a jump when it assumes that art implies 'genius':

> The postulated product is none other than the product of genius, or, since genius is possible only in art, the *product of art*.[8]

Schelling, one feels, had never taught a creative writing workshop. But he was, of course, using his terms in particular ways. For Schelling, the principle of 'genius' involves the workings of the unconscious *with* those of the conscious mind, and so solves the problem of artistic imagination: the old 'where do you get your ideas from?' writers know so well.

It's obvious how appealing a philosophy which dignified the mixing of conscious and unconscious thought would be to Coleridge: a poet whose relationship with dream, drugs, alcohol and their creative results is well documented.[9] For Schelling, a total artwork would allow all forms of artistic knowledge to operate at once, and remove the limits genres set on the mind. The trouble with the conscious mind, the mind that is at work in philosophy, is that it is necessarily subjective: or as we would say now, reflexive. Because artistic knowledge includes the work of the unconscious as well as this conscious mind, it is the only human activity which is equal to the possibility of complete knowledge:

> this unknown, which here brings objective and conscious activity into unexpected harmony, is none other than that Absolute which contains the universal ground of the pre-established harmony between the conscious and the unconscious.[10]

Wagner took a step forward from process to product, and used *Gesamtkunstwerk* in a not-unrelated way, to express the need he perceived for an organic, unselfconscious and fully integrated work of drama; one that flowed from the Greek sense of participative catharsis.[11] Today, his essay 'Art and Revolution' would probably be framed as a critique of art's commodification by global capitalism, and its consequent reduction to mere entertainment. 'Art' is supposed to bring society to its senses and remind it of the importance of Nature, and 'the Brotherhood of Man':

> only *Revolution*, not slavish *Restoration*, can give us back that highest Art-work. [...] If the Grecian Art-work embraced the spirit of a fair and noble nation, the Art-work of the Future must embrace the spirit of a free mankind, delivered from every shackle of hampering nationality.[12]

In this moment Wagner manages to be both left-wing and essentialist. It seems a virtuoso feat; until the march of italics catches the reading eye, and reminds one how just this kind of will to redistribution, rather than actual belief in equality through difference, would less than a hundred years later combine with an essentialist view of the 'deserving' in National Socialism. He goes on:

> Only the *Strong* know *Love*; only *Love* can fathom *Beauty*; only *Beauty* can fashion *Art*. [...] Art is Beauty energized.[13]

However, in the same essay, Wagner suggests that the total art work is also a remedy for difficulties with genres of performance. The problem, as he sees it, is that performance is divided:

> into the two opposing classes, Play and Opera; whereby the idealizing influence of music is forbidden to the Play, and the Opera is forestalled of the living heart and lofty purpose of actual drama. Thus on the one hand the spoken Play can never, with but few exceptions, lift itself up to the ideal flight of poetry; [...] On the other hand, the Opera becomes a chaos of sensuous impressions jostling one another without rhyme or reason [...][14]

'Art and Revolution' seems to suggest that such divisions can be remedied by a unified purpose, one which provides a work with a unified vision (although the essay doesn't actually spell this out). What Wagner does say clearly is that, without the discipline of this overarching vision, a libretto becomes prosaic and music decorative. Joined-up vision seems to be equal to a larger scale of meaning. The challenge of opera *as a genre* is to create transcendent scale and so meaning – the very largest of gestures – and *Gesamtkunstwerk* meets that challenge. Wagner also argues that all the elements of opera must be thought up together – as indeed the constituent parts of a single vision would be – since without musical thought, the 'book' cannot be poetry, and without words to add denotative meaning, the music can't do serious work.

His companion essay, 'The Artwork of the Future', is a much more sophisticated and lengthy work than 'Art and Revolution', and moves towards a philosophy of the will, which Wagner calls 'Necessity'. It is, though, no *ars poetica*; nor might we reasonably expect it to be, since Wagner is explicitly eschewing the notion of craft in favour of an idea of art. Friedrich Nietzsche's reception of this thought and of the operas themselves, in *The Case of Wagner* (1888) – and the Nietzsche-reception which has in turn followed that work – make these essays and their associated ideas a well-trodden path. Nevertheless this fierce separation struggle between the philosopher and his former mentor tested a number of ideas about music and poetry to destruction.

For Nietzsche, the priority Wagner gives to language demonstrates that he is '*not* a musician by instinct'.[15] His 'style' is 'theatrical rhetoric, a means of expression, of underscoring gestures, of suggestion, of the psychologically picturesque'[16] rather than something made in and out of music. Nietzsche locates the compromise that he believes Wagner's operas demand from their constituent elements in what he sees as this failure of the composer's imagination. The music of Wagner's operas, he argues, is compromised and made the servant of language – that is, of representation. But language itself is also compromised, as it is reduced to rhetorical gestures: 'His music becomes language, drama's handmaiden' and '*he has increased music's capacity for language to the point of making it immeasurable.*'[17] Wagner's 'theatrical rhetoric' is flawed, for Nietzsche, because the composer is no playwright: he is 'not enough of a psychologist for drama'.[18] It is also flawed because it *is* merely drama, that untranscendent form: 'Theatre is the revolt of the masses.'[19] (Though Nietzsche arguably ignores the degree of intimacy between poetry and narrative that *Gesamtkunstwerk*'s compositional process entails.) For a true musician, Nietzsche believes, music would be enough in itself: 'As a matter of fact, he repeated a single proposition all his life long: that his music did not mean mere music. [...] "*Not mere* music" – no musician would say that.'[20] Whatever its emotional source this recognition of the conflict of interests between music and poetry in opera is salutary. But does 'the case of Wagner' in fact differ from that of Ivor Gurney who, as we saw in Chapter 7, was both a poet and a composer of the first rank, and who did sometimes, but only rarely, compose both the words and music for his songs?

As if in responding to this, Nietzsche allies thought with melody, on the grounds that both are effectual, and nail their colours to the mast. The true musician, or writer, will plump for and create form: one aspect of this form is that it can be experienced, whether by a reader or a listener. It can give pleasure; it can also communicate ideas. For Nietzsche, a key reason that 'Wagner's art is sick' is that it mystifies, refusing both to communicate and to invest in aesthetic experience.[21] He paraphrases – or is that parodies? – the Wagnerian position:

> Above all, no thought! Nothing is more compromising than a thought! Rather the state preceding thought, the throng of yet unborn thoughts, the promise of future thoughts, the world as it was before God created it – a recrudescence of chaos. Chaos induces intimations.
> To speak the language of the master: infinity, but without melody.
> [...]
> *Principle:* melody is immoral. *Proof:* Palestrina. *Practical application: Parsifal.* The lack of melody even sanctifies – [22]

Nietzsche's rhetoric here resembles nothing so much as Guido d'Arezzo inveighing against *musica ficta*. Possibilities and alternatives loosen the clarity of musical and philosophical thought. A melody is music made graspable, much like a philosophical idea. But Nietzsche's idea, not fully expanded in either the original essay, its two Postscripts or its Epilogue, suggests a hinterland of associated possibilities. A melody is a conceptual, and conceptualisable, entity: like a philosophical proposition.

But is it also *purposive*? To do philosophy, which is what Nietzsche says Wagner's music resists, is to enquire or to investigate: and these are activities whose purposes are set from their outset.

We saw in Chapter 3 how the phrasal breath is a connected *series* of pitches or words. Is part of that single line of connections – which we might call a trajectory – an innate purposefulness say, rather like a sense of destination? Does a phrase in some way set out to be a phrase? As we saw in Chapter 6, the parameters set by grammar in language, and by key or other pitch orientation in music, seem to suggest it does. And in both cases, as we saw in the same chapter, phrase-making seems to have to do with making sense; with the work of art as meaning-making. Related to the idea that breath is a *measure* of meaning is that other, even more suggestive, notion; that *melody is itself* semantic. As we saw, it's not just that we hear the phrasal unity of whatever can be said before the breath runs out; but that such rhythmic, meaningful units have an aural character of their own; that they are a *meaningful melody*, as it were a 'song without words'.

Nietzsche goes further still in his attack on Wagner's operatic 'style', which he claims is the result of a series of failures on the composer's part. His Wagner not only lacks musical instinct and fails to write good drama. He also fails to create an 'organic form', and it's to deny and obfuscate this 'incapacity' that he has created his 'style'.[23] It is certainly true that 'style' is what we remember about Wagner's total art work. In letters, Claude Debussy – like Nietzsche, ambivalent about his mighty peer – saw the German as 'the victim of his own system: in spite of a quartet of tubas and all the trumpets in the catalogue, the result is none the richer for them.'[24] Writing to his friend the great violinist Eugène Ysaÿe in 1896, he is frank about the effects of having 'Wagner's transatlantic abundance hurled back at me', leaving the French composer 'looking like some poor devil who simply couldn't afford his [...] contrabass tubas.'[25] Such comments remind us how key to Wagner's style is the scale on which he liked to work. It's hard to ignore the practical implications, for one's posture as well as one's pocket, of the five hours of *Parsifal*, or the fifteen of the *Ring* cycle.

Grandiose scale characterises Wagner's concepts in such a thoroughgoing way that it almost seems to be their *point*. In a telling throwaway, Debussy also refers to 'Wagner's bombastic metaphysics', and it is this 'bombast', with its suggestion of collateral damage, that summons up the way Wagner treats words, narrative, music, staging and the operatic occasion alike as mere elements in one overarching creation.[26]

For Nietzsche, the problem with this is not the over-reaching; instead, it is of a mystifying 'holiness [...] among philosophers this is [...] a sort of shutting the gate at the point where *their* world only begins – [...] To say it more politely: *la philosophie ne suffit pas au grand nombre. Il lui faut la sainteté.-*'[27] In other words, Wagner's elision of the categories of words, music and other artforms creates an opium for the masses. Nietzsche calls his former friend and mentor 'this old magician', and coincidentally we find Debussy describing a portrait of Wagner, by the Belgian artist Henry de Groux, as 'looking like an old, cynical magician, guarding his secret'.[28]

Philosophical ideas – such as those aired in this chapter – need not be *true* to the world around them. They don't need confirmation by the material world to be interesting, or even useful. But one doesn't have to be a follower of Schelling, a Nietzschian or a Wagnerite to see how significant ideas about a total artwork might be *for* art. They highlight the piecemeal, partial nature of artistic genres and of the individual works that make up those genres. The forms of art – in this case, of music and poetry – are contingent, and man-made. However necessary the medium of which they're composed is to their identities and ways of working, these identities are not in themselves essential.

Understanding of this fact has traditionally hung back from, yet hung around, schools of composition and poetry like a kind of bad faith; what Peter Porter, in another context, memorably called 'The Smell on the Landing'.[29] For if the very identities of poetry and music are not fixed and essential, there is no *essential* form that either must take. And so the arguments between schools of music and poetics can only be based on choice and intention. However thoughtful these choices and intentions may be in their own terms – they could include, for example, a commitment to freedom of thought under censorship, a desire to respond to catastrophe, or a belief that only writing from personal experience is honest – they are made beyond, and beyond the nature of, poetry and music themselves. Perhaps this is why, as we'll see in the next two chapters, form is the site of such violent struggles within both music and poetry.

Notes

1. Karl Friedrich Eusebius Trahndorff, *Aesthetik oder Lehre von der Weltanschauung und Kunst,* (Berlin: Maurer, 1827). Richard Wagner, 'Beethoven', in *Die Hauptschriften,* Ernst Bücken (ed.) (Stuttgart: Kremer, 1956), p. 282.
2. See David Roberts, *The Total Work of Art in European Modernism* (Ithaca, NY: Cornell University Press, 2011).
3. Barbara John, 'Gesamtkunstwerk' in *See This Sound* website, http://www.see-this-sound.at/compendium/abstract/41. Retrieved 9/1/16.
4. Percy Bysshe Shelley, 'Mont Blanc' in *Percy Bysshe Shelley,* Fiona Sampson (ed.) (London: Faber, 2011), p. 12.
5. 'Mutability' in ibid., p. 5.
6. Samuel Taylor Coleridge, *Biographia Literaria: Annotated Edition,* Adam Roberts (ed.), in *The Edinburgh Critical Edition of the Major Works of Samuel Taylor Coleridge* (Edinburgh: Edinburgh University Press, 2014).
7. Friedrich Schelling, *System of Transcendental Idealism* [1800], Peter Lauchlan Heath (trans.) (Charlottesville: University Press of Virginia, 1978).
8. Friedrich Schelling, 'from *System of Transcendental Idealism*', Albert Hofstadter (trans.), in Albert Hoftstadter (ed.), *Philosophies of Art and Beauty* (Chicago: Chicago University Press, 1964), p. 365.
9. Schelling's notion of the unconscious itself was foundational; he may even have been the first to coin the term. For an extended study see: Matt Ffytche, *The Foundation of the Unconscious: Schelling, Freud and the Birth of the Modern Psyche* (Cambridge: Cambridge University Press, 2013).
10. Hoftstadter, *Philosophies of Art and Beauty,* p. 364. Schelling solves the problem of imagination in rather the way that early Christian thinkers solved the problem of revelation: which they saw as, rather, a problem of how to understand that secular and pre-Christian philosophy had some good in it. Philosophy, Justin Martyr (c. 100–165 CE) and Clement of Alexandria (c. 150–215 CE) concluded, was good as far as it went, but necessarily partial since it lacked access to Christian truth. 'Justin Martyr on Philosophy and Theology' and 'Clement of Alexandria on Philosophy and Theology' in Alister E. McGrath (ed.), *The Christian Theology Reader* (Oxford: Blackwell, 2001), pp. 4 and 5–6.

11. I am standardising the spelling because this is a discussion of a shared concept of *Gesamtkunstwerk*.
12. William Ashton Ellis (trans.), *Richard Wagner's Prose Works*, vol. 1 (London: Kegan Paul, Trench, Trübner & Co, 1892), pp. 53–4. http://petrucci.mus.auth.gr/imglnks/usimg/6/6a/IMSLP94177-PMLP194194-RWagner_Prose_Works_Vol1.pdfretrieved23/2/15
13. Ibid. pp. 57–8.
14. Ibid. pp. 43–4.
15. Friederich Nietzsche, *The Birth of Tragedy and The Case of Wagner*, Walter Kaufmann (trans.) (New York: Vintage, Random House, 1967), pp. 172–3. One thing we do learn is that Wagner himself completed all the libretti for the *Ring* cycle *before* he started work on the music.
16. Ibid.
17. Ibid. p. 173.
18. Ibid. p. 175.
19. Ibid. p. 183.
20. Ibid. p. 177. The true writer, too, would rise to the challenge of language, which is to say thinking.
21. Ibid. p. 166.
22. Ibid. pp. 167–8.
23. Ibid. pp. 170–1.
24. Claude Debussy, 'Letter to Charles Levade, 4 September 1903' in *Debussy Letters*, François Lesure and Roger Nichols (eds), Roger Nichols (trans.) (London: Faber, 1987), p. 140.
25. Ibid. p. 87. 'Letter to Euène Ysaÿe, 13 October 1896'.
26. Ibid. p. 172. 'Letter to Louis Laloy, 10 September 1906'. Contrast this with the way an admirer like Proust pictures Wagner's compositional process as much more an affair of happy accidents of memory; and how this, too, is a reflection on the writer's own work.
27. Nietzsche, *The Birth of Tragedy and The Case of Wagner*, p. 163.
28. Nietzsche, *The Birth of Tragedy and The Case of Wagner*, p. 160. Debussy, 'Letter to Robert Godet, 18 December 1911' in *Debussy Letters*, p. 249.
29. Peter Porter, 'The Smell on the Landing' in *Once Bitten, Twice Bitten* (London: Scorpion Press, 1961), p. 41.

Chapter 10

The Consolations of Tradition

Since the millennium, certain trends in Anglophone poetry have echoed the 'turn' in Western art music away from what we might think of as mid-century 'scholasticism' towards such conventional musical rewards as readily detectable patterning, or euphony. Artistic credibility and a response by non-specialist audiences no longer appear inimical. It has once again become possible to develop serious original work using traditional verse forms such as the ballad (which we saw at work in Chapter 6), or musical tropes as familiar as the rising or falling scale on which Arvo Pärt's famous *Fratres* is built.[1]

This shift, from the complex and unfamiliar to material that is distilled and empirically accessible, makes us ask whether it is cultural conditioning, or some innate human capacity, that lets us experience certain tropes as more accessible than others. (Recent work with MRI scanning shows that the experience of reading poetry 'lights up' areas of the brain associated with music, but not always those associated with reading prose.[2]) But quasi-scientific questions like these address the causes rather than the character of art music and poetry, and so fall outside the scope of this book. I'm trying to map music onto poetry, not onto the brain. Instead, in this chapter I'll look at similarities between the ways in which traditional forms are used and experienced in poetry and music.

Fratres was written in 1977, though it continued to be revised and re-arranged until 1992. But in poetry it's the last two decades in particular that have seen a revival of influential work in strict forms such as the sonnet. The artforms are out of step with each other. But this time lag also reflects a relative lack of urgency to the changes under way in verse. Poetry was never as wholly immersed in a 'new scholasticism' as was Western art music. To date there have always remained pathways and schools within which Anglophone verse could practise conventional compositional techniques. For example, North American verse has arguably been more successful than the British tradition at developing traditional 'musical' resources within free verse. While recognisably formal projects have flourished within the US *vers libre* tradition, in Britain its adoption has sometimes seemed more like a breaking of the old 'bonds' of full rhyme and strict metre than the introduction of new sounds. (One source of this feeling may be the creative irruption of oral traditions within British culture during the seventies and eighties. Poets of first- and second-generation Caribbean descent, though as various as Linton Kwesi Johnson and Grace Nichols, united in bringing *vernacular* traditions into *literary* verse.[3])

Supporting and even exaggerating this tendency, UK critical and educational reception has focused largely on poetic imagery, as well as to a lesser extent on the sensory pleasures of vocabulary. This *content-led* approach has come to dominate the delivery of poetry by schools and universities.[4] Education may always be at least a decade behind art practice, but it exerts a disproportionate pressure on that practice, since it's frequently the only access even the British intellectual 'elite' has to contemporary poetry. British poems are thus generally understood as being 'about' something. They are written from a context that assumes they either describe, or contain a 'message'. For example, 'Warming the Pearls' by Carol Ann Duffy is usually taught as a positive representation of female intimacy; while her 'Prayer' becomes a poem about the democratisation of culture.[5] These readings of two works from the GCSE syllabus are not inaccurate. But Duffy could equally be taught as a highly sophisticated poet, the inheritor of a key English elegiac tradition running from Thomas Hardy by way of Philip Larkin: a poetry related to hers in scale and tone, and in the concerns it addresses. Like Duffy's personal lyrics, Hardy's own often touch on baulked love, including retrospective love for his dead wife Emma, as in the poem 'The Voice'; and use the local and everyday to speak to society and the state of the world.[6] 'In a Time of the Breaking of Nations' watches a field being ploughed: an activity then as quotidian as is the child's piano practice in Duffy's 'Prayer'.[7] Poems of sexual regret thread Larkin's work too: from the early 'Wants', first published in *Twenty Poems*, to 'Wild Oats', from *The Whitsun Weddings*.[8] Like Hardy and Duffy, he conjures a whole society from what is local and familiar: a music stool, tarmac back lanes, housewives marooned on housing estates.[9]

Even poets writing as early and as influentially, in the postwar British shift away from strict metrical form, as Ted Hughes (*The Hawk in the Rain*, 1957) and Sylvia Plath (*The Colossus*, 1960) are image-led.[10] Both were astonishing image-coiners. Partly as result, it's surprisingly hard to bring to mind, or to the ear, the characteristic *rhythm* of a Plath or Hughes line, although passage after passage is astonishingly memorable. This is not so strikingly the case with contemporary North American verse. To think of C. K. Williams (1936–2015) is to think immediately of the urgent, urging way that short qualifying phrases allow him to sustain his lines' exceptional length.[11] Conjure the work of W. S. Merwin (b. 1927) and what comes to mind is a line that starts *in medias res* and remains 'aloft', untethered by punctuation, throughout the poem.[12] The mind's ear can recall the open-toned, short-ish lines of Donald Hall (b. 1928), or the slightly longer and less evenly matched lines, still characterised by open vowels, of his somewhat younger contemporary Robert Hass (b. 1941).[13] In each of these cases, free verse has been developed into a particular *sound*scape.

That may in part be a legacy of North American Modernism. From 1933 to 1956, the Black Mountain College theorised and practised free verse as a form that, they believed, could be more authentic than strictly formal verse to the embodied human composing or hearing that poetry. Charles Olson's famous essay 'Projective Verse', which we looked at in Chapter 3, was in fact published before he joined the Black Mountain faculty: the School's influence was spread far beyond its campus by a number of distinguished poets and practitioners from the other arts, as well as by the seven issues of the *Black Mountain Review* (1954–7).[14] For Black Mountain poets, free verse wasn't the absence of form, but a new, organic series of forms; which might be related to breathing, walking or meditation.[15]

A third possible reason for the generally greater freedom and formal experimentation within North America free verse is that the continent lacks the long British tradition conflating those who are allowed to publish verse with those who have received an elite education. (We saw in Chapter 8 how significant membership of this club was for a poet like Geoffrey Chaucer.) North American poetry has long embraced influences from oral and popular traditions. Walt Whitman's psalmic *Leaves of Grass* (whose first edition appeared in 1855) is no less redolent of liturgy, and of the rhetoric of popular preachers and wayside political speakers, than is Allen Ginsberg's *Howl*, written exactly a century later in 1955.

Despite all this, a handful of British poets do elaborate new forms within free verse. Characteristic of John Burnside's poetry is the long, single 'breath slur' with which he extends his lines by stepping them. His 2014 collection is even titled *All One Breath*.[16] A Burnside line sets out from the left-hand margin in the usual way; then, as if to create a caesura, both full of tension and opening up a pause, it may 'step' down to the next, not returning to the margin but continuing where the line above left off. Some of these 'steps' have a feel of qualifying clause or parenthetical comment; not quite asides, since they move the narrative main line of thought along, they work like 'gear-changes' into another pitch or tone which, as gear-changes will, can create momentum rather than put a brake on it.

A comparable effect – of stepping down, or aside, into another tonality – occurs in Western art music when the first violin, that icing on the cake of any ensemble, falls silent for a passage. At the opening to the *Presto Finale* of Felix Mendelssohn's *String Octet* Op. 20, the movement's first statement – heard initially on the cellos – passes between instruments in the form of a fugue. A fugue is, in a sense, repeatedly beginning. The 'top', audible line of each new entry restates its opening material. As we saw happening in the Grosse Fugue in Chapter 5, this creates a kind of aural 'blanket stitch', reaching back repeatedly to whatever has just been stated. Yet here the young composer creates the effect not of hampered progress but of vigorous momentum, as 'scrubbing' quavers set up the opening, then clothe the arrival of his main figure of striding, stepped chord minims (see Fig. 10.1):

Figure 10.1 Opening of the last movement of Mendelssohn's *String Octet*

Fugues oscillate between the phrase just heard and its current iteration; between then and now. They're peculiarly predictive: each statement carries with it the implication of forthcoming restatement. Since an intrinsic property of music and verse is chronologic sequence, forms that play with that temporal order are as significant as they are unusual. Such play is a form of reflexivity: the music steps outside itself, doing more than simply pass 'innocently' through time. The fugue *acknowledges* that music is temporal, and that what is happening right now has a causal relationship with what has just happened or is about to happen. Many, if not all, forms could be read as a way of generating *what comes* next. This is true whether that relationship is highly obvious, as in a rondo, or relatively more incorporated into a range of influential elements, as in sonata form. Fugue doesn't make a more direct allusion to time than does a rondo: both use repetition. But it does so more proximately: the figure is no sooner stated than it gets restated. The recapitulation, or return, that is part of sonata form is even more differentiated both by temporal distance – we get to it after a 'development' and by the translation of some of its material to another key – and can be so 'incorporated' into the lengthy preceding development that it goes undetected by the untrained ear.

In fugue the individual lines of the polyphony, the moment just gone, and the one just happening are all held in mind together. John Burnside's stepped lines set up a similar process of mental superimposition. That stepped-down alignment between the first phrase and the second *shows* (both ear and eye) that they belong together, and this belonging together makes them at the same time, and respectively, nostalgic and prospective. Held in mind at once, they bounce off each other, and this becomes the motor of entire poems:

> [...]
> and how, on a morning like this, with our everyday lives
> suspended
>   in these white parentheses
>
> we start again from scratch: the coming night;
> the ferry that runs to the island;
>   the sullen ice;
>
> the shapes we have scarcely noticed, bearing us on
> to all we have yet to become
>   to the blank of a future.[17]

But Burnside's use of formal patterning within free verse reflects at least in part his interest in North American poetics. It remains unusual in British free verse, which as a result turns more frequently to traditional forms than does contemporary work from across the Atlantic. Nevertheless the difference is always one of degree. Contemporary US poets who work in strict form include Marilyn Hacker and the Irish émigré Paul Muldoon. But I'm concentrating on strict form in British verse because it's where the 'turn' towards such forms is most clear-cut.

Among forms undergoing a revival in Britain are the sonnet, iambic pentameter and – especially in creative writing work-shops – more recent imports such as the pantoum and ghazal. Practitioners of the latter include Mimi Khalvati, who is not only a poet of the first rank but a leading teacher of strict form. Her ghazals aren't particularly designed to underline her own cultural heritage: she was born in Tehran but has lived in the UK since the age of six. Instead, they describe environments or explore relationships, and their use of repetition creates a con-tinually self-modifying pattern that articulates a particular *sensibility*. The words that close each couplet of a ghazal must rhyme with the poet's own 'signature' in its final line. Although the first-time reader doesn't yet know what form this signature will take – kenning, pen-name or sobriquet – the whole poem anticipates it and so feels 'enclosed' by the poet's presence. Khalvati's very first ghazal was a love poem, and plays on the doubled 'mi' or 'me' of 'Mimi' and the doubled 'me' of 'you and me'. 'If you are the rhyme and I the refrain, don't hang /on my lips, come and I'll come too when you cue me' says the second of its eight couplets; while the final one says:

> Be heaven and earth to me and I'll be twice the me
> I am, if only half the world you are to me.[18]

Iambic pentameter has also been gaining in popularity, out-growing its history as the form favoured by Shakespeare and John Milton. Nowadays, we're as likely to hear in it the edu-cated, conversational tones of W. H. Auden, or Tony Harrison's note of anti-Metropolitan political seriousness. These two poles of contemporary British poetry aesthetic – the fastidious Senior Common Room and Northern working-class popular culture – have between them redeemed iambic pentameter from a dead end as poetic 'costume drama'.[19]

The form that's seen the greatest revival, the sonnet, is itself a native of iambic pentameter. Sonnet form seems to be resurgent for a number of reasons, and *as* a number of different things. This resurgence may be British, but North Americans using the form include both Robert Pinsky and C. K. Williams. Perhaps the most portable of the Classical and Romantic forms, sonnet's fourteen lines make it short enough to memorise with relative ease. It doesn't last as long as the three-minute pop song (though it probably contains more words), but some of its functions are perceptibly similar. The sonnet, a 'little song', belongs in the lyric tradition. While this tradition carries a trace of what was briefly called subjectivity, it's also concerned with 'songlike' or nice-*sounding* form. The ubiquity of global popular culture means many contemporary poets, especially those of the middle generation and younger, have their musical formation almost exclusively from non-art music. For these writers, the sonnet's scale and role seem, among traditional forms, particularly recognisable and so accessible. The conventional structure of the pop lyric, with its bridge section and chorus that turn the opening material, is even loosely related to the sonnet *volta* or turn.

In 2015, when the musician-poet Don Paterson published *40 Sonnets* of his own, he had already translated Rilke's *Orpheus* sonnets, edited a sonnet anthology and produced a study of Shakespeare's sonnets.[20] This level of commitment to one formal cause is extreme, but other contemporary poets work in related ways. Michael Symmons Roberts's *Drysalter* (2013) responds to the *Book of Psalms* in its themes and concerns, but is numerologically related both to that *Book* and to sonnet form, since each of its 150 poems is fifteen lines long. The experience of a fifteen-line poem, especially of its self-enclosure and scale, echoes the sonnet, though the poems in *Drysalter* don't as a rule make a sonnet turn. Nevertheless, the ear notices length, and asks *what could not be fitted* into fourteen lines. The fifteenth line of any poem is significant just because it exceeds the sonnet: as if it counterbalances or comments on the previous fourteen lines, somewhat as an alexandrine comments on the metre of the preceding lines. Poems that stop at fifteen lines – and also, for analogous reasons, those of thirteen and twelve – are paying a 'slant' homage to sonnet form.[21]

Tensions between conventional and innovative elements are a characteristic of the contemporary sonnet; which may itself be syllabic, unrhymed or use four-stress lines. These creative tensions help build the richness of the artform. Commercial verse has a notorious tendency to repeat itself – finding several ways to say 'I love you', for example – but literary poetic material often undergoes a kind of *modulation*, in the musical sense. It's 'worked over' by being passed through another element. In music this element is a new tonality; in poetry, it's often thematic but can be something formal, such as a new or unexpected technique.

The work of American poet Robert Pinsky (b. 1940) shows how readily such 'modulating' new material can be made to seem not external but intrinsic. His broadly narrative poetry repeatedly looks over its own shoulder to other times and places. Born Jewish in New Jersey during the Second World War, Pinsky often refers to European ancestors whose culture and experience he uses to 'triangulate' – and thus, paradoxically, to make more 'real' – his own American experience. 'Not what they were' is the informal refrain to a late poem 'In Berkeley', which asks, 'We hungry generations [...] Did you think we wanted / To be like you?'[22] Sometimes this poem's 'Volunteers, escapers, not what they were' are European plants and flowers removed from their original context. At others they are people: Malcolm X, a 'Sufi mother and child', the poet himself. 'I flicker and for a second / I'm picking through rubbish / To salvage your half-eaten muffin, one hand / At my ear to finger a rill of scab.' That 'I flicker' is lightly done, with the accustomed ease of a poetics that hasn't undergone radical renovation since the poet's debut in 1966. A number of Pinsky's earliest poems were written in iambic pentameter. Some, like 'Library Scene' (written in pentameter, but not in iambs), used full rhyme. In this poem, the familiarity of the form creates a sense of completion, even though other times and places are in play:

Someone is reading in a deepening room
Where something happens, something that will come

To happen again, happening as many times
As she is reading in as many rooms.[23]

Formal tradition offers British poets the resources of other times and places, too. Some translate, or create homages to, an earlier poet: as Don Paterson does with Rainer Maria Rilke's *Orpheus* sonnets, or Tom Paulin does with a range of different poetries in *The Road to Inver*; where he turns Classical and German Romantic texts alike into Irish verse.[24] When a poet goes further and takes traditional form into their own new work, it becomes highly audible. The more unexpected – or contrasted with other elements – it is, the more audible it becomes. Poems like Sean O'Brien's comic 'The Plain Truth of the Matter', on the probity of liking marmite, or Don Paterson's tragic 'The Swing', in which a male narrator thinks about the child his partner is aborting, sting with their contemporaneity *because* their sound is traditional and the contemporary content creates a piquant contrast. ('The Swing' is in ballad form, with slant ABAB rhymes and characteristic alternating four- and three-stress, residually iambic, lines; the two quatrains of 'The Plain Truth of the Matter' are in four-footed iambic meter.[25])

If traditional form provides a 'piquancy bonus' for today's poets and their audiences, in contemporary music a related recognition of the extra dimension created by recognisably traditional form seems to underscore the work of two highly influential composers – Arvo Pärt and John Tavener – whose experiments with musical mysticism have played a significant role in the 'turn' art music has made towards such formal elements. Born before the mid-point of the last century, both found themselves to be religious composers at a time when professed religion was no longer at the heart of the European cultural mainstream. Arvo Pärt's mature style, which he calls *tintinnabulation*, emerged under communism and the secular, Soviet occupation of his native Estonia. In order to achieve it, his own work underwent a pioneering version of music's shared 'turn' away from tone-row serialism: which he first employed in 1960's *Nekrolog*, developed into full-blown serialism by the time of 1963's *Perpetuum mobile*, and combined with collaged quotations in the early 1970s. The British composer John Tavener converted to Orthodox Christianity in 1977; we can speculate that his religious 'turn' may have been heightened by the serious illness that dogged his adult life. Both composers borrow from minimalism, while eschewing its tight-wound repetitions, to compose music that simultaneously reveals its engagement with the values of the past, and displays a stripped back contemporary language. Works like Pärt's *Cantus in Memoriam Benjamin Britten* (1977) and Tavener's *The Protecting Veil* (1989) emphasise an arc of musical thought; an *and then … and then*. Both use a single line with bare, sometimes ostinato, chords moving beneath it, both maintain a marked difference in pitch between that line and those chords, both frequently use rising forms and an instrument straining against its technical limits, and both embrace an extreme slowness that suggests a breath being held.

To see the work this language does, we only have to compare Pärt with the earlier Olivier Messiaen (1908–92), that great European Modernist who was also an avowedly Christian composer. Messiaen's chromatic language was also in its own time revolutionary, although (as we saw in Chapter 4) it also arose from the work of his predecessors, including other more 'accessible' French chromaticists, like Claude Debussy, Gabriel Fauré or Maurice Ravel, whose work was largely completed before the Second World War. The more than sixty years that Messiaen served as organist at La Trinité in Paris encompassed not only the Second World War but the period of Catholic Renewal culminating in the Second Vatican Council, convened in 1962. French Catholicism of this period was shaped by overlapping struggles between ultramontanism's belief in the primacy of the Vatican, and Gallicanism's faith in the separation of civil powers; between *ressourcement* (a return to theological sources) and *aggiornamento* (bringing the Faith up to date); and between the Solesmes model of Gregorian chant and participative para-liturgies. For all the personal modesty that may have become a man of faith, the sumptuous dissonances and shifting textures Messiaen uses demonstrate an unquestioning confidence in his occupation of both the Catholic religious and the artistic mainstream. They're a sign not of counter-cultural revolution but of battles already won.

Pärt's compositional language, on the other hand, can be seen as a response to a cultural and musical emergency whose provisions must be utterly rethought and rebuilt. His is a transitional practice carried out on shifting terrain: *camping sauvage* instead of a bourgeois dwelling. His 'turn' to traditionally fundamental elements – such as unisons and parallel motions, traditional instrumentation, euphony and liturgy – first appears in the cluster of works composed around the time of his emigration to the West, which include *Cantus in Memoriam Benjamin Britten* (1977), *Spiegel im Spiegel* (1978) and *De Profundis* (1981).

The fact that Pärt's hollowed-out harmonic world produces a clarity and simplicity that appeals to 'cross-over' non-specialist audiences may or may not demonstrate something about the power of traditional form. It is absolutely beside my point. In any case, these responses aren't a homogeneous entity. Religious believers, and that section of the often-secular cultural intelligentsia who enjoy minimalism, for example as an extension of jazz-fusion, are generally discrete communities.[26] There is certainly no automatic link between spirituality and any particular musical or poetic form. Since the mid-twentieth century, the two leading protagonists of Anglican verse, T. S. Eliot and Geoffrey Hill, have both produced highly wrought Modernist poetry that explores the difficulties, rather than the accessibility, of spirituality. Interviewed in *The Paris Review*, Hill is explicit about how Eliot's notion of impersonality influenced works such as his 'The Mystery of the Charity of Charles Péguy' (1983). He also gives a defence of complexity:

> the German classicist and Kierkegaardian scholar Theodor Haecker [...] argues, with specific reference to the Nazis, that one of the things the tyrant most cunningly engineers is the gross oversimplification of language, because propaganda requires that the minds of the collective respond primitively to slogans of incitement. And any complexity of language, any ambiguity, any ambivalence implies [...] an intelligence working in qualifications and revelations ... resisting, therefore, tyrannical simplification.[27]

For a popular-spiritual poetic 'fix' in any way equivalent to Pärt or Tavener, we must return to the best-selling North American Pulitzer Prize winner Mary Oliver. Nothing could be further from Eliot and Hill. Her somewhat ecological, even lightly pantheist, spirituality is non-denominational, and she writes free verse. Her book titles, which include *White Pine* (1994), *Blue Pastures* (1995), *West Wind* (1997), *Blue Iris* (2004), *Red Bird* (2008) and *Swan* (2010), make the lucid directness of this project clear.

It is Jaan Kaplinski, the leading poet among Pärt's Estonian countrymen and his junior by six years, who offers a link between Oliver and Pärt. Kaplinski started as a strict formalist and moved into meditative free verse and prose poetry – influenced partly by Buddhist philosophy, partly by ethnographic interests – in the 1980s, just after Pärt's 'turn'. The resulting poetry is highly accessible, both intellectually and aesthetically, in ways similar to Oliver's. Elsewhere, however, their work differs. Oliver's shorter-lined poems are *visibly* in the portable lyric tradition. They deal with a spontaneous reaction to a single moment: something that allies them to the subjective element within the traditional lyric project. Kaplinski produces verse whose often long lines sometimes lengthen 'all the way' into prose poetry, and consistently vary *within* each of the collections he produced between the two versions of his *Evening Brings Everything Back*, published in respectively 1984 and 2004.[28] The literal, denotative meaning of poetry has exposed its writers to even more direct censorship, such as that practised by the Soviet regime, than musicians risk. It's not surprising, then, that Kaplinski's walks in the forest can sound more like solipsistic retreats than calls to shared values. The long poem *The Soul Returning*, written between 1973 and 1975, makes this explicit, asking 'do you / hear / my / silence / do I / hear / your / voice'.[29]

But, just as Oliver and Kaplinski are only part of what's going on in contemporary verse, so Pärt and Taverner are not the only mid-twentieth-century composers whose work ushered in the radical openness of musical postmodernity. Also key to this shift was the formally related discipline of minimalists, like Steve Reich (who was born one year after Pärt, in 1936) and Philip Glass (one year younger again), to which we'll turn in the next chapter. Since the sixties, their pared-back sound – tellingly first known as the New York Hypnotic School – has been adopted by a number of composers. Among these, one of the best-known is John Adams (b. 1947).[30] Though not a full-blown minimalist, Adams has been specific about his reaction against what he saw as the deadening effect of the serialism that still dominated the academy when he was a student at Harvard.[31] Postmodernity, interpreted as artistic laissez-faire, has also permitted the more expansive, contrasting lyricism of younger composers like the

Scottish Catholic James McMillan (b. 1959), or the English composers Mark-Anthony Turnage (b. 1960) and Thomas Adès (b. 1971). A formal musical vocabulary which expressly includes both *expressionism* and a notion of *beauty* is now centre stage.[32]

This wholesale 'turn' in music is significantly weightier than the more scattered, though still significant, shifts in contemporary Anglophone poetics. As we'll see in the next chapter, it has chiefly been achieved not by a series of conversions within individuals' compositional sensibilities but by the wholesale relinquishment of *number* as a determining element in key compositional areas. That number creates formlessness because its use is *implicitly aleatoric* – that is, *non-intentional*, even if not always truly random – is one of the counter-intuitive lessons of twentieth-century musical culture, as we'll see in the next chapter.

Notes

1. Arvo Pärt, *Fratres* (London: Universal Edition, 1991). http://www.universaledition . com / Arvo - Paert / composers - and - works / composer/534/work/2544. Retrieved 2/1/16.
2. 'The experience of reading varies markedly between differing texts which may be, for example, primarily informative, musical, or moving. [...] Using fMRI, we examined brain activation in expert participants reading passages of prose and poetry. [...] The experience of reading contrasting texts is associated with differing patterns of brain activation, the emotional response to literature shares ground with the response to music, and regions of the right hemisphere are engaged by poetry.' Adam Zeman, F. Milton, A. Smith and R. Rylance, 'By Heart: An fMRI Study of Brain Activation by Poetry and Prose', *Journal of Consciousness Studies* 20:9–10 (2013), pp. 132–58. http://www.ingentaconnect.com/content/imp/jcs/2013/00000020/F0020009/art00008. Retrieved 24/1/16.
3. I've written about this cultural transmission and adaptation, and its influence on British free verse forms, elsewhere. Fiona Sampson, *Beyond the Lyric* (London: Chatto & Windus, 2012), pp. 94–119.
4. In its official guide on 'How to write an A* GCSE poetry response', the *Times Educational Supplement* writes that an A* essay on poetry 'is characterised by a confident engagement' with the themes, ideas, relationships and technical 'construction of the poems'. Note the order in which these requirements are given. 'How to write an A* GCSE English Literature Poetry Response' in

Times Educational Supplement on-line teaching materials. Created 30 December 2009. https://www.tes.com/teaching-resource/how-to-write-an-a-gcse-poetry-response-6031386. Retrieved 28/8/15.

5. Carol Ann Duffy, 'Warming Her Pearls' from *Selling Manhattan* (London: Anvil Press, 1987), p. 58. Carol Ann Duffy, 'Prayer' from *Mean Time* (London: Anvil Press, 1993), p. 52.

6. Thomas Hardy, 'The Voice' in *Selected Poems*, David Wright (ed.) (Harmondsworth: Penguin, 1978), p. 378.

7. Ibid. pp. 282–3.

8. Philip Larkin, 'Wants' and 'Wild Oats' in *Collected Poems*, Anthony Thwaite (ed.) (London: Faber, 1988), pp. 42 and 143.

9. It's noteworthy that the UK's first woman laureate is part of this masculine tradition.

10. Both debuts belong to the 1950s. Sylvia Plath *The Colossus and Other Poems* (London: Faber, 1960). Ted Hughes, *The Hawk in the Rain* (London: Faber, 1957).

11. C. K. Williams, *Collected Poems* (New York/Newcastle upon Tyne: Farrar, Straus and Giroux/Bloodaxe, 2006).

12. W. S. Merwin, *Migration: New and Selected Poems* (Port Townsend, WA: Copper Canyon Press, 2005). (The book won the US National Book Award for Poetry.)

13. Donald Hall, *White Apples and the Taste of Stone*: *Selected Poems 1946–2006* (Boston and New York: Houghton Mifflin, 2006). Robert Hass, *The Apple Trees at Olema* (Tarset: Bloodaxe, 2011).

14. The *Review*'s editor was Robert Creeley.

15. See Chapter 3.

16. John Burnside, *All One Breath* (London: Cape, 2014).

17. John Burnside, 'Responses to Augustine of Hippo', *Gift Songs* (London: Cape, 2007), p. 9. In recent years, he has moved increasingly away from stepped lines; tellingly, he returns to the technique for the title poem of his 2014 collection *All One Breath*.

18. I am grateful to Mimi Khalvati for permission to quote this ghazal, which is uncollected although it has featured on the A-level syllabus.

19. Sean O'Brien himself is arguably the nexus of these traditions. Raised in Hull and now living and working in Newcastle, he writes with a socio-political commitment that joins him to the Harrison–W. S. Graham anti-Metropolitan tradition. Yet he was educated at Cambridge and had a lifelong friendship with the older Australian poet Peter Porter (1929–2010): the transmitter, in Britain, of the Audenesque tradition of highly cultured and discursive talking verse. It's a tradition with which O'Brien's work, particularly in the thoughtful argumentation of books like *The Beautiful Librarians*, is also in dialogue. Sean O'Brien, *The Beautiful Librarians* (London: Picador, 2015).

20. Don Paterson, *40 Sonnets* (London: Faber, 2015). Don Paterson, *Reading Shakespeare's Sonnets* (London: Faber, 2010). Don

Paterson, *101 Sonnets: From Shakespeare to Heaney* (London: Faber, 1999).

21. Arguably, that 'slant' makes the homage all the more pronounced: just as a 'slant' rhyme may be more conspicuous than full rhyme because it sets up an oscillation between rhyming and not-rhyming.

22. Robert Pinsky, *The Figured Wheel* (Manchester: Carcanet, 1996), pp. 11–12.

23. Ibid. p. 238.

24. Don Paterson, *Orpheus: A Version of Rainer Maria Rilke* (London: Faber, 2007). Tom Paulin, *The Road to Inver* (London: Faber, 2004).

25. Sean O'Brien, 'The Plain Truth of the Matter' in *November* (London: Picador, 2011), p. 34. Don Paterson, 'The Swing' in *Rain* (London: Faber, 2009), pp. 6–7.

26. As it happens, both audiences are in their own ways highly influential, since they include both proselytising faithful, and the scholars and journalists who are our cultural commentators.

27. http://www.theparisreview.org/interviews/730/the-art-of-poetry-no-80-geoffrey-hill. Retrieved 28/8/15.

28. Jaan Kaplinski, *Selected Poems*, Jaan Kaplinski with Sam Hamill, Hildi Hawkins, Fiona Sampson (trans.) (Tarset: Bloodaxe, 2011).

29. Ibid. p. 218.

30. Tom Johnson, 'Changing the meaning of static' in *Village Voice*, September 7, 1972. This was also the article which seems to have contained the first use of the term 'minimalism'. Edward Strickland, quoted in Richard Kostelanetz and R. Flemming (eds), *Writings on Glass: Essays, Interviews, Criticism* (Berkeley and Los Angeles/ New York: University of California Press/Schirmer Books, 1997), pp. 114–15.

31. Michael Broyles, *Mavericks and Other Traditions in American Music* (New Haven, CT: Yale University Press, 2004), pp. 169–70.

32. I use the term 'expressionism' not 'expressiveness' to establish the link with the art-historical term for a particular formal school and set of intentions.

Chapter 11

Radical Measures

In recent years, the idea of 'the poem' has been pulled in polarising directions. In the last chapter, we began to see how an ideological debate is under way that echoes what's taken place in Western art music since the middle of the twentieth century. This is not just a question of style. Poetic 'sense', already a complicated, unstable concept, is being challenged and transformed.

As we saw in Chapters 5 and 6, poetry has traditionally used language in ways that allow a 'surplus' of implied or possible meanings and sensory experiences to pull against its grammatically and semantically coherent literal or 'surface' meaning. Nevertheless, as I argued in Chapter 8 poetry is a *communicative* discourse, one that anticipates an audience; and this remains the case even if that audience is purely Ideal: conceived of as posterity, or God, for example.[1] As readers and writers, we use this intrinsically public, shared identity of poetry as a form of communication as a marker of semantic coherence. In other words, our default approach to a poem is *expecting it to make sense*. Because of this, we 'puzzle over' passages that we don't understand. For even grammatical coherence doesn't by itself necessarily generate sense. 'The cat is green' may be a surreal image, but it makes sense in a way that 'The oven glove is automatic' does not.

But some contemporary verse has reversed the roles of these latent and surface 'meanings' so that uncertainty *itself* – along with an open field of semantic resonances, and the effects of sound divorced from communication – *are* what its grammatical and other structural elements 'tell' the listener or reader. The Language poets, strongly associated since the 1960s with the

West Coast in the US and with Cambridge in the UK, create work that foregrounds uncertainty in a number of ways: for example by using found texts (Charles Bernstein, in 1978 the influential co-founder and editor of *L=A=N=G=U=A=G=E* magazine, quotes jargon, corporate language and questions from his Chinese translator); writing collaboratively (as Lyn Hejinian does in *Leningrad* (1991), a book-length work partly co-authored with Russian poets); or setting up aleatoric language games (the Connecticut poet Charles O. Hartman has even published a study of computer-generated poetry).[2] Some of the techniques they use, including cutup, collage and concrete poetry, date even further back, to writers at work in the 1920s – including the Surrealists in Europe, and poets like Charles Reznikoff in the US – and are between eighty and ninety years old.

What these approaches have in common is that they avoid using the exploratory line of thought to build a poem. Among the terms practitioners use for these techniques are 'innovative' (clearly out of date) and the slightly more credible 'postmodern'. Yet both terms understate the radicalism of this move. Uncoupling language – and verse – from its *communicative* function is not merely an innovation within the artform, but contributes to a whole other genre – the tradition of the text as physical object – which is particularly strong in visual art practice, from the great tradition of Islamic calligraphy to the Futurist moment in poster art. Even postmodernity doesn't collapse the identities of disciplines: postmodern architecture produces *buildings* – structures that can be entered and inhabited – while postmodern theoretical prose deploys the conventional apparatus of grammatical and meaningful statement.[3]

To understand how radical the Language poetry move really is, I'd like to revisit the 'turn' in Western art music which I described in Chapter 10. One way to talk about what happened to music in the twentieth century is to say that it changed its relationship to number. That change started with the Second Viennese School, whose composers followed Arnold Schoenberg in using the twelve-tone 'row', or 'series', in serial music in the two decades after 1923. The intervention of the Second World War meant that several of the school's members, among them Schoenberg himself, made their way to the US, and promulgated their techniques on the other side of the Atlantic. Members of this second generation included the Czech-born Ernst Krenek and Heinrich Jalowetz. By the 1950s, serial music was being widely written by, among others, Igor Stravinsky and Milton Babbitt in the US, Luciano Berio and Luigi Dallapiccola in Italy, and Pierre Boulez in France. Even Witold Lutosławski, sequestered behind the Iron Curtain in Poland, experimented briefly with serial music in the 1950s before developing his own variant, twelve-tone rows which operated as scales.[4]

The individual row or series of each piece of serial music places the twelve semitones of the octave in its own particular order, which it then repeats for the rest of the piece. This creates a dense, determining structure for pitch, and so eliminates an aspect of compositional choice. Some serial composers also use a 'duration row' which determines the length of notes. In 1946 Milton Babbitt wrote his PhD dissertation on *The Future of Set Structures in the Twelve-Tone System*, basing his analysis on his own practice of applying serial technique to every aspect of a piece, and articulating a thoroughgoing mathematical and theoretical system to codify this technique into 'set', 'pitch-class' and 'interval-class'.[5] Shortly afterwards, in 1949–50, Olivier Messiaen also made a brief foray into thoroughgoing serialism when he applied it to dynamics and mode of attack as well as pitch and duration in 'Mode de valeurs et d'intensités' from *Quatre études de rythme* for solo piano.

What exactly *is* so radical about this? After all, number has always been a musical element. Counting is part of musical culture. You can't make rhythm of any kind – whether it's a two-step march, the 7/8 time of traditional Balkan music or a South American tango – without *counting* out pattern. We saw in Chapter 2 how numerical proportion is a key musical structuring device. It counts stanzas in song, measures the sections in sonata form, and codifies a minuet in three-time. Number also characterises pitch. Western tonality's 'circle of fifths' is better described in arithmetical terms than tested on the vibrating violin string – where, as we saw in Chapter 2, it doesn't quite 'add up'.

At first, serialism must simply have seemed to free up this picture. Now key pitch relationships could be reset for every new piece, when the composer selected its 'tone row'. The composer could play God by replacing the independently existing physical relationships of the harmonic series with the conceptual relationships of his row. Rhythm and duration, too, could be freed from convention, and from the limits of a time signature. But rows – though they can be varied by inversion or reversal – are neither developmental nor generative. They include no mechanism for shifting from one to another, or building relationships between or within them. Aleatoric music offers a similar hope of freedom, and creates similar limits. Like serialism, it generates forms which are arbitrary not only in their relation to the physical world but in their determining effect at every compositional moment, as number cuts across and preempts the *and then . . . and then* of music. In pieces systematically predetermined by numerical 'settings' there is in effect no need to *do* the piece in extension. Since we can already know what will happen, its *chrononomie* has been collapsed, and the contract with the Ideal or individual performer and audience is cancelled.[6]

This rupture is revealed by resistance: the perceived difficulty of relating to, or taking pleasure in, such music. Yet while music which seems to eschew the 'difficulty' and density of serialism has gained in popularity, number has remained important to composers and their audiences. As we saw briefly in the last chapter, minimalism's iterative, hypnotic performances put the contemporary interest in number to its own uses. The phased iterations Steve Reich made famous in a series of pieces from 1965's *It's Gonna Rain* to *Drumming* (1971) seem able both to work by compositional *feel* – since numbers of repetitions are not, for example, geometric – and to build a 'story arc' in ways similar to a chaconne, using repeated material as a basis for variation. Minimalism's exploitation of the resources of repetition reflected contemporary practice across the arts. Andy Warhol's famous series of silkscreen prints of iconic objects and portraits first started appearing in the early 1960s[7]. Martha Graham (1894–1991) followed by Pina Bausch (1940–2009) and many others, have created a vocabulary of (repeated) contemporary dance gestures, just as classical ballet earlier created and repeated its vocabulary of *pliés*, *jetés* and *fouettés*, from which to build full-length pieces.

Minimalist music did not at first appeal primarily to

traditional Classical concertgoers so much as to new young audiences, who might not comfortably have seen themselves figured in the contexts of art music. These new audiences found one could 'lose oneself in the music' in a different way from that possible in Western Classical music up to and including Modernism (a way which incidentally prefigured Trance music and the Rave movement). Minimalism's here-and-now experience of the iterated phrase turned the participating consciousness constantly back to itself, in a kind of musical solipsism.

Western art music is culturally specific, but the culture it's specific *to* – the 'West' – is, despite such generational differences, both more geographically extensive and more monolithic than any single contemporary poetics. Art music may not be the only thing, or even the main thing, being listened to from Tokyo to New York or from Dublin to Buenos Aires. But in any given year, the same kind of music is being played in concert halls across this vast region. Different kinds of poetry, on the other hand, are to some extent protected from each other by 'meaning'. A poem in Armenian can't be read by someone who only knows French, and Australians may have a hard time of it with contemporary Finnish verse. This throws up many practical, intellectual and creative questions, around translation and publishing in particular, but does mean that it's possible for a variety of poetics to coexist even within today's globally connected world. No single contemporary poetic development – even one led by the well-resourced scribblers of North America – can quite become hegemonic.[8]

This coexistence of poetics means that within contemporary Western poetry – and in fact even within Anglophone verse – practices analogous to those from both before and after the 'turn' in Western art music are to be found. Today, both austerely numerological verse, and writing that is recognisably from the lyric tradition, are being written and read (albeit by their own 'communication communities', to borrow Alasdair MacIntyre's term).[9]

It's surprising that, among these, the extreme of contemporary poetics associated with reliance on number, and with the abandonment of communicable meaning, should see itself as inheriting the Beat mantle. In the 1950s, even as art music tightened the elective bonds of serialism, Beat poetry was displaying a passionate desire to communicate. The rhetoric of Allen Ginsberg's *Howl* (1956), one of the movement's founding texts, includes hyperbole – in both diction and catastrophising imagery – vastly extended sentence structures, repetition and incanted lists.[10] We might even feel that the result of all this is *over*-communication. Like fellow Beats William S. Burroughs (1914–97) and Jack Kerouac (1922–69), Ginsberg resorted to the surreal and the shocking in an attempt to *épater* the American bourgeoisie – but also to communicate with them. Beat poets would have been astonished to find themselves co-opted to the social isolationism of work that abandons communication. After all, they weren't merely iconoclasts – they didn't go round burning books – but *writers* who challenged the poetic status quo precisely in order to articulate new ideas about society and to involve new audiences within that society. They felt they had *things to say*. To hear a recording of Ginsberg in old age singing William Blake is to realise how deeply he saw himself as part of the same prophetic tradition as his eighteenth-century precursor.[11]

But contemporary poets writing at the other extreme – who take a view of poetry as *purely* intentional communication, even at the expense of acknowledging such musical elements as form – also feel they inherit the Beat mantle. Writing in free verse, they see themselves as descending from the Beats by way of Confessionalism. Ginsberg's with-one-bound-he-was-free refusal of the academic, and beyond it of many carefully, even arguably too-craftily wrought musical formal effects, is read by these poets as a new, immediate honesty.[12] Today, influential British poets working in free verse include Simon Armitage, who became the Oxford Professor of Poetry in 2015. An advocate for what we might call 'the common-sense reader', Armitage reminds us of the importance of poetry's 'fourth wall' of poetry: that it has an audience. He is active in enlarging audiences for poetry: collaborating on radio programmes, writing public art commissions, and taking long-distance walking trips during which he gives readings in exchange for bed and board.[13] As this energetic practice makes clear, creating pleasure is not intrinsically elitist or reactionary – but rather the reverse. Working with forms such as the lyric, that have been used in other times and places, is not the same as making any culturally elitist claim about the 'eternal verity' of those forms, or their associated cultural traditions.[14]

Despite the great variety of contemporary poetics, and the radical extent to which the more numerological forms, like language poetry, develop *beyond* the boundaries of poetry itself, number remains important to the majority of contemporary poets and composers. Just why is it so tempting? Abstraction – being released from the obligations of the realist contract – offers the challenges and scope of engagement with apparently limitless possibility, yet making is always limited by intention. This is not to confuse process with product, but to remember that each man-made object is a particular kind of thing, and its coherence comes from being that thing: Guido d'Arezzo's 'single plane'.[15] The limits on abstract art, of whatever genre, are to be found *within* the artwork itself. An obvious example of this is scale. A painting, or a piece of orchestral music, *is* a particular size. Its boundaries are neither infinite nor porous, however radically open it may be to interpretations. This is even true of a piece like John Cage's *ASLSP* (*As Slow as Possible*), designed (as its title suggests) to be played as slowly as possible and which, in one contemporary performance on a specially constructed organ in the ruined St Burchardi Church in Halberstadt, Germany, begun in 2001 with a 17-month rest, is scheduled to last for 639 years.[16] Although the witness's experience of the actual artwork, if not the concept of it, is of *almost* infinitesimally slow-moving time, even this performance is not infinitely extended. Nor is it infinite 'as it goes'. It doesn't simultaneously include every possible permutation of pitch, duration and instrumentation. D'Arezzo's *musica ficta* is also 'fictional music', works not written and those which cannot exist.

Despite this, abstract form can appear almost infinite in its possibilities: an extreme case of the choice that can cause paralysing compositional anxiety. Writer's block, according to Zachary Leader's eponymous 1990 study, is a state of mind for which the French and Germans have no term.[17] It's arguable whether the condition even exists; although the neurologist Alice W. Flaherty claims, in *The Midnight Disease* (2004), that literary creativity is the function of a specific brain area, and so both composition and block may be caused by actual changes in brain activity.[18] Sure enough, few report-writers have claimed to suffer from block. Yet creative writers do report a terror of the blank page: the blogosphere is alive with the term 'blank page syndrome'.[19] Samuel Taylor Coleridge called it 'an indefinite indescribable Terror'.[20] 'Yesterday was my Birth Day,' he wrote in his notebook in 1804, when he was thirty-two. 'So completely has a whole year passed, with scarcely the fruits of a month. – O Sorrow and Shame [...] I have done nothing!'[21]

A turn to number might seem as much a way to manage this anxiety as an aesthetic or intellectual choice. Unexpressive and non-denotative, number is a system which doesn't need to be developed by the composer or poet but is pre-existing; and which, within its own field, is as absolute as Western tonality (which is to say, not entirely). For the poet, it offers the attraction of being additional to language's denotative functions – when for example it counts the number of feet in a line – even though, as we've seen repeatedly, non-denotative aural elements may in fact be part of what language *means*. The poet who doesn't feel she has 'anything to say' can at least feel she has a *way* to start. For the composer, the whole new set of compositional techniques it offers help fill up the blank score before a note has been composed.

At the same time, the costs of using number appear low. Just as music can make additional use of it in minimalism without 'going all the way' into serialism, so poetry can use number in ways that fall short of *quantitative verse*. The development of one of these ways of counting, syllabic verse, is associated with Modernism: unsurprisingly, given that movement's concern was the materials from which artworks are made. Early adoptors of Anglophone syllabics include Dylan Thomas and Marianne Moore – as well as the (admittedly non-Modernist) W. H. Auden. Because English is a stress-timed language – rather than syllable-timed as, say, French or Japanese are – its syllables don't create a regular, audible music; and so English syllable-counting poetics arise not from oral tradition but from within literacy.

It's both the power and the shortcoming of Anglophone syllabic verse that it is counter-intuitive. Although not strictly inaudible – since syllables are after all units of *sound*, not groups of unsounded letters – the form doesn't produce audible patterns because the ear doesn't know where the line ends. The visual cue of the line-break, as it's laid out on the page, guides the *eye* towards reading the form. The ear glimpses syllabic pattern only when line ends are marked by rhyme, or by regular line-end or half-line (hemistich) stresses; and often the only concession English language syllabic verse makes to the line is not to break a word across it. However, the pure iambs of Dylan Thomas's 'The Rod Can Lift its Twining Head' mean this rhyming poem carries regular numbers of syllables as well as of stresses per line. The two stanzas of 'In My Craft or Sullen Art' are composed of seven-syllable lines which aren't quite so well signposted. But they are at least discrete phrases, end-stopped by meaning:

> In my craft or sullen art
> Exercised in the still night
> When only the moon rages
> And the lovers lie abed
> With all their griefs in their arms[22]

In the tradition that descends from W. H. Auden by way of Peter Porter, the 'hidden' metre of syallabics allows verse to sound discursive, even conversational, rather than sprung by the tight 'musicality' of either strict metre or free verse that has been composed on the ear. Porter's 'A Minatory Submission' uses ten-syllable lines, with occasional slippage:

> Desire to overcome the vanity
> Of soul is what drives humans on to sex –
> Just so the mariners of an Inland Sea
> Declare when shown the ocean's vast complex.
> We are so inward that we find ourselves
> Matching bits of bodies from top shelves:
> I see my partner; nobody sees me.[23]

Though this is punctuated according to grammatical and semantic need, the lack of musical punctuation makes it *sound* as if it is not, and the result successfully invokes an involved, in-turned tone, as of someone thinking to himself.

Syllabic verse cues the reading eye at some times, the musical ear at others. But quantitative verse that is seen rather than sounded ranges further afield from sound and sense. Concrete poetry and cutups create shapes on the page that, although they *may* illustrate what the poem says, are 'scanned' by the eye independently of the language those shapes carry. Characters become units of ink as much as words. Their oscillation, between 'colouring in' a shape and being read as sound and sense, creates a stimulating visual rather than sonic experience. This undoes the chronologic relationship between poetry and time, and moves the experience of such 'texts' into the simultaneous plane of the visual.[24]

But contemporary quantitative poetry *can* be both aurally dynamic and (so) chronologic. The French sound poet Patrick Dubost uses a whole range of one-off patterns such as numbered lines, aleatoric performace, list and syllogism structure and staccato, musical delivery. His verse is recreated in live performance, but also makes stimulating semantic sense both on the page and 'out loud'. Dubost's performances are based on phasing (my term, which I'm using in the Reichian sense). A rhythmic text is repeated and overlapped to build dense patterns of multiple voices, as well as to obscure – but not deconstruct – meaning. The poet uses his hands to conduct himself as he reads. His performances are metronomic, the percussive sounds of the words deeply pleasurable. French is a syllable-timed language, so each syllable *is* a 'tick' of clockwork regularity. The listener's experience and pleasure oscillate between the poem's meaning-bearing and its curious unison polyphony. It's probably no coincidence that Dubost trained and worked for much of his adult life as a mathematician and that his education in the arts was musical, not poetic.[25]

Dubost's solo performances are accompanied by tape loop; he also encourages ensemble performances in which audience members are each allocated a particular phrase with which they can choose to join in. They can also choose how many times to repeat it. In other performances, an ensemble chooses from a range of phrases, but can't utter them until they've been performed by Dubost himself. In every case, the individual phrases or sentences form a whole that *makes sense*. Dubost's texts have often-conceptually challenging things to say, and *argue through* these using language and thought in a 'joined-up', chronologic way. It matters what's said *when* because each statement only makes sense in context. There's nothing unusual about this; it's how most texts work. In other words, Dubost's poetry *works with* duration even while it plays with it. His phased repetitions act like a stuttered enunciation, but an enunciation nevertheless, of the text. 'Some propositions written at the end of 1996 to be read in 1997 and So As Not To Die' opens:

1. I write so as not to die.

2. Each year I look at the world with a little more tenderness, so as not to die.

and ends:

96. Throw money out the windows so as not to die, then go very quickly down into the road to retrieve your money and so as not to die.

97. On paper, we talk quietly, with just the hand moving and a very few neurons active. Minimal consumption of energy. Writing is the most economical thing to do in order not to die.

98. One does one's hair every morning so as not to die.

99. There we are, in the present, planted like oaks, with only language to stop us dying.

100. Today is a perfect day not to die.[26]

Dubost performs at poetry and at contemporary music venues, and another way to think about his poetics is as unpitched music – like Steve Reich's *Clapping Music*, for example. But it's his use of *semantic* structures extended through time – in other words, of language used *as* language – that deepens this 'music' in ways that are not simplistically nostalgic for the 'expressive' qualities of, say, Romanticism.

Number, then, can undermine or enhance the relationship poetry and music have with time and with meaning. It always plays a determining role, but not necessarily an overdetermining one, in these genres. The radicalism of the mid-twentieth century's experiments with quantitative artforms seems ultimately to do no more than place us back aboard our original train of thought, running through time and space at measureable speed. But we have one more stop before that train reaches its destination.

Notes

1. Chapter 8's Ideal Reader is an audience in this sense.
2. Charles Bernstein, 'A Test of Poetry' in *My Way: Speeches and Poems* (Chicago: University of Chicago Press, 1999), pp. 52–5. Lyn Hejinian, *Leningrad: American Writers in the Soviet Union* (San Francisco: Mercury House, 1991). Charles Hartman, *The Virtual Muse: Experiments in Computer Poetry* (Hanover, NH: Wesleyan University Press, 1996), see especially pp. 54–64.
3. I've written elsewhere about perceptions of poetic radicalism: Fiona Sampson, 'The Experimental Dilemma', *Primerjalna Knjizevnost*, Ljubljana, 37:1 (2014), pp. 261–70. Though proponents are fewer in Britain than they are in the US, they are often university based, and so able to exert a disproportionate influence on the non-specialists who pass through their hands. In North America, the school colonises publishers such as Green Integer, and campuses including the University of California. Green Integer publish *The PIP Anthology of World Poetry of the 20th Century*, a multi-volume revisionist project edited by Douglas Messerli, Green Integer's publisher himself. On the publisher's relevant web page, a long list of international poets living and dead appears, introduced by a note which makes clear how wide-ranging this ambition is: 'Posted below is a listing of poets we plan to include in our upcoming volumes of the PIP Anthologies. [...] We also invite readers to send us complete biographies of poets from our list [...] We also will consider other names of poets readers may want to suggest for inclusion in our overall listing.' http://www.greeninteger.com/pip_poet_biographies.cfm. Retrieved 29/8/15.
4. Steven Stucky, *Lutosławski and his Music* (Cambridge: Cambridge University Press, 1981). P. 63 quotes Lutosławski, speaking in 1957, '[I]t is difficult to conceive of a more absurd hypothesis than the idea that the achievements of the past several decades should be abandoned and that one should return to the musical language of the nineteenth century [...] The period of which I speak may not have lasted long [...] but all the same it was long enough to do our music immense harm.'
5. Though the dissertation was unpublished at the time, and Babbitt's influential thought was initially disseminated by his compositions and his other critical writing. Milton Babbitt, *The Function of Set Structures in the Twelve-Tone System* (Princeton: Princeton University Press, 1992). Cf. Larry Sitsky (ed.), *Music of the Twentieth Century Avant Garde: A Biocritical Sourcebook* (Westport, CT: Greenwood Press, 2000), pp. 17–18.
6. In the next chapter we'll take a closer look at the process of co-creation in which they are involved.
7. Andy Warhol's first New York solo pop art exhibition was hosted

at Eleanor Ward's Stable Gallery November 6–24, 1962. The exhibit included the works *Marilyn Diptych, 100 Soup Cans, 100 Coke Bottles* and *100 Dollar Bills.*

8. North American poets do appear to be better-served financially, and in terms of marketing and other benefits such as prizes, than those from other countries, but US critics are not yet 'the world's policeman': not least because they seem relatively uninterested in work from the rest of the world. The Pulitzer Prizes for Letters, for example, are (apart from journalism and history categories) still not open to non-US writers, though North Americans have long been eligible for UK prizes. According to the prize regulations for books published in 2015, the Prizes' ninety-ninth year: http://www.pulitzer.org/files/entryforms/2016lbbn.pdf. Retrieved 29/8/15.

9. Alasdair MacIntyre, *After Virtue* [1981] (London: Bloomsbury Academic, 2013).

10. Allen Ginsberg, *Howl: Original Draft Facsimile, Transcript, and Variant Versions, Fully Annotated by Author, with Contemporaneous Correspondence, Account of First Public Reading, Legal Skirmishes, Presursor Texts, and Bibliography,* (London and New York: HarperCollins, Harper Perennial Modern Classics Series, 2006).

11. And a prophetic role for the poet would be both a familiar and a loaded one for this Jewish writer. Although, as the writer and radio producer Tim Dee, who recorded Ginsberg's singing, has remarked, the singing itself sounds like nothing so much as Ivor Cutler.

12. As we saw in Chapter 6, Confessional poetry is peculiarly vulnerable to this construction.

13. http://www.simonarmitage.net

14. Though musicians have a tendency to utter *bien pensant* bunkum about a 'universal language', forgetting that while the *instinct to* music may be universal, the forms musics take are culturally specific.

15. As we saw in Chapter 4.

16. http://www.aslsp.org/de/home.html. Retrieved 29/8/15.

17. Zachary Leader, *Writer's Block* (Baltimore: Johns Hopkins University Press, 1990).

18. Alice W. Flaherty, *The Midnight Disease: The Drive to Write, Writer's Block, and the Creative Brain* (Boston: Houghton Mifflin, 2004).

19. http://www.explorewriting.co.uk/blankpagesyndrome.html. Retrieved 29/8/15. Even Wikipedia is not convinced by the authority of its sources, commenting on itself amusingly: 'Blank page syndrome is similar to writer's block,[how?] but is not a psychological term.' https://en.wikipedia.org/wiki/Writer%27s_block. Retrieved 29/8/15.

20. Samuel Taylor Coleridge 'October 22 1804', in *The Notebooks of Samuel Taylor Coleridge*, vol. 2: *1804–1808*, Kathleen Coburn (ed.) (Princeton: Princeton University Press, 2002).

21. Ibid.

22. Dylan Thomas, 'In my Craft or Sullen Art', in *The Collected Poems of Dylan Thomas*, John Goodby (ed.) (London: Weidenfeld & Nicolson, 2014), pp. 176–7.

23. Peter Porter, *Better Than God* (London: Picador 2009), p. 27.

24. As we saw in Chapter 4, one of the earliest and best-known examples often given of concrete poetry, George Herbert's 'Easter Wings', is really no such thing. The 'wing' shape of the lines is in fact a rhythmic, *aural* discipline, which gives the poem formal 'bite'. http://www.poetryfoundation.org/poem/173626. Retrieved 10/1/16.

25. http://patrick.dubost.free.fr/index2.html; https://www.youtube.com/watch?v=jJNnRC056E8;https://www.youtube.com/watch?v=2QuiXOZ9rjk; https://www.youtube.com/watch?v=oDpwQ7J2ah8.Retrieved 29/12/15.

26. My translation. Original in *Cela fait-il du bruit?* (Elme: Voix éditions, 2004), pp. 35–46.

Chapter 12

Performance: The Role of the Audience

As I write this, on an InterCity Express racing through snowy Austria, my gaze is repeatedly drawn to the woman sitting opposite me. Her mini-skirt and thigh boots create an eccentric ensemble with her deeply wrinkled pensioner's face. She holds the headphones of an old-fashioned Walkman tight against her ears as if to squeeze even closer to an experience that leaks out, anyway, in the high notes of an operatic aria. It must be on maximum volume. Her eyes are closed; her expression is shockingly private. Who's to say why she's moved – or why by Guiseppe Verdi? The point is that she must listen to the thing itself – the moving soundscape that takes her with it as it happens – in order to *be* so moved. She doesn't have this ecstatic expression because she's thinking *about* the opera. She's listening: recreating each number as it's recreated in her in a boundary-less to-and-fro between her pleasure and the pleasurability of the music. Clearly and overwhelmingly, her experience has 'meaning' and, though I don't share her feelings about Verdi, I know for myself what that is like. (And so, I suspect, do you.)

Tastes vary: mine from yours, and both of ours from day to day. What I fancy for supper tonight may not be what I fancy tomorrow. You tell me your favourite poem is Rudyard Kipling's If', and I find this inexplicable. Something tells us that this mutable criterion, taste, isn't quite enough when it comes to thinking about poetry or music. We feel resistance to the equality between choices that it suggests. Our *experience* is more wholehearted than this. In the contemporary poetry world, commitment to any particular school of poetics tends to be treated as an *ethical* virtue or failing. The language poetry uses about itself in reviewing and puffery bears this out. Terms like 'authentic', 'searching', and of course the notorious 'teaches us what it is to be human', are common currency.

And it's not just 'professional' indulgence. We all tend to listen to music, and read poems, as if they are (or are not) *true to* something. The teenager's passionate adherence to a single kind of music – something Seventies films from *Saturday Night Fever* (1977) to *Quadrophenia* (1979) tried to enoble – is a paradigm of how taste in music and books comes to be the signifier of an entire moral and social identity. Coming of age novels exploit this key to characterising their protagonists with a regularity that suggests how consistent the experience is. In Johann Wolfgang von Goethe's *The Sufferings of Young Werther* (1774), the eponymous young Romantic is shaped by reading Romantic literature; a fashion with which the 'entry' for 'June 16, 1771' in Book One, in which his hero first talks to the beloved Lotte, makes hay.[1] In *Du côté de chez Swann*, the first volume of Marcel Proust's *À la recherche du temps perdu*, the fictional Vinteuil *Sonata* is set up as an arguably more thoroughgoing mnemonic even than the more famous madeleine.[2] In *My Struggle*, a sextet of novels some see as a contemporary response to Proust, the contemporary Norwegian writer Karl Ove Knausgård details how his adolescent self was internally shaped and externally defined by the music he listened to.[3]

It's hard not to blame the Romantic moment – which conflated a new way of writing with a new sensibility, as Goethe did in *Werther* – for at least some of this. In 1821, Percy Bysshe Shelley wrote, in 'A Defence of Poetry', that:

> Poetry is the record of the best and happiest moments of the happiest and best minds. [...] A Poet, as he is the author to others of the highest wisdom, pleasure, virtue and glory, so he ought personally to be the happiest, the best, the wisest, and the most illustrious of men.[4]

But a more recent example of the 'true faith' approach is Raymond Carver in 'One More':

> So there it is. Nothing much else needs be said, really. What
> *can* be said for a man who chooses to blab on the phone
> all day, or else write stupid letters
> while he lets his poems go unattended and uncared for, abandoned –

or worse, unattempted. This man doesn't deserve poems
and they shouldn't be given to him in any form.
His poems, should he ever produce any more,
ought to be eaten by mice.[5]

And I realise my own working life has been full of roles based
on just such beliefs about the 'true' excellence of artworks.
When I was a violinist, my job was to find what was good in a
piece of music, and present that to an audience. If a professional
performer can't 'get' a piece of music well enough to do this, the
failing is held to be in her, not in the piece. Later, working vari-
ously as an editor, reviewer, translator and teacher of poetry,
my task became to discriminate between 'strong' and 'weak'
pieces of writing – in order to avoid, or at least try to improve
on, the latter.

This belief that what 'works' is *in* the poem or piece, not in
the eye of the beholder, goes far beyond any professional role.
It's what we all do when we recommend a book saying, 'It's
really good'. In the final chapter of *this* book I'd like to suggest
that this level of investment in music and poetry occurs *because*
they are experiential forms. They happen when they're being
experienced. This in turn suggests two mechanisms at work.
First: if it *is* experiential, our experience *co-creates* the song or
poem, and as co-creators we're involved and invested in it to a
particular degree. Second: since what is experienced can't be
paraphrased, neither can experience itself. What happens, and
what happens *to me*, are uniquely coterminous: and in this sense
my experience *is* part of the piece or poem itself.

The big shift this requires is for us to think of music and
poetry as *practices* – things done – whether that 'doing' is
carried out over centuries by anon, in a matter of weeks by a
well-known writer, or in the three minutes it takes to read a
poem. These practices are *intentional*. And they're *teleological*,
because they have in mind a particular kind of thing to be done.
In the *thin* version offered by traditional cultural readings,
however, music and poetry tend to be viewed not as practices,
but simply as texts. Thus objectified, they run the risk of being
reduced to something inadvertent, symptomatic either of a
culture at large or of individual psychopathology. I learnt to
distrust this approach during the decade I spent working in

health and social care. To treat the creative writing of, for example, people institutionalised by long-term care as a mere symptom was very precisely to miss its meaning.[6] At its worst, pathologising the author allows the reader the 'upper hand' in an open field of interpretation, one that's unanchored in – because it *trumps* – any evidence of *textual intention* such as poetic form. And this is the first step towards 'disciplining' creativity when it's seen as 'disorderly'. The notorious Stalinist-era diagnoses of 'sluggish schizophrenia' and 'paranoid reformist delusion', given to Soviet writers whose work wasn't regarded by that regime as sufficiently wholesome, arise from a unique and poisonous moral and political motivation. But they are simply exaggerations of this pseudo-diagnostic approach.[7]

Indeed the history of visual 'outsider art' tells this same story in reverse. From its first exploration in the 1920s by psychiatrists Walter Morgenthaler in Bern and Hans Prinzhorn in Heidelberg, through second generation research by the artist Jean Dubuffet and Leo Navratil, the psychiatrist who founded the Artists' House at the asylum in Gugging near Vienna, the work of self-trained, often under-educated 'outsider' artists whose vision is unusual – and sometimes even visionary – has gradually become understood as *art brut*. Dubuffet's term is still used today to mean, in his words:

> Works produced by persons unscathed by artistic culture, where mimicry plays little or no part (contrary to the activities of intellectuals) [...] a completely pure artistic operation, raw, brut, and entirely reinvented in all of its phases [...][8]

This is not empty sentiment. The meaning of poems is their practice and use – *as poems*. As we saw in Chapter 3, verse written by adults with severe learning difficulties is no different from any other in this respect. To miss textual indicators of intention like line-breaks, in writing by people with long-term health issues (whether or not they write within a clinical care setting) is to miss its writerly capacity:

'Lost for Words'

You see I could
I could speak
I could speak a few words

Some strange
Some strange half felt sentiment
I could
I could try
If only I could make the connection
The connection
Connection between thought
Between thought and sound
Sound
That's it
Sound
A collection
A collection of
Of what? Yes that's it
A collection of vowels
To string
To string
To string a sentence
A sentence together
To connect
To make
To make some sort
Some sort of contact
A statement
A statement to
A statement to the effect
To the effect
To say
To say
I am still alive![9]

I keep returning to just a handful of the hundreds of poems written in the years I worked in health and social care. As well as being fine pieces of writing, these are ones I have authorial permission to quote. And that authorial ownership is part of the *meaning* of this rhythmically sophisticated, mimetic poem by Sue, who wrote it soon after emerging from several months of being mute.

So viewing poems and music as intention-laden practices is a *thicker* model than seeing them as simply texts. It's also thickened up with consequence. Most human practice is accompanied by, and even entails, the desire to do it well. This is as true of parenting as it is of road-building. In the arts, the desire to define what 'works' artistically, and why, must originally have been a makers' anxiety. Traces of it remain in the formalised braggadocio of compositional contests from rap battles to the Welsh Talwrn y Beirdd, and Prince of Poets and Millions' Poet, the generously funded televised contests run in the United Arabic Emirates for classical Arabic and Bedouin verse respectively.[10] But once communities are large enough to support – that is, pay – rival artists this anxiety becomes public. The competing papal and royal commissions that play such a formative role in the Italian Renaissance, and that Giorgio Vasari's *Lives of the Artists* report on from his near-contemporary perspective, reveal the anxiety of patrons about finding the best art with which to immortalise themselves.[11]

The questions these anxieties pose comprise the well-trodden territory of aesthetics: *What is an artwork; and who can judge it, and how?* Recorded aesthetic theories date back to Plato, four centuries BCE, who wrote on craft versus inspiration in *Ion*, beauty in *Hippias Major* and imitation in Book X of *The Republic*.[12] Today's approaches range from an analytical philosophy of beauty as an objective quality, developed by Guy Sircello in the US, to a hermeneutic account of how shared contexts produce shared judgements by the Canadian Gregory Loewen.[13] Such sophisticated formulations are themselves a branch of cultural activity, the outcome of particular cultural conditions. We can see this when we contrast them with our ignorance about how the preliterate producers of Neolithic art thought about what they were doing.[14]

But even an aesthetic theory has to found itself. It can be explicitly a posteriori, and define – perhaps with greater precision and elegance than has hitherto been the case – what is celebrated as art, or as good art, in the culture in which it finds itself. This is the approach critics often take. Brian Sewell, long a staple of the London *Evening Standard*, was a mercurial example of the value of close-reading work in one's own terms. The Australian critic Robert Hughes was another: the essays collected in his *Nothing If Not Critical* made authoritative definitions of current and recent projects and movements.[15]

Alternatively, aesthetic theory can attempt to *impose* a metaphysics of art, turning away from actual current practice and referring to what it sees as enduring values, such as truth or beauty. The problem with this approach is that age-old sceptical child's question, *Who says?* The aesthetic theorist, however brilliantly conscientious, is a situated individual, and so his thinking about art must necessarily be at least implicitly a posteriori. And yet this is very close to our intuitive relationship with music and poetry. Many of the most influential aesthetic theories have taken this approach, and have often served to galvanise change in artistic practice. That great British nineteenth- and twentieth-century succession of artist-thinkers – John Ruskin (1819–1900), William Morris (1834–96) and Eric Gill (1882–1940) – secured changes in values, practices and artistic products that is no less significant for having been subsequently overtaken by a global art-market.[16]

One successor to Ruskin, Morris and Gill was Bernard Leach (1887–1979), who launched the twentieth century's British studio pottery movement. In his *A Potter's Book* (1940), he quotes a Japanese colleague, 'Mr Kawai of Kyoto', as saying that people recognise what is good work 'with their bodies'.[17] Leach's opening chapter, a manifesto called 'Towards a Standard', repeatedly uses the term 'intimacy'. He talks about the near-familial intimacy of craftsmen working together in a studio. (Perhaps this isn't surprising given that he also founded a pottery dynasty whose members included his son David and his third wife Janet.) Elsewhere, he identifies the 'intimate feeling' that handmade objects have for whoever uses them. Poems are also handmade, of course, and so is music (except the kind composed on mixing desks). Leach's argument about this 'intimate feeling for material and form' assumes a similarity between the potter, who 'know[s] out of his body the nature of' his materials, and his pot's user. That assumption of similarity is not dissimilar to the one song posits between singer and listener. Leach's notion of intimacy, of a *togetherness* of the maker and his audience, is too good not to borrow for music and poetry. It reminds us that these practices are shared by everyone who takes part in them – whether they're writing a poem for the parish magazine, choosing the music for granddad's funeral or performing at the Wigmore Hall.[18]

As this is a human-centred way to think about music and poetry, it's not surprising that it helps us to see them as, primarily, experiences. But what happens if we start from the other direction, and ask what remains when that human presence is removed from either genre? The first thing we notice is that, when they're not being uttered or read, played or heard – including silently, 'on the page' – pieces and poems are simply *not happening*. The *idea of* them may be happening when we think *of* them: *I need to go practice Shostakovich Five*; *I think I'll teach James Merrill's 'The Changing Light at Sandover'*. But this isn't the same as *thinking through* them. The name of a work is not that work, but simply a mnemonic for it. I'd have to be able to 'run through' a tune or a poem 'in my head' to be able to say that I *remember* it.

The marks on paper (or an illuminated screen) that fill up a book or a score don't 'do' the poem or piece, but are a set of instructions *for* 'doing it'. As the French composer Pierre Boulez says, in *Boulez on Music Today*:

> There is also – though I mention it only as a reminder – a form of paraphrase which consists in the graphic transcription of the notated symbols of the score. This boils down to a summary transposition of results already established [...] a marked weakening is noticeable between the work and its description.[19]

It's the same with devices for storing *performances*. Wax cylinders, cassettes, LPs, CDs, even the digital Cloud, are all material records of performances of pieces, but *are not* the pieces they can, when 'played', release. The mobile of thread and CDs my neighbours hang in their kid's bedroom *is just that*: not a symphony, but a disc of polycarbonate.

Because music and poetry happen in being done, time places both makers and audiences in the same relationship as each other to a piece of music or poetry. Musicians understand the impersonality implicit in *making a piece happen* since, unlike poets, they are trained as *performers*. Even the early education of most composers is in playing an instrument.[20] (Relatedly, musicians make an important distinction between *practising* – work they do by themselves on learning how to play difficult passages – and *rehearsing*, that is 'running through' the whole piece with the complete ensemble.) As we saw in Chapter 1, our shared experience takes place on a single plane. (Which is not to say that we compose poems and pieces at their eventual speed: but is to say that we are building *temporal objects* as we do so.) But there are no tempo marks for reading, and those for musical performance are often only approximated to, so what remains unchanged from occasion to occasion is not exact duration, but that other manifestation of temporal existence, the sequential unfolding that, as we saw there, Igor Stravinsky calls *chrononomie*.

Artistic impersonality is a familiar concept; one we readily trace back to T. S. Eliot. But the equalising effect the temporality of music and poetry has on makers and audiences alike brings a different principle of impersonality into play. We also saw in Chapter 1 how a few poets 'read' from memory, dispensing with – to borrow the term from Michel Donaghy, one of the chief exponents of this tricky feat – the 'scaffolding' of a book and a lectern.[21] In doing so they become less, not more, present. Awareness of the intervening reader – as someone who turns a page, rustles papers or puts on reading glasses – creates distance between the audience and the poem. When that awareness is replaced by the poem itself, spoken as if 'directly' from memory, we're more likely to *hear* (only) text. The (relative) absence of a performing personality also makes room for each individual audience member to experience the poem *for themselves.*

It's for this reason that musicians perform from memory wherever possible. And there's more than one way to remove such intrusions, even from poetry. Some years ago, I worked on a commission to produce a poem for a park in High Wycombe, where it was inlaid as a winding *path* into some paving. Stone-carver Alec Peever carved the letters of my poem at just the right size for reading at walking pace. Any larger, and the words might have been too 'quick' for pedestrians; any smaller, and they might have disrupted the rhythm of walking – or been left unread.[22]

Another example of how these chronologic objects 'do their thing' impersonally – or apparently without us – is the way a musical or poetic phrase survives as an earworm. In Mark Twain's short story 'A Literary Nightmare', earworm sufferers can gain relief if they 'infect' someone else with that worm. Interestingly Twain, writing as early as 1876, used a pre-existing jingle as his earworm – 'Punch brothers! Punch with care! Punch in the presence of the passenjare!' – and I wonder whether he wasn't himself infected by that jingle and trying to wish it on to us.[23]

In my earliest research, when I worked with health service users like the women of St Cross House whom we met in Chapter 3, I worked with the idea that all discourses define themselves.[24] What makes a poem be a poem? It does what a poem does; and so on. There's an aroma of late Wittgenstein (and a risk of circularity) to this thinking, and at that time I was indeed interested in both late Wittgenstein and late Heidegger, because both refute the innocence of language. Each of them reminds us that language is a thing in itself, and not merely an extension of its individual user. Although this seems obvious to poets, who needs must grapple with the medium, the point is under-expressed in thinking *about* poetry.

Of course, these aren't the only philosophers to make this kind of point. (Among others who do so, Paul Ricoeur's hermeneutics excavate the secret life of language, and Friedrich Nietzsche argues that language is the scaffolding that gets us to an apprehension, but is not itself the content of that apprehension.[25]) Nor can one 'be' *both* a Heideggerian and a Wittegnsteinian. For the Ludwig Wittgenstein of the *Blue and Brown Notebooks* and the *Philosophical Investigations*, language *is* its use; and though there might be errors in usage, and foolish ideas had *within* language, questions of authenticity to anything outside this use, such as to a world it claims to describe, do not arise.[26] For Martin Heidegger, particularly after *the turn* (*die Kehre*) which he started to make in the 1930s, language – not *being* whatever it thinks about – is doomed to inauthenticity; although using it while bearing this in mind does approach authenticity. Poetry, which acknowledges its own relinquishment of the realist contract, is therefore important; and he himself resorts to it – partly in order to think *about* poetry.[27]

In fact, I'm neither a Wittgenstenian nor a Heideggerian. I believe that philosophy *thinks*, not that it *knows*. I do so despite understanding that this isn't particularly the way of the world: which is for different ways of thinking and talking to compete. For example, in the world of poetry, to return to where we started, different schools of poetics busily disparage each other. So, next, I researched the notion that the way poetry defines itself is in contradistinction to other discourses. This means that a discourse is always in the process of constructing itself, and this returns us to our picture of poetry as a practice.

But it's a practice in which audiences participate. Certain poets are peculiarly committed to staging the reader's or listener's experience. Percy Bysshe Shelley was fascinated by movement and change and wanted to generate them himself, not only as a schoolboy chemist or adult revolutionary but in his verse. So his long lines rush onward, speeded along by extended sentences, piled-up adjectives, and toppling lists. The entire first section of his 'Ode to the West Wind', for example, is one long breathless sentence (even if he does cheat a little, using colons to override the cadences of closure):

> O wild West Wind, thou breath of Autumn's being,
> Thou, from whose unseen presence the leaves dead
> Are driven, like ghosts from an enchanter fleeing,
>
> Yellow, and black, and pale, and hectic red,
> Pestilence-stricken multitudes: O thou,
> Who chariotest to their dark wintry bed
>
> The winged seeds, where they lie cold and low,
> Each like a corpse within its grave, until
> Thine azure sister of the Spring shall blow
>
> Her clarion o'er the dreaming earth, and fill
> (Driving sweet buds like flocks to feed in air)
> With living hues and odours plain and hill:
>
> Wild Spirit, which art moving everywhere;
> Destroyer and preserver; hear, oh hear![28]

The helter-skelter forces the reader to participate in this versification, since to speak these lines is to become literally breathless. French philosopher Hélène Cixous calls this kind of writing a 'strategy of velocity', and it places Shelley in a radical countertradition to realist, descriptive or confessional poetry. (Other writers in this tradition include both his German Romantic older contemporary Friedrich Hölderlin (1770–1843), celebrant of the 'on-rushing word' and, much later, the twentieth century's Beat poets.[29])

A very different verison of the significance of audience in co-creating poetic practice is the figure of the public poet. Community and national spokes-poets seem to arise at times of shared difficulty: war, the establishment of a state, government by dictatorship. They remain relatively rare: though a poet witnesses his community, that community may not witness the poet. Few of the poets Stalin identified as threats to his regime were rabble-rousers. Even Osip Mandelstam's famous 1933 satire on Stalin, 'Kremlinskii Gorech' ('Kremlin Highlander', the poem which led to his final arrest and death), was only read to small groups of friends. But a poet like the Palestinian Mahmoud Darwish (1941–2008) is created through dialectic with a community who wait for, memorise and quote the poems that 'their' poet writes *for* them: that's to say, in the knowledge that they do so. Darwish, who was seven when his family fled Galilee for Lebanon, only to return to Acre a year later, led a politically and poetically situated life. As a young adult he lived in Haifa and was a member of the Israeli Communist Party, went to Moscow to study, joined the Palestine Liberation Organization, and was forbidden to return home until 1995, when he settled partly in Ramallah. His poetic fate was sealed on 1 May 1965, when he read 'Identity Card', a poem from what was only his second collection, *Leaves of Olives*, to a crowded Nazareth cinema. Each stanza of this poem repeats: 'Write it down: I am an Arab.'

The reading caused a near-riot and within days the poem had been disseminated throughout the Arab world. Darwish became a kind of Palestinian National Poet, a role that seems to have been non-negotiable. In a 2002 interview with the American poet Nathalie Handal, Darwish said, 'I thought poetry could change everything, could change history and could humanize, and I think that the illusion is very necessary to push poets to be involved and to believe, but now I think that poetry changes only the poet.'[30] But while he may have wished to step back, his audience would not let him do so. As he says in *Mural* (2000), his book-length poem of elegy and exile:

> And the poet says: Take my poem if you want,
> there's nothing in it for me besides you,
> take your 'I'. I will complete exile
> with the messages your hands have left for the doves.
> Which one of us is 'I' that I may become its other?
> A star will fall between speech and writing,
> and memory will spread its thoughts ...[31]

This version is from a beautiful, complex translation by Palestinian-American poet Fady Joudah. In a translation by

Rema Hammami, a (female) Professor of Anthrolopology in Ramallah, and John Berger (possibly of relevance here is that Berger is British, of Jewish descent, and living in France), the fusion of lover, reader and country is both more explicit and more intimate. Translation is arguably the closest form of reading, and the differences in these versions highlight how the reader co-creates the poem:

> Take back the poem if you want
> for me there's only you in it
> Take back your 'I'
> The exile will be complete with what's left of handwriting written
>   for the carrier pigeons
> At the end which me am I in us?
> Of the two of us
> let me be the last
> A star will fall between the written and the said
> A memory will lay out its thoughts ...[32]

Yehuda Amichai (1924–2000) is a national poet on an older model: he remade what had been newly promoted to the national tongue into a literary language, and in so doing declared and developed its capacity for complex thought and for sustaining contemporary culture. His verse works – like that of Mihai Eminescu (1850–89) in Romania, France Prešeren (1800–49) in Slovenia, or Adam Mickiewicz (1798–1855) in Poland – to validate the newly created or contested state.[33] Amichai's personal relationship with Hebrew sums up this process of 'naturalisation': he himself started life as the German-speaking Ludwig Pfeuffer, learning Hebrew as religious texts in Würzberg, Bavaria.

In another example of translation as co-reading, here is his An Old Toolshed', in a translation by Assia Gutmann. German-born, she had come to Britian from what was then Palestine by way of Canada: you can just hear her non-native speech in the unresolved grammatical knot of the second stanza:

> What's this? This is an old toolshed.
> No, this is a great past love.
>
> Anxiety and Joy were here together
> in this darkness
> and Hope.

Perhaps I've been here once before.
I didn't go near to find out.

There are voices calling out of a dream.
No, this is a great love.
No, this is an old toolshed.[34]

There's more than one type of ambiguity here. I love the oscillating opening and closing image (and the way that, in opening and closing the whole poem, it oscillates round that, too). But I suspect that spatial ambiguity in the second stanza – between 'been *here*' and '*go* to find out' – is in fact grammatical.

So is the value of a poem or piece of music simply *personal* preference rather than consensus, the norms of 'good taste' – or even received usage? Do I think *true* 'good taste' has some kind of ontological status, of the kind that Wittgenstein claims for language use? No: that's not the case I'm making. My point is smaller and, as Bernard Leach would say, more 'intimate'. It is simply that whatever's *there*, in a piece of music or a poem, is something we co-create each time that work happens, whether sitting alone over a book at the kitchen table, or turning to a national poet for inspiration.

One way to say this might be that experience is something that cannot exist without us, but that is built into verse and music *so as to be released by* us. It is not raw time, but it is a temporal element that we are the measure of – and that is also the measure of us. Their experiential nature is what makes poetry and music chronologic; and experience is what locates us as ourselves. It matters, finally, that *we* are on the metaphorical train as it passes through the landscape it is part of.

The window's open and a dusty smell of hay fills the compartment. A flock of cranes passes overhead in their long straggling V formation. Just round the bend I can see the station approaching us: three apple trees with whitewashed boles, a bench, and the one-room building outside which the station master stands holding up his flag. It's time to stop. And so we do.

Notes

1. Johann Wolfgang von Goethe, *The Sufferings of Young Werther*, Stanley Corngold (trans.) (New York: W. W. Norton, 2012).

2. Marcel Proust, *À la recherche du temps perdu* [1913] (Paris: Gallimard, 1954).

3. Karl Ove Knausgård, *My Struggle 1: A Death in the Family*, Don Bartlett (trans.) (London: Vintage, 2013).

4. Percy Bysshe Shelley, from 'A Defence of Poetry'. http://www. poetryfoundation.org/learning/essay/237844.   Retrieved   10/1/ 16.

5. Raymond Carver, *A New Path to the Waterfall* (London: Harvill, 1990), p. 96.

6. T. S. Eliot, 'The Dry Salvages: II' line 94 in *Collected Poems 1909–1962* (London: Faber, 1974), p. 208.

7. Anatoly B. Smulevich, 'Sluggish Schizophrenia in the Modern Classification of Mental Illness', *Schizophrenia Bulletin* 15:4 (1989), pp. 533–9. http://schizophreniabulletin.oxfordjournals. org/content/15/4/533.long Retrieved 30/8/15.

8. Jean Dubuffet, 'L'art brut préféré aux arts culturels', in Jean Dubuffet, *Prospectus et tous écrits suivants*, vol. 1 (Paris: Gallimard, 1967), pp. 201–2. Quoted in Charles Russell, *Groundwaters*, (Munich, London, New York: Prestel, 2011), p. 18.

9. Sue, Kingfisher Writing Group Salisbury, Salisbury Arts Centre/ Artscare, 1999.

10. http://www.bbc.co.uk/programmes/p024prnf

11. Giorgio Vasari, *Lives of the Artists* (Mineola, NY: Dover, 2005).

12. He also included passages on rhetoric and on inspiration in *Phaedrus*. Plato, *The Dialogues*, Benjamin Jowett (ed.). http://oll. libertyfund.org/titles/166. Retrieved 30/8/15.

13. Guy Sircello, *Love and Beauty* (Princeton: Princeton University Press, 1989). Gregory Loewen, *The Use of Art in the Construction of Personal Identity: A Phenomenology of Aesthetic Self-Consciousness* (Lewiston, NY: Edwin Mellen Press, 2012).

14. Some of this work featured in an exhibition the British Museum called *Ice Age Art*: *The Arrival of the Modern Mind*, British Museum 7 February – 2 June 2013. We might argue that their work *itself* is what they were thinking.

15. Robert Hughes, *Nothing If Not Critical* (London: Collins Harvill, 1990).

16. They were largely concerned with the individual maker as practitioner. Thus Ruskin in 1853 in *The Stones of Venice*:

> No good work whatever can be perfect, and *the demand for perfection is always a sign of a misunderstanding of the ends of art.*
> This is for two reasons, both based on everlasting laws. The first, that no great man ever stops working till he has reached his point of failure. [...] Of human work none but what is bad can be perfect, in its own bad way. [...] The second reason is, that imperfection is in some sort essential to all that we know of life. It is the sign of life in a mortal body, that is to say, of a state of progress and change.

The Genius of Ruskin: Selections from his Writings, John D. Rosenberg (ed.) (Charlottesville: University Press of Virginia, 1998), p. 183.

17. Bernard Leach, *A Potter's Book*, 2nd edn (London: Faber, 1945), p. 17.
18. That this is a very broad artistic 'way' is a whole other, and I believe wholly positive, story.
19. Pierre Boulez, *Boulez on Music Today*, Susan Bradshaw and Richard Rodney Bennett (trans.) (Faber: London, 1975), p. 17.
20. In her history of the National Youth Orchestra, its founder Dame Ruth Railton recalls how aspiring young composers and conductors would be invited to make up the percussion section in order to learn orchestral music-making. Ruth Railton, *Daring to Excel* (London: Secker and Warburg, 1992).
21. As we saw in Chapter 1. Michael Donaghy, *Wallflowers* (London: Poetry Society, 1999), pp. 17–20.
22. Jack Scruton Memorial Garden, High Wycombe, 1999. www.wycombe.gov.uk/Core/DownloadDoc.aspx?documentID=3016, pp. 5–6. Retrieved 30/8/15.
23. An earworm can haunt the mind without changing anything else in it. This worries critics of poetry's, and instrumental music's, 'relevance'. Yet all sorts of things – shopping lists, political convictions, worries about a friend living with cancer – can equally be held in mind, without necessarily having any influence on each other. This doesn't make any of them less meaningful *in themselves*.
24. In particular, I wanted to make the case that people in community settings were truly *doing poetry*, even if what they wrote wasn't necessarily publishable. My PhD ('Towards a Theoretical Foundation for Writing in Health Care', Radboud University, Nijmegen, Netherlands, 2001) and the publications that followed it, especially: Celia Hunt and Fiona Sampson, *The Self on the Page* (London: Jessica Kingsley, 1998) and Celia Hunt and Fiona Sampson, *Writing: Self and Reflexivity* (London: Palgrave Macmillan, 2006).
25. Friedrich Nietzsche, *The Gay Science*, Bernard Williams (ed.), Josefine Nauckhoff and Adrian del Caro (trans.), in *Cambridge Texts in the History of Philosophy* (Cambridge: Cambridge University Press, 2001). Paul Ricoeur, *Hermeneutics and the Human Sciences: Essays on Language, Action and Interpretation*, John B. Thompson (ed. and trans.) (Cambridge: Cambridge University Press, 1981).
26. Ludwig Wittgenstein, *The Blue and Brown Books* (Oxford: Basil Blackwell, 1989). Ludwig Wittgenstein, *Philosophical Investigations*, G. E. M. Anscombe (trans.) (Oxford: Basil Blackwell, 1989).
27. Martin Heidegger, 'The Thinker as Poet' in *Poetry, Language, Thought*, Albert Hofstadter (trans.) (New York: Harper Colophon, 1975), p. 13.

28. *Percy Bysshe Shelley*, Fiona Sampson (ed.) (London: Faber, 2011), p. 35.
29. Hélène Cixous, *So Close*, Peggy Kamuf (trans.) (Cambridge: Polity Press, 2009).
30. Mahmoud Darwish, interviewed by Nathalie Handal, 'Mahmoud Darwish: Palestine's Poet of Exile' in *The Progressive*, http://progressive.org/node/1575. Retrieved 30/8/15.
31. Mahmoud Darwish, 'Mural' in *If I Were Another*, Fady Joudah (trans.) (New York: Farrar Straus and Giroux, 2009), p. 105.
32. Mahmoud Darwish, *Mural*, Rema Hammami and John Berger (trans.) (Verso: London, 2009), pp. 13–14.
33. Romania formally became a nation-state with that name in 1862 and Israel in 1948, while Poland was actually partitioned in the years to 1790.
34. Yehuda Amichai, *Love Poems: A Bilingual Edition* (Tel Aviv: Schoken Publishing House, 1986), p. 47.

Index

EU Authorised Representative:

Easy Access System Europe Mustamäe tee 50, 10621 Tallinn, Estonia

gpsr.requests@easproject.com

Printed and bound by CPI Group (UK) Ltd, Croydon, CR0 4YY

26/05/2025

01882795-0001